ISRAEL

Is It Good for the Jews?

RICHARD COHEN

Simon & Schuster
New York London Toronto Sydney New Delhi

Simon & Schuster
1230 Avenue of the Americas
New York, NY 10020

First Simon & Schuster hardcover edition September 2014

SIMON & SCHUSTER and colophon are registered trademarks of Simon & Schuster, Inc.

For information about special discounts for bulk purchases, please contact Simon & Schuster Special Sales at 1-866-506-1949 or business@simonandschuster.com.

The Simon & Schuster Speakers Bureau can bring authors to your live event. For more information or to book an event, contact the Simon & Schuster Speakers Bureau at 1-866-248-3049 or visit our website at www.simonspeakers.com.

Interior design by Aline Pace

Jacket design by Henry Sene Yee

Manufactured in the United States of America

10 9 8 7 6 5 4 3 2 1

Library of Congress Cataloging-in-Publication Data is available.

ISBN 978-1-4165-7568-9
ISBN 978-1-4165-8427-8 (ebook)

Dedicated to the memory of Mona Riklis Ackerman
Born Tel Aviv May 22, 1946
Died New York, December 5, 2012
She loved Israel. She loved being Jewish

Contents

CONTENTS

ISRAEL

Is It Good for the Jews?

———————————

1

The Great Mistake

The greatest mistake Israel could make at the moment is to forget that Israel itself is a mistake."

That sentence, tossed off under deadline pressure, was the "lede" to a column I wrote for the *Washington Post* in the summer of 2006. Israel was then involved in yet another of its inconclusive miniwars, this one with Hezbollah to the north. Three years later, it would turn on Hamas to the south, pummeling Gaza, and then do it again in 2012, albeit stopping short of a ground invasion. As always, Israel applied its acknowledged doctrine of disproportionate force, using airpower, with its inevitable loss of civilian life.

The world looked on in horror—yet it had looked the other way when the frequent wayward rocket, fired from Lebanon or Gaza, wobbled over the border and killed the occasional Israeli. Few looked, either, at the nighttime ritual of Israeli parents attempting to comfort frightened children in whose imaginations the odds of being struck by a homemade rocket went from near astronomical to dead certainty. If the siren went off, if the blimp hovering over the woebegone town of Sderot in the south detected an incoming rocket, a resident then had only about thirty seconds to make it to a shelter. This is a heart-pounding dash for a young person. For the elderly, it's a near impossibility.

Israel was "an honest mistake," I wrote, "a well-intentioned mistake, a mistake for which no one is culpable, but the idea of creating a nation of Jews in an area of Arab Muslims (and some Christians) has produced a century of warfare and terrorism of the sort we are seeing now. Israel fights Hezbollah in the north and Hamas in the south, but its most formidable enemy is history itself."

The word *mistake* was itself a mistake. Yet I could find no other that expressed what I meant: not fault, not wrong, not evil, not awful, but, yes, a mistake: a belief that somehow the Arab Middle East would politely make way for European Jews, that an oasis of white Europeans could be established in a vast desert of Arabs, that a bit of colonialism—never mind that there was no home country—could endure despite being something of an anachronism, a dinosaur hatched way too late.

There was an instant reaction to what I had written. Even in the prosaic black-and-white type of a newspaper, the word *mistake* had a Day-Glo quality to it. It blinded, it dazzled. On the internet, it seemed incendiary. It provoked sane people to write insane emails, and for months afterward, kind people, using the tone of voice reserved for children or the mentally feeble, asked if I had indeed written what they had heard I had written—I am read, apparently, via rumor—and if so, it was just plain a pity. I had, it seemed, gone nuts.

At the same time, a disquieting sort of applause came my way. Needless to say, the odd anti-Semite checked in via email, making the usual whacko references to Jewish power and Jewish wealth and Jewish malevolence. This sort of stuff is easy to dismiss because it is so loony.

More troubling—infinitely more troubling—were the congratulations I received from friends, colleagues, and acquaintances who you would have thought—that is, *I* would have thought—were either supportive of Israel or, at the least, not hostile to it. But what oozed out, what was suggested or inferred or implied, was that they had finally met a Jew who acknowledged the truth about Israel. They exhibited relief, since they must sometimes wonder about an innate, hopefully imperceptible, feeling about Jews—not, of course, anti-Semitism, that's for sure, but a something, a feeling, a suspicion that worried them plenty.

For the fact of the matter—or rather, the *feeling* of the matter—was that Israel had been acting so *Jewish*. No longer was it a Paul Newman-ish place, a land of blue-eyed Jews in inverted sailor caps who were always the underdogs, but a place of arrogant, pushy, smart, and duplicitous people. They had made the metaphorical leap from renters to landlords. They were turning down the heat on the Palestinians, replacing 100-watt hallway bulbs with 60s and then 40s, squeezing the hapless and innocent Arab, diminishing his standard of living and fueling the cycle of violence that erupts with biblical regularity—a time for peace and a time for war.

Security concerns, always an excuse for the inexcusable, became the standard, all-purpose rebuttal. Did the world appreciate Israel's situation? Did it understand the sort of neighborhood Israel lived in? Did the world understand what had to be done? Did the world even give a damn? The world offered criticisms. Many Jews heard something else: anti-Semitism.

Israel seemed both to care about world opinion and not to care about world opinion. It seemed suffused with self-righteousness; so stoked on a distant victimization that it could not see what others were seeing: the victim had become the bully. It had been years since the cruel-but-necessary had been necessary at all. It seemed rather that the West Bank roadblocks were often arbitrary, imposed because they could be imposed. Israel had become not just the Jewish State, but a very "Jewish state," irritatingly sanctimonious, querulous, and justifying it all with invocations to the past.

But these critics were constrained from being openly critical. Impatience with Israel might seem like anti-Zionism, which might seem like anti-Semitism, which definitely would put the critic in pretty awful company. Israel was always the odd man out, the exception to the rule. It could not be discussed as, say, France could be, and criticized for what it did without convening a posse and beating the bushes for an ulterior motive: anti-Semitism, pro-Arabism—something like that.

I agreed with much of this criticism. In countless columns over the years, I had condemned the Israeli occupation of the West Bank and Gaza Strip. I had been to both areas, as well as elsewhere in the Arab world, and I had written over and over again that by becoming an occupying power, Israel had lost its moral monopoly. Its Arab enemies might be dictatorships or monarchies, and the various Palestinian organizations might be corrupt and astonishingly violent (the 1972 Munich massacre of eleven Israeli Olympic athletes, for instance), but not only had they achieved underdog status, they had achieved it retroactively. Even the 1948 War of Independence, in which the newly created State of Israel was attacked by five Arab nations, was recast as a virtual sucker punch—a cakewalk in which a modern, muscular, coldly efficient army easily dispatched an inchoate and pitifully thin invasion force. The Jews won because they were always going to win—or, as some would have it, because Jews always manage to win.

So I plunged into this book. I would explain what I meant by "mistake." I would tell the story of where Israel went wrong and how Israel went wrong. I was a frequent visitor. I had been to yeshiva as a kid, and then, after the third grade (by which time I was fluent in Hebrew), I transferred to an after-school program where I continued my Hebrew and religious studies. I had been bar mitzvahed; an Orthodox affair in which the Torah was unrolled and the intimidating silver pointer, a veritable finger of God, placed in my hand, and I was firmly guided over the ancient text, a cursive Hebrew lacking the diacritical vowel signs with which I was familiar. Panic engulfed me, but I did okay. It was a cloudy day, but at that moment, my mother said, the sun came out. Some said it was coincidence.

The point is that I knew my stuff: my Hebrew stuff and my Israel stuff and my Arab stuff and my Judaism stuff. In addition, I knew my Jewish history, and, above all, I knew my Holocaust—board feet after board feet of books about this monumental crime. The Holocaust has become my theology, my own black eschatology. If I could understand it, if I could understand how so many people murdered so many other people, if I could even understand how they could watch Jews starve to death or rot of disease or kill their babies before their eyes—the whole panoply of horrendous, inexplicable cruelty—then I might know something about people and evil but also about this God who permitted it all; this *just* God who showed no justness at all. I would keep looking.

First, though, I had to brush up a bit—just a bit, I thought. I cracked this book and that, and this book or that led me to yet another book and, often, to a footnote, which led to a document that at one time might have been virtually irretrievable, but now, with a click of the computer key, could be summoned from the vast research library in the cloud. I read and I read and I learned and I learned. Some was familiar, much was new, and some was familiar but forgotten—things I didn't know I knew. Slowly, inexorably, I fell in love. What a marvelous people these Jews were! What magic and what genius and what drama and what tragedy!

As for the story of Israel, it was not true that the Paul Newman-esque depiction of it was not accurate. It was—more or less. More true than false. The state was built, it was true, in total and sometimes arrogant disregard of the Arab people who lived there. But it had been built by many people who wished

4

no actual harm to those Arab people and who sometimes thought, innocently enough, that what they built—and the way they built it—could benefit the Arabs. In the meantime, their own determination to smash the ghetto culture led to an insistence that they do their own labor. This meant the dislocation and dismissal of the Arab farmworker or industrial worker—a galling hardship for these victims of muscular Zionism who were understandably reluctant to sacrifice their measly livelihoods to build a state for a bunch of Europeans.

The Palestinians were what we might now call collateral damage—just in the way. They were Middle Easterners somehow trapped in a place that was intended (by others) as an extension of Europe. These Jews were not going to become Middle Easterners, virtual Arabs, as were those Jews who lived elsewhere in the region, but Europeans—emancipated ones at that—brimming with modernity and all sorts of weird ideas: the communal raising of children, for instance, not to mention a distinct lack of modesty among the women. These were people who felt compelled to establish a university and a symphony orchestra—to re-create both the learning centers of Europe and its café culture. Their achievements were stupendous, but maybe the most stupendous achievement of them all was the revival of the Hebrew language. They leaned over the Torah, the Talmud, and the other holy books and breathed air into the collapsed lungs of a dormant language so that it became fit for the synagogue and the bedroom.

They did make the desert bloom. They did drain the Hula swamp. They did erect that Bauhaus wonder, Tel Aviv, on nothing but sand and dreams. They did organize an army from scratch and made it formidable. They did build some of their own weapons, and they did fight tenaciously, and they did have among them leaders who espoused tolerance and respect for their enemy, the Arabs—and spit in the eye of history and the hard lessons learned about the efficacy of ethnic cleansing.

Ethnic cleansing worked, and it was commonly practiced: much of Europe had been made ethnically neat, with ethnic Germans herded back to Germany, Ukrainians sent packing from Poland, and so on. But these sentimental Jews, intoxicated on the theories of Karl Marx and the impractical requirements of Judaism, were besotted by the charms of the common man, even when he was the enemy. They often treated the Arabs roughly, sometimes inhumanely, but remonstrated by their leaders and nagged by the precepts of Judaism and Jewish culture, they stopped well short of what others had done in that era and earlier. Israel today is one-fifth Arab, and not because of immigration.

Over all this history, like the volcano that formed the island, loomed the

Holocaust. It was immense, impossible to see around or over, but before and after—before Auschwitz, Treblinka, and, just to give one person recognition, the murder by the Nazis of Sabina Spielrein, one of the first female psychoanalysts, shot in 1942 along with her two children by an SS death squad—were two distinct periods that were instrumental in the creation of Israel. These periods have become increasingly obscure (as the Holocaust emerged and pronounced itself separate from World War II), as if there is no room in memory for them all and as if the Holocaust was, by itself, responsible for the creation of Israel. In a sense, that's true and remains true, but the dead, no matter how many millions of them, were incapable of creating a state. Only the living could do that.

The first period is the era from the end of World War I to the beginning of World War II. It is significant not only for what happened, but for what it portended. The collapse of the Prussian, Russian, Austro-Hungarian, and Ottoman Empires caused a concomitant rise in nationalism and, because Jews were seen everywhere as "other," anti-Semitism. Poland, a veritable Jewish homeland within Europe, became increasingly anti-Semitic. It implemented oppressive laws and regulations well before the arrival of the Nazis. The Poles hated the Nazis, but too many of them hated the Jews as well.

Poland's anti-Semitic measures were a product of Polish democracy—or, if democracy is not quite the right word for the authoritarian government of Marshal Józef Klemens Piłsudski, then certainly the will of the people. The reigning monarchs of central and eastern Europe—the emperor, the kaiser, the czar—had been anti-Semites to one degree or another, but they'd had no need to cater to the far stronger, irrational, and downright homicidal hatred of the mob. With the fall of the monarchies, the situation changed dramatically. Democracy came straight at the throat of Jewry, and Jewry, with America having sharply limited immigration, needed a place to go. Palestine, with a minuscule but already well-established Jewish community, went from being an aspiration to a haven.

The second period, the post-Holocaust era, pales next to what directly preceded it, but its importance lies in the fact that it was unfolding in what we might now call real time. The Holocaust had ended, but the killing of Jews continued. In Poland alone, some 1,500 were murdered within two years of the war's end. The actual number remains in dispute—it may be less than 1,500. Not in dispute, however, is that the authorities were often indifferent to what was happening, and the Roman Catholic Church, a Polish institution of immense moral authority, was downright sympathetic to the murderers. As good

Christians and anticommunists, they thought they had a beef. Jewish communists were flocking back from their safe haven in the Soviet Union. They would do to Poland what, in the popular imagination, they had done to Russia itself.

The post-Holocaust era found most of the Jews of Europe not only homeless but effectively stateless as well. This was particularly the case for those from Poland, which had been the European Jewish heartland (over three million Jews before the war), but it was true for other Eastern European Jews. Many if not most of them had no desire to once again live among neighbors who often had either been complicit in the Holocaust, indifferent to it—or, with the occasional murder and pogrom—seemed intent on continuing it.

Several hundred thousand Jewish refugees were on the move—rousted first from their homes by the Nazis and then fearful of returning on account of pogroms, episodic violence, and a reluctance to live among neighbors who, both literally and figuratively, were walking the streets in clothes stolen from Jews. Most of Europe's dispossessed Jews were eventually housed in displaced persons camps located in Germany or Austria and administered by the American military. Where should they go? Where could they go? Not to America, which had become immigrant-phobic and suspected, moreover, that embedded in that raggedy collection of Jews were more than a few communists. Not back to their home countries. That was out of the question.

So, where? As it happens, they were asked—a survey. The Jews answered: Palestine. Overwhelmingly, they wanted to be among their fellow Jews. They wanted to be safe—although they recognized that Palestine was disputed territory and risky. They wanted, mostly, to be out of Europe, and it was their enormous claim on Western sympathies and the growing realization that they could not stay and had to go, that capped what Theodor Herzl, the founder of modern Zionism, had set in motion not even fifty years before. It was not the dead of the Holocaust that produced Israel, it was the survivors. Try telling *them* that they had made a mistake.

On August 2, 1914, a camera seemed to catch Adolf Hitler attending a rally in Munich's Odeonsplatz to cheer the outbreak of World War I. He is in a huge throng, highlighted in contemporary prints of the photo, hatless. He has that familiar shock of black hair, that peculiar and now infamous mustache. He seems to be cheering, and soon, of course, he would be off to the war he wanted so much and which would cost the lives of some two million Germans, but not—in a rebuke to God—his own. (The authenticity of that photo has recently come into dispute.)

Much of recent history is in that one picture. Within a mere twenty years, the swastika would fly from all the buildings on the Odeonsplatz. A twelve-hour drive today from there is Poland, where my family, including my mother, was still living. "Run! run!" I want to yell. "Come to America! That man in the crowd wants to kill you."

My mother, two years old at the time, made it to America almost seven years later. So did her immediate family. On my father's side, most were already in America, and some came much later: my great-uncle Leo, for instance, who sold his photo studio in Warsaw and went to Detroit. But those who stayed all perished—machine-gunned on the edge of town or murdered at Treblinka, a Nazi death camp in the gloomy forest. Also in that picture is Israel. It did not exist at the time, of course, but its creation was substantially the result of what happened that day in the Odeonsplatz.

Hitler, as much as Herzl, created Israel.

Had there been no First World War; had the mad Gavrilo Princip not been where he was not supposed to be; had he not chanced upon the car bearing the Austro-Hungarian Archduke Franz Ferdinand and his consort, Sophie; had he not shot the couple dead; had Germany not gone to war; had Hitler not survived the trenches; had the Allies invaded Germany itself and thrashed it so thoroughly that neither it nor any stab-in-the-back theory could have survived the defeat; had a madman not taken absolute control of the most powerful state in Europe; had he not bizarrely set out to kill all the Jews he could find anywhere he could find them; had the Jews of Europe not found themselves unable to go to America—as millions had already done—had they not been locked out of Palestine as well, doors closing all over the world, "coffin boats" loaded with refugees steaming frantically from port to port; had they not been murdered, in groups and one by one, until an Everest of bodies reached so high that it polluted heaven itself; had they not died by gas and bullet, by blow and disease, by starvation and fatigue, by depression and suicide, and then, when it all seemed over and the gates to the camps were thrown open, by the hands or clubs or pistols of their former neighbors; had history not stumbled and fallen, crashed and veered, tilted and turned; had the accidental not become the inevitable—had all this and more not happened; had six million souls expired the usual way, often in the pain that is the reward of life itself, then Israel, little Israel, would not have happened. But then after so many years of isolated murders, occasional pogroms, and bizarre restrictions—in Romania, during the interwar period, Jewish medical students were forbidden to work on gentile cadavers—the diligent Germans had organized a European killing machine that left the continent bereft of Jews and not particularly remorseful, either.

I cannot quite bring myself to yell "Run, run" where Israel is concerned, but that is where my logic takes me. There is a catastrophe looming, not inevitably, but possibly—maybe even probably. The impossible, the unimaginable, has already happened, but as we shall see, the conditions for a repeat, an echo—at the very least, *an attempt*—are ripening. The means toward this end, the ominous march of science that enabled Nazi Germany to murder with unprecedented efficiency, has enabled relatively poor countries to assemble arsenals of nuclear weapons. The laws of probability warn that some of these might either be used by their owners or—lost or stolen—fall into the hands of terrorist groups of the sort that behead people in the name of all that is holy. These groups hate Israel. These groups hate Jews.

Israel is the product of history's most murderous century. As a nation, Israel is a battered child. It is therefore difficult to reproach Israelis for their occasional cruelty, for their wavering resolve to expel the Arabs from their land, for their fierce determination to prevail no matter what; or to demand that they learn nothing from the past, forget everything from their past, and become—if it comes right down to it—the patsies of all history. The criminally insane had ruled Europe, and madness was official policy. What is amazing, what remains just plain extraordinary, is not that this madness produced even more madness but how, for the most part, it did not. And Israel is asked to, and sometimes does, give up land, a strategic advantage, so that others may be rid of this problem.

I had been brave to write that Israel was a mistake. I was told that over and over again. I had stood up to my own people and told the truth. The impolitic truth. I was dismayed by this reaction. I love my own people. I love their inadvertent insistence on defying political correctness and not to be like everyone else and instead be intellectually distinct, different. I love them for their disproportionate number of Nobel Prize winners, Pulitzer Prize winners, composers and lyricists, revolutionaries and reactionaries, for their great, incalculable wealth, for being merchant bankers, merchants, bankers, but rarely tellers. I love them for their wit and their sense of humor. I love them for their Judaism, their contribution to Christianity and Islam, ungrateful sons both. I love them for persevering. I love them for the enemies they have made, and I love them for surviving. I love them wistfully, for they are fading as a people and a force. The American Jewish community, more than half of the world's Jews, is shrinking. It assimilates and then assimilates some more. Jews had once been 4 percent of Americans; they are now under 2 percent, falling toward 1 percent and increasingly less preoccupied with Israel and less certain about what to do about it.

The creation of Israel was a product of its time and the product as well of a whole lot of what-ifs and odd circumstances: remorse and the fleeting marriage of philosemitism with a benign anti-Semitism. Theodor Herzl, Chaim Weizmann, and the other early Zionists understood that they could enlist bigotry and myth, the wealth and power that could be seen but particularly the wealth and power that could not be seen, in their cause. They were powerful beggars, coming to the crowned heads of Europe and to various chancelleries, hats in hand, while behind them, unseen and unheard, was a richly imagined army of bankers and financiers, writers and revolutionaries, conspirators in league with Masons and communists and industrialists. The power of the Jews lay not only in what they could do but even more in what others *thought* they could do.

Following the war and the Holocaust, anti-Semitism was out of victims and somewhat out of steam. It needed a breather, and in that odd and totally uncharacteristic moment, even the anti-Semitic Joseph Stalin supported the creation of the Jewish state, if only to vex Britain and gain a foothold in the Middle East. It was a window, cracked open as if to air out the stench of Auschwitz. The Soviet Union would soon resume its anti-Jewish ways, supporting the Arabs out of anticolonial brotherhood as well as reactionary Russian Jew hatred, but for that one historic moment, it seemed to forget who it was and what it believed and endorsed the creation of Israel.

Everything had come together: Western antipathy toward the odd and unlikable Arabs, Stalin's weird support, and, of course, that wonderful, almost unreal, historical moment when the United States was flush with oil and the Middle East merely important but not yet essential.

At the same time came a powerful ripening, a maturation, a virtual eruption of political, economic, and cultural power that is only now beginning, imperceptibly, to ebb. The American Jewish community, having been divided over both the wisdom and—for want of a better word—the *Americanism* of Zionism, came bursting out of the ghetto with its political muscles rippling. Give us Israel, it demanded—and Harry Truman, neck and neck in the presidential election of 1948 with the Republican Thomas Dewey, did.

And so Israel was created, beckoning the remnants of European Jewry (and, a bit later, those from Arab countries) into a supposedly safe place that wasn't safe at all. Many of the world's remaining Jews were collected—*herded* may be a better word—into a little country and within that country, concentrated in a vast urban area so compact that a single awful weapon could nearly complete the task of Hitler. It was, you can now see, a mistake.

2

The Founder

The founder of modern Israel would not have liked modern Israel. He would have considered it much too religious, too socialistic, too obsessed with Jerusalem, too Middle Eastern, too informal, and much too Jewish. He would have been stunned, and none too pleased, to find that the lingua franca was Hebrew (he much preferred his beloved German), and given the present circumstances, it's possible that he would have chosen to reside somewhere else. The country that Theodor Herzl created is not the country he had in mind.

What he envisioned was a Middle Eastern version of Vienna: many Jews, some Arabs, lots of palms, and, somehow, coffeehouses galore. In fact, were it not for the presence of so many repugnant Jews, German composer Richard Wagner himself might have felt at home in Herzl's Israel. In one of history's little jokes, it was Wagner's soaring music that provided the score for Herzl's activities.

Herzl wrote *Der Judenstaat* while stoked on the music of that arch-anti-Semite whose operas were performed frequently in Paris. "Only on those nights when no Wagner was performed did I have any doubts about the correctness of my idea," he wrote in his diary. After one performance of *Tannhäuser*, he settled on the idea of having an opera house in Israel.

In addition to opera houses, Herzl wanted cafés—"I shall transport over there genuine Viennese cafés"—and versions of Vienna's and Berlin's prestigious newspapers. Although he would have preferred the new nation to speak German, he was open to French or English. The one language he ruled out was Hebrew. "Who among us has a sufficient acquaintance with Hebrew to ask for a railway ticket in that language?" he wrote. As far as Herzl was concerned, Hebrew was the language of the synagogue, vaguely oriental and somewhat backward. It would have no place in his Jewish state. When he closed his eyes, he saw Vienna.

Herzl's creation, his "Jewish state," might be a state and would certainly be Jewish, but it would not be a *Jewish* state. It would, in fact, be nothing like what it would become, what with the outsized role played by religious political parties, government subsidies to religious institutions, exemptions for the very pious from military service—and, above all, the fierce religious motivation of some West Bank settlers and their conviction that they are doing what God wants.

As for the latter-day veneration of Jerusalem, a squalid little city that Herzl did not give a hoot about, he would have been either mystified or appalled, probably both. As a capital, he preferred Haifa: scenic, secular, and in Herzl's day, with a minuscule Jewish population. It may seem now that Jerusalem was the raison d'être for the very existence of Israel—as it says in Psalm 137:5, "If I forget thee, O Jerusalem, let my right hand wither"—but to the early Zionists, not the least of them the founder, Jerusalem was hardly worth a limb. Chaim Weizmann, Israel's first president, chose not to live there, and although David Ben-Gurion, the first prime minister, insisted on the symbolic centrality of the city, he too chose to live elsewhere. (He retired to the Negev Desert.)

Tel Aviv, the city of German expatriates, Bauhaus architecture, and robust secularism, was almost precisely what Herzl had in mind for his Israel. His Israel would not in the least way be religious. It would be, in fact, like Herzl himself: without religion to speak of. This Israel would be a place free from religious discrimination, free from all the usual European restrictions and quotas—universities, professional associations, and so on—free from opprobrium, and free, of course, from the threat of anti-Semitic violence. It would, in short, be a place where a Jew could be a free Jew, a proud Jew, a totally unfettered Jew, but it could also be a place—and this was most important—where a Jew could be free *not* to be a Jew.

Since Herzl largely defined his Judaism as not being a Christian, Jewish identity would lose its force and become virtually meaningless. Where there were few Christians and many Jews, Jews could be like Christians were in Europe—and Christians, it goes without saying, would be left alone. Under those conditions, Herzl could be what he already felt he was: a German-speaking citizen of the larger German-speaking world.

Herzl was one of those Jews driven mad by being Jewish. It's hard to appreciate such a malady now; it belongs to a distant era of fainting and vapors, smelling salts passed under the nose, neurasthenia, and a feverish sexual intensity produced, paradoxically, by stern Victorian codes of behavior and dress. (The immensely popular Austrian Jewish writer Stefan Zweig remarks in his memoir, *The World of Yesterday*, how covering the body from head to toe sexualized the least sexual parts of the body.)

For a secular Jew such as Herzl, being a Jew meant a suffocating oppression, a yearning to be merely a citizen of *Mittleuropa*, that swath of the continent where German was spoken, where Wagner was adored, where Goethe was read, and for which Heine always pined. This was its own cultural nation. It stretched east from the French border to Prague or Breslau, in what is now Poland and called Wroclaw. It was a country within a country—within several countries, actually: kingdoms such as Prussia or Bavaria or just sections of cities, like Prague or Warsaw, where the language of the most prestigious coffee-houses was often German.

In the important cities, German was the language of both the elite and progressive Jews. That diligent employee of the Worker's Accident Insurance Institute for the Kingdom of Bohemia, Franz Kafka, spoke and wrote in German, although he was also fluent in Czech. Herzl's family came from Hungary, but they spoke German. They considered themselves Germans, proud Germans, overly proud Germans. They loved the language. They loved the culture. They were entirely besotted. Their son felt no different: "I am a German Jew from Hungary, and I can never be anything but a German."

In a way, it's odd that Charles Darwin had to go all the way to the Galápagos Islands to formulate his theory of evolution. He thought that the extreme isolation of those islands, coupled with the absence of predators, had allowed the wildlife of the Galápagos to evolve in distinctly unique ways. But had this Englishman merely crossed the Channel, he might have found a similar sort of adaptation when it came to Jews.

The first adaptation would have been that of Jews themselves to a millennium of religious persecution. Its consequences were great, both to Jews and to their gentile neighbors. Jews were hemmed into ghettos where they developed a language and a culture of their own. Much of it was based on what gentiles must have seen as their odd, recalcitrant religion with its invidious rejection of Jesus Christ as the Messiah. Some of it was simply the product of hundreds of years of ghetto life, of persecution—of fear of the stranger and what he might do and, too often, did.

Persecution forced Jews into moneylending (usury), which was useful to the general community but odious just the same, and from there into the nimble manipulation of money and figures—interest rates and such. Jews were pushed into commerce, which had little prestige and no glory. They were barred from all sorts of professions and, in Russia, even from the civil service, and so they found that the best boss, the most benign, was themselves. Since they could not work for gentiles, since they could not work for the government—Jews made up less than 2 percent of Poland's civil servants and less than 1 percent of Weimar Germany's—since they could not teach in the public schools, and since the army was closed to them except as conscripts, they worked for themselves. They were shopkeepers and artisans, often in the garment trades and often in home workshops and almost never in agriculture, mining, or industrial work.

The result was a paradox. A web of discriminatory regulations, practices, and traditions kept many if not most Jews in poverty but enabled a few to become rich. A farmworker could not better himself materially, especially if the farm he worked was not his. But a shopkeeper, a moneylender, a merchant, or even a carter whose son would become Rudolph Cohen of New York City could amass some wealth and then some more wealth and then, in a generation of hard work and parsimony, maybe riches.

Jews were particularly well situated to exploit the capitalistic energy unleashed by the Protestant Reformation of the sixteenth century. They could make use of their intellect, of what the pen could do on paper, instead of what the sword could do to flesh or the plow to soil. In time, with the emergence of capitalism, these traits would become essential and would make certain Jews rich, but they somehow provided even the impoverished masses with the knack of succeeding in other fields: law, medicine, science, music, literature, and, of course, journalism.

Lifting the boot from the neck of Jews in western and, later, central Europe, produced an explosion of talent and brilliance that was simply stunning. Stefan

Zweig, an example of both, wrote that "9/10ths of what the world celebrates as Viennese culture in the 19th century was promoted, nourished or even created by Viennese Jewry." In Vienna itself, every tenth person by 1880 was Jewish—and, with the highest rate of conversion in Europe, desperate not to be—and many in Vienna and elsewhere were echoing Wagner's earlier complaint that Jewish culture had corrupted German culture. He published his essay "Judaism in Music" in 1850, when he was living in exile in Zurich, Switzerland, and not yet the musical titan he was to become. But Wagner kept his nose to the anti-Semitic grindstone, overcoming his friendship with individual Jews to incessantly warn about Jews in general until his death in 1883. He was determined, he said, to "emancipate German culture from the yoke of Judaism."

Herzl's was the new face of the European Jew. A journalist like so many others, he was one generation removed from the shtetl, the Jewish ghetto or village, moving away from it at warp speed and on his way, like so many other Jews, to the ultimate in assimilation: conversion. Herzl himself stopped short, but countless others did not, and this presented anti-Semitism, if not the anti-Semite, with a problem: What do you do with a Jew who is no longer a Jew?

Herzl was a man possessed, and such a man is dangerous—or great. He was a psychological mess, miserable in his marriage (and miserable to his wife), fixated on young girls, in the manic grip of one scheme or another, and, pathetically, a touch anti-Semitic. When it came to Jews, he liked only those like himself: urbane, sophisticated, assimilated—Jewish only by designation, not by religious conviction or lifestyle. And while he could not quite bring himself to convert to Christianity, he nevertheless urged that other Jews do so. His thinking was coldly logical: no more Jews, no more Jewish problem.

Herzl did not use the term "Jewish problem." Instead, in *Der Judenstaat* (*The Jewish State*) and in his other writings, he employed its functional equivalent, "the Jewish Question." This and similar phrases were later made infamous by the Nazis and associated with mass murder. It had no such connotation in Herzl's day. It presupposed that the "question" was not solely one of religious or ethnic bias—not one of perception—but also of religious or ethnic behavior or appearance. In other words, while anti-Semites could certainly be blamed for the occasionally shabby treatment of Jews like Herzl or for snubbing that erstwhile Jew Benjamin Disraeli, the former British prime minister, they could be pardoned for how they felt about eastern European Jews, especially the religious, with their weird garb, customs, and appearance.

Appearance was not all that separated the caricature of the Jew from the ordinary gentile. There was also the matter of behavior: their perceived loudness, their allegedly shady business practices, their supposedly disproportionate numbers in the underworld, and, of looming importance, their preponderance in the radical political parties of the day.

Today we might call this "blaming the victim" and hoot Herzl out of the hall for political incorrectness. After all, if you close off certain occupations to members of a group, then, of course, crime becomes attractive to them. If you deny them the protection of the law or if the law itself becomes an instrument of persecution, then, of course, they will have contempt for the law.

The sociological explanations go on and on, but at the end of the nineteenth century, sociology itself was yet to come. It was then mostly undisputed that Jews acted and looked like Jews simply because they were Jews. Herzl, something of a deracinated Jew, might not have argued.

The late Israeli historian and biographer of Herzl, Amos Elon, found several examples of Herzl expressing ugly opinions about his coreligionists. From his diary: "Yesterday grande soiree at the Teitels'. Some thirty or forty ugly little Jews and Jewesses. No consoling sight."

After visiting the beach at Ostend, Belgium: "Although there are many Viennese and Budapest Jews here, the rest of the vacationing public is very pleasant." What makes these observations particularly jarring, if not incomprehensible, is that they were contained in a letter to his parents, Viennese Jews. They were originally from Budapest themselves—although clearly of the right sort.

It was obvious to Herzl that anti-Semitism did not exist in a vacuum, the inventive concoction of the paranoid, but seemed to be a natural, even understandable, response to the Jew himself, to certain Jews in particular, and, above all, to Jews when they were numerous. "Wherever it [anti-Semitism] does not exist, it is brought in together with Jewish immigrants," he wrote. "We are naturally drawn into those places where we are not persecuted, and our appearance there gives rise to persecution. This is the case, and will inevitably be so, everywhere, even in highly civilized countries—see, for instance, France—so long as the Jewish question is not solved on the political level. The unfortunate Jews are now carrying the seeds of anti-Semitism into England; they have already introduced it into America."

The modifier *unfortunate* does little to take the sting off Herzl's snooty observation. He ignored the fact that anti-Semitism was quite capable of existing even when deprived of its oxygen, Jews. It had done so in England, for instance. From 1290, when Edward I banished Jews from his kingdom, to 1656, when Oliver Cromwell let them back in, there were no Jews at all in England. And yet sometime between 1596 and 1598, William Shakespeare was able to conjure the greatest, most complex, most fascinating of all anti-Semitic stereotypes: the repellent Shylock of *The Merchant of Venice.*

By Shakespeare's time, the avaricious, heartless Jew was already established as a stock character. Just a few years earlier, Londoners could have seen Christopher Marlowe's *The Jew of Malta,* with its hideous Jewish caricature, Barabas—yet another merchant. With both Shakespeare and Marlowe, their Jew was only partly their creation. He was also an anti-Semitic stereotype. Shylock's palpable humanity was not, as some insist, a way of showing that the Jew, too, was human, but served a useful theatrical purpose (pure evil is dramatically uninteresting) and as a warning: the Jew could both look and act like anyone else. If you pricked him, he did indeed bleed.

Herzl must have had the hardest time coming to grips with anti-Semitism. In his day, it was still religion based: a loathing of the Jews for their rejection of Christ and for His crucifixion. Added to that was the matter of ethnicity. The classic Jew, the stereotypical Jew, was a bearded fellow who spoke an odd language (Yiddish), dressed exotically, and practiced a mirror-image religion: Sabbath on Saturday instead of Sunday. He was perverse and engaged in all sorts of perverse endeavors, everything from moneylending to outright criminality. But Herzl was none of those things. He dressed like the proper Viennese. He spoke a proper German. He practiced no religion to speak of, and Saturday was just another day to him. He saw himself as German. Surely the world would see him the same way.

To that end, Herzl joined a dueling society while at the University of Vienna and actually fought a duel. By the 1890s, though, university and sporting clubs throughout the empire were not only closing their membership to Jews but also refusing to duel with Jewish clubs. To win was hardly to gain honor; to lose was ignominy beyond endurance. The new and rising social enmity toward Jews was, as Herzl himself might have guessed, a response to the influx of eastern Jews into Vienna and the rise of nationalism.

The first wave of the new anti-Semitism coincided, appropriately enough, with the death of Richard Wagner in 1883. It was then that Herzl abandoned his efforts to be a proper, assimilated (Jewish) German, and resigned from his dueling society. It was becoming clearer and clearer that no Jew, no matter how accomplished with the saber, could ever attain what the dueling scar (*Renommierschmiss*) represented: admission into the university's elite and, thereafter, into the highest levels of German and Austrian society. To save his son, Hans, from this fate, he refused to have him circumcised—a sacred obligation for a Jewish parent. Herzl knew exactly what he was doing. He was rejecting an identity that would "sour and blacken his [Hans's] life as mine has been soured and blackened."

Herzl was wrong on that score. Being a Jew was unrelated to religious belief or practice. Jewishness was a condition of birth, a crushing affliction. If one were religious, then that was one thing, and piety must have brought solace, if not clarity. But particularly for secular, assimilated Jews, being Jewish was some sort of noneradicable stain, a birth defect that could never be rectified. Marcel Proust, himself the grandson of a Jewish currency speculator, likened Jews to homosexuals: in certain salons, both were regarded "with sophisticated curiosity."

By the late 1800s, European anti-Semitism was taking off at a gallop, propelled by the growth of nationalism and the expansion of democracy. The old anti-Semitism had been replaced by one designed to appeal to the rabble. Many forces were at work, and no two nations were the same, but in Vienna, something very important happened. The year was 1887, and Karl Lueger was running for mayor.

Lueger was an affable demagogue, a nimble politician who responded to the influx of eastern Jews into Vienna by adopting anti-Semitism as the central plank of his platform. He ran for mayor three times, and each time was blocked by Emperor Franz Joseph I from claiming his prize. The old emperor had spent a lifetime juggling the ethnic animosities and ambitions of Austria-Hungary's countless peoples. Lueger went after the Jews, and while the emperor might not have cared much about them, he did care a great deal about the principle of the thing—the threat to ethnic equilibrium—and so he squashed Lueger and his ugly movement over and over again. The third time, though, an exhausted Franz Joseph acquiesced. In 1897 Lueger took office.

For the next thirteen years, Lueger was mayor of the capital city—and a good mayor he was. He modernized the municipal water system and in other ways prepared the infrastructure that allowed Vienna to grow and prosper. He also recognized and exploited the immense power of anti-Semitism, made all the more politically potent by the growth and enfranchisement of the lower and middle classes.

Lueger was a particularly dangerous anti-Semite if only because he might not, at heart, have been one. The Austrian historian Brigitte Hamann quotes the merchant Sigmund Mayer as telling Lueger, "I'm not blaming you for being anti-Semitic; I'm blaming you for *not* being anti-Semitic."

Not only was Lueger a personally charming man whose actual policies represented no threat to the Jews, but among his personal friends were several Jews. When confronted about this, Lueger famously replied, "I decide who's a Jew."

Stefan Zweig, yet another Jew whose religion was German culture and who was undoubtedly feeling a bit uneasy himself at the influx of eastern Jews into Vienna, recalled Lueger's tenure with equanimity: "His city administration was perfectly just and even typically democratic." In fact, Zweig—normally a keen observer of his times—managed to sleepwalk through those years in Vienna without, as he put it, "the slightest suppression or indignity as a Jew." (When, in 1942, he committed suicide while in exile in Brazil, it was because he had been reduced by the Nazis to being nothing more than a Jew—or so wrote Hannah Arendt, the acerbic German-Jewish philosopher and émigré to America.)

Either way, authentic anti-Semite or merely repugnant opportunist, Lueger was a despicable fellow. His language, when it came to Jews, was harsh and ugly. He invoked all the usual insect metaphors: locusts and such. And he did not shy from rhetoric suggesting that the only good Jew was a dead Jew. Lueger showed other European politicians how anti-Semitism could be harnessed for victory at the polls. It was in this era that August Ferdinand Bebel, a founder of Germany's Social Democratic Party, dubbed anti-Semitism "the socialism of fools" because it had an even greater political punch than the promise of an eight-hour day and holidays at the beach.

Hitler, living in Vienna at the time, cited his debt to Lueger even though, as he ruefully acknowledged, Lueger was a hopelessly old-fashioned Jew hater and did not define Jewishness biologically. As far as Lueger was concerned, a splash of water—baptism—could cleanse the Jew of all that made him despicable. Hitler differed with that but nevertheless credited Lueger as a mentor. With

Lueger, anti-Semitism became an inextricable part of right-wing politics. Hitler believed; Lueger did not necessarily believe, but Hitler believed that Lueger did.

From then on, it would not do merely to keep Jews out of the best clubs; a Hamburg dockworker was not likely to care about that. It was now necessary to take harsher measures that would satisfy the rising nationalistic desire to be one people. At the same time, the old, customary anti-Semitism still thrived.

The Jew was despised for not being a Christian as well as for a host of despicable personal characteristics, everything from lechery to avarice to a magical way with money, and, increasingly, what seemed like a genetic disposition toward radicalism. There were so many reasons to hate Jews, so many reasons to punish them. Anti-Semitism was the most adaptable, plastic, and malleable of all conspiracy theories. To the believer, it explained so much. In fact, it explained almost everything.

Many Jews tried converting. After an awkward transition period, that worked, and the societies of central Europe abounded with erstwhile Jews, some of them generations removed from Judaism. In Germany, former Jews could become army officers, whereas actual Jews were restricted to the reserves. Still, a kind of taint lingered.

Moses Mendelssohn came to the gates of Berlin in 1743 as a pious Jew with a desire to further his religious education. His eldest son lapsed into no religion at all, and his grandson, the musical prodigy Felix, was baptized and raised a Christian. Nonetheless, even though Felix popularized the music of J. S. Bach, wrote sacred music himself, married a minister's daughter, and was so thoroughly and unquestionably a Christian that he was buried in a church graveyard, he never was able to shake his Jewish identity—not in his own time; not, certainly, in the Nazi period; and not even in our own. (In Jiri Weil's darkly comic 1960 novel *Mendelssohn Is on the Roof,* the Nazis order that a bust of Mendelssohn be removed from the roof of the Prague concert hall. The SS, told to choose the bust with the biggest nose, selects Hitler's favorite, Richard Wagner.)

Gustav Mahler, too, tried to slip the skin of his Jewishness, converting to Catholicism out of indifference to Judaism and for compelling career reasons. As the personification of precisely what Wagner so despised—the Jewish modernist—Mahler was routinely vilified in Vienna's robust anti-Semitic press until he eventually left his post at the Vienna Court Opera. Not only did his conversion to Catholicism not matter much to his contemporaries, but it has hardly mattered to subsequent generations, either. He is still a Jewish composer, although the modifier *Jewish* has gone from an epithet to an inferred explanation of his anguish, his genius—even the supposed hint of a klezmer band in his First Symphony. At the very least, it adds to his aura.

Almost anywhere in central and eastern Europe, being a Jew was becoming more and more onerous, a nagging low-grade fever. Herzl certainly suffered from it. His father had amassed a small fortune in finance and had largely left his Judaism, but not his Jewish identity, behind. For the son, though, this vestigial identity was an affliction. It not only set Herzl apart from the rest of German-speaking society but also marked him as related to the bizarre, pious Jews of eastern Europe, the very ones who were moving west and taking up residence in Vienna and Berlin—an alien people, speaking a ghetto tongue, working at demeaning trades, having no loyalty to the state (which had so recently oppressed them), and belonging not to a nation but to a tribe of their own.

Herzl's Zionism was really his second pass at solving the Jewish problem. The first had been a zany scheme to have all Jews convert to Christianity: to rescue his fellow Jews, Herzl concocted a grandiose plan for a mass conversion. It would be a gigantic, moving event presided over by the princes of the Roman Catholic Church, including the prince of all the princes: the pope in Rome. Herzl even had the venues picked out. In Vienna, the event would take place precisely at noon at St. Stephen's, the city's cathedral, where the emperor came annually on Corpus Christi to lead his nation in prayer. Significantly, one Jew who would not convert to Christianity, who would attend and lead other Jews to the cross but dramatically stop short, was Herzl himself. Conversion was not for him.

Herzl was not insane—just a trifle mad. What made him so was the plight of his fellow Jews and his times. His great awakening came when his employer, Vienna's (Jewish-owned) *Neue Freie Presse,* made him its Paris correspondent, and he wound up covering the treason trial of Alfred Dreyfus. The army captain was the stiff, humorless, reluctant personification of modernity, but a mere pawn in a fight between French progressives and conservatives. The trial consumed France, stirring up squalls of anti-Semitism that Herzl saw, with horror and uncanny prescience, as a harbinger of the whirlwind of barbarism to come. The trial of Dreyfus did not take place in backward Russia but in France, arguably the most liberal and progressive country on the European continent. It was France that had toppled its monarchy, had beheaded its king, had given the world "Liberty, Equality, Fraternity," had taken the Church down a peg or two, and even—for a while—had changed the names of the months. France had emancipated its Jews—a community of only fifty thousand—granting full citizenship in 1791, while the others states of Europe, including Britain, had not yet done so. The fact that Dreyfus was an army officer said something about France; in Germany, that was not yet possible.

And yet Dreyfus was degraded. His sword was broken, his epaulets ripped from his uniform, his reputation sullied, his career ruined, and his health broken—all because he was a Jew.

In *Der Judenstaat,* Herzl concluded, "The Jewish question persists wherever Jews live in appreciable numbers." As it turned out, France did not have "appreciable numbers" of Jews—maybe 2 percent of the general population—but it did have some prominent ones (the de Rothschilds, above all), and, more to the point, it did have a reactionary and embattled Roman Catholic Church. What alarmed the Church and reactionary France in general was the threat posed by modernity. For this, the dour, virtually charmless Dreyfus was in some sense the perfect representation. Where once officers might be chosen for their place in society, for their charm and connections, they were now the product of an examination—and Dreyfus scored very high indeed. But he was not, as you might suppose, the lone Jew in an army of Catholics and maybe a few Protestants. In *Why the Dreyfus Affair Matters,* Louis Begley tells us there were some three hundred Jewish officers in the French army at the end of the nineteenth century. Five of them were generals.

Dreyfus embodied yet another caricature: the Jew as unstoppable nerd. In fact, a member of the panel that examined him when he completed his military studies gave him high marks for his technical knowledge (19 out of 20), but an insulting zero for his military bearing. This was an attempt to keep Dreyfus from being assigned to the general staff, where, as a Jew, he was distinctly not wanted. He might be smart, he might test well, and he might even be brave. He was, though, simply not French.

Dreyfus went off to Devil's Island, and Herzl went off to write. He must have identified mightily with the wretched man. They had both chosen to make their way in the gentile world: Herzl as a writer, Dreyfus in the more exotic military. They were both forced to confront the fact that what they considered the least significant part of their being—not their talent, not their industriousness, not their impeccable morality, but their altogether irrelevant Jewishness—was to others the most relevant.

To Herzl, Dreyfus proved the utter futility of believing that progress would help the Jews, save the Jews—free the Jews from restrictions, quotas, hostile looks, and, of course, from having to *be* Jewish. He got so much wrong. He was so thoroughly a European of a particular time, a denizen of *Mittleuropa* who shared its assumptions of cultural superiority, so blithely dismissive of what were to become the Palestinians, and so certain of his right to simply buy or finagle a piece of the Middle East without so much as a by-your-leave from the people who lived there, that his genius is easy to overlook. What he got right overshadowed all the rest. He sensed the coming calamity, not in the brooding way that Kafka did (or is thought to have done) but in an immensely practical way. He realized that only the Jews could save the Jews. "The hand of fate shall also seize Hungarian Jewry," he later wrote to a Jewish member of the Hungarian parliament. This was 1903, a year before Herzl's death. He concluded his warning with these words: "There is no escape."

3

Anti-Semitism:
A Gift to the Jews

In 1898 Theodor Herzl hurried from Vienna to Palestine to meet with the German kaiser, Wilhelm II. This was to be their second meeting. Their first, in the Ottoman capital of Constantinople, had left Herzl buoyant. Wilhelm had reacted enthusiastically to the idea of establishing a Jewish entity in what was then Ottoman-ruled Palestine. To this end, the kaiser volunteered to use his presumed influence with the Ottoman sultan, and, in exchange, Herzl would use the considerable wealth of international Jewry both to compensate the kaiser for his troubles and to upgrade Palestine. The kaiser mentioned the need for more water. Herzl, without hesitation, said in effect, No problem. The Jews will pay for it.

"Well, money you have plenty," Wilhelm told Herzl. "More money than any of us."

In his diary, Herzl says the kaiser tapped his boot with his riding crop—a bit of Prussian exuberance, apparently.

The meetings had aspects of a comic opera. The kaiser had pitched his tent in an empty lot on Jerusalem's Street of the Prophets. (The two men had met barely a week earlier at a spot south of where Tel Aviv is now located.) Despite literally being surrounded by Palestinians, Herzl and Wilhelm conducted themselves as if those very people did not exist at all. No mention was made of them, and no mention was made, either, of other Arabs with an interest in the future of Palestine. Those included the Syrians and the Egyptians and, deep in the Arabian Desert at the time, the Hashemites, who would someday rule Iraq and Jordan. (Also missing, of course, was that desert chieftain, Abdul al-Aziz ibn Abd al-Rahman Al Saud, who would displace the Hashemites as custodians of Mecca and Medina and become the king of a country he named after himself.) As was the custom, the locals were excluded and their fates discussed—if not decided—by one colonial power (Germany) attempting to act for another (the Ottoman Turks) by dealing with the presumed agent of a third (the Jews of Europe).

Even for that era, the kaiser had taken matters one step too far. The sultan was not quite as compliant as he thought. The Muslim Turks were simply not going to turn over Jerusalem to the Jews. The sultan, with what must have been some impatience, made that clear to Herzl over and over again. Abdul-Hamid II's full title was His Imperial Majesty, the Sultan Abdülhamid II, emperor of the Ottomans, Caliph of the Faithful—and it was the last bit that thwarted Herzl. The Ottoman monarch, like the pope, had religious as well as temporal obligations. He was caliph, self-proclaimed leader of all Muslims, and while in reality that did not amount to much—he was widely ignored, was hardly a religious scholar, and could claim no descent from the Prophet Muhammad—he nevertheless was the custodian of Islam's three holy cities, one of which was Jerusalem.

The importance of Jerusalem can hardly be overstated. It was not just another historic Muslim city, such as Damascus or Baghdad, but the city from which Muhammad ascended to heaven. From AD 610 to AD 623, Muslims prayed facing Jerusalem. It was only later that Mecca became the religion's focal point, but Jerusalem never lost its importance or, after it became the capital of Israel, its power as a cause in its own right. Herzl might as well have been asking the pope to sell Vatican City. His offer was both preposterous and insulting.

Still, the Ottomans were desperate; maybe some sort of deal could be made. The so-called Sick Man of Europe was wheezing, and the diplomats of Europe were pacing, like greedy heirs, waiting for the old man to expire. The 1878 Treaty of San Stefano that followed a Russian-Turkish war had jarred Bulgaria loose from the Ottoman Empire. The empire was shedding possessions, and just about everything seemed to be in play. Who would get what remained of Constantinople's territories? Who would get the Middle East, with its increasingly important waterway, the Suez Canal? Who would get Lebanon and the prestige of protecting its Christians? Indeed, who eventually would get Palestine and the Christian holy places, the goal of so many Crusades? All during the nineteenth century, hunks of the Ottoman Empire had been pried free. Why not arid, worthless Palestine?

Herzl had come to his meetings with the kaiser with mostly empty pockets. He had little more than his own personal wealth and whatever funds his associates could raise. All together, they had access to some money, but nowhere near what it would take to buy a piece of the Middle East, even if it were for sale. The storied rich Jews of Europe—and there were some—were almost to a man opposed to Herzl's mad scheme, and some were downright hostile to it. In France, the mightiest Jew of them all, Baron Rothschild, repeatedly snubbed him. In fact, the publication of *Der Judenstaat* produced mostly a collective yawn among Herzl's own assimilated and increasingly secular Jews of central and western Europe—and those who were not bored were irate. In certain circles, Herzl himself was seen as a bit of a crackpot. One of Herzl's friends, Dr. Emil Schiff, urged him to burn the manuscript, and that most renowned of Viennese Jews, the eminent Zweig himself, referred to Herzl's masterpiece as "this obtuse text, this piece of nonsense."

Theodor Herzl possessed immense self-confidence, and he was both an accomplished and industrious writer. But his greatest talent was his ability to see over the horizon, to somehow intuit what was coming for European Jews. In his own milieu, his apprehension was hardly universally shared. For most wealthy and influential Jews, things were only getting better. Barriers were falling, restrictions being repealed or eroded. Being a Jew was turning out to be not such a bad thing—not as good as being a Christian, but a long way from being deprived of life, liberty, and whatever could be hidden in the mattress. Foreshadowing what many Israelis later saw as the infuriating apathy of western Jews after the creation of the State—oodles of donations sent, but very few people—the assimilated Jews of enlightened Europe wanted only to assimilate some more. The horror that Herzl saw coming at western Jewry remained invisible to them.

The kaiser, however, accepted Herzl for what he wasn't: the face of rich European Jewry. He was unaware that Herzl's true following did not live west of Potsdam, but east of it. The helpless, hapless, downtrodden, and flat-broke masses of eastern Europe were Herzl's most appreciative audience. Among them were some scattered rich, but in the main, the Jews of the Pale of Settlement, of the shtetl, the town, the village, and the ghettos of the larger cities, lived poorly and often illegally. Here there was, imperceptibly, a stirring, a yearning to escape from an empire that was taunting history by becoming increasingly oppressive. These Jews were Herzl's fodder, but he hardly knew they existed.

In the Russian Empire, Jews were relegated to the Pale of Settlement, the considerable area that Catherine the Great had established for her despised Jewish subjects. The Pale encompassed portions of what is now Poland, Lithuania, Ukraine, Belarus, and parts of (western) Russia itself. By law, Jews were forced to live there (exceptions were granted), and even within the Pale, parts—including whole cities—were off-limits. Jews were barred from certain professions, professional schools, even grade schools.

This was no *Fiddler on the Roof* existence: genteel poverty, rich family life, and the occasional song. This was a life of grinding poverty, of filth and disease, of furious adherence to tradition and antipathy to progress—of a Jewish culture shaped by hatred and fear and determinedly xenophobic. The creation of the Pale was rooted in the standard religious and cultural hatred of Jews. But it had a utilitarian aspect, too. By keeping the crafty Jew out of Moscow or Saint Petersburg, the government shielded Christian Russians from economic competition.

Russia at the time was two countries—or *at least* two countries. Whatever it was for Russians or Ukrainians or Poles or ethnic Germans, it was something else for Jews. The country was not tacitly anti-Semitic or effectively anti-Semitic; it was legally, formally, and quite proudly anti-Semitic.

Still, not even Russia was impervious to modernity. Change was under way. Its agent at one point was the czar himself, Alexander II. He had come to the throne in 1855, and, defying expectations, this onetime martinet became a reformer. Most significantly, in 1861 he freed the serfs. That was two years before Abraham Lincoln issued the Emancipation Proclamation, freeing slaves in a nation, the Confederate States of America, over which he had no authority.

For Jews, Alexander II turned out to be not quite a Lincoln. Still, he made a difference. The previous czar, Nicholas I, had expanded the practice known as Cantonism. The original system had been established by Peter the Great in

1721 to provide for the military education of young boys. Under Nicholas I, the system was used to take Jewish boys as young as eight and forcibly induct them into the army for a period of twenty-five years. The boys were treated cruelly and usually compelled to convert to Christianity.

The Jews of Russia lived in dread of their children being abducted by bounty hunters or seized by the military. During that period, the heartrending wail of the concluding prayer of the Yom Kippur service, *Ne'ilah,* was often a plea to God to save the souls of the boys ripped from the community and never expected to return. Alexander II abolished the system. As far as is known, it had produced exactly one Jewish officer: Herzl Yankl Tsam, drafted as a seventeen-year-old and made captain forty-one years later. He never converted.

In 1881 Alexander II was assassinated. A handful of Jews were implicated in the plot, and the result was the usual anti-Semitic mayhem. In all, over two hundred Jews were beaten to death, and the new government set about reversing Alexander's reforms. Alexander III was an uncomplicated anti-Semite. As far as he was concerned, his father's reforms had been a debacle. Among other things, the new liberalization had enabled Jews to infiltrate the cities and compete in business with Russians. That could not be tolerated.

Russia persisted in hurling back progress. In 1891 all of Moscow was made off-limits to Jews; those already in the city were required to return to the Pale. A series of anti-Jewish laws were promulgated. Jews were prohibited from buying or leasing land, from moving from their shtetlach to the towns, and from doing business on Christian holy days. Quotas were instituted—in schools, in professions, in the civil service. By 1887, the quotas for high school and college were reduced to 10 percent within the Pale and 5 percent outside the Pale. In practice, this meant that many Jews could go no further than elementary school. For the young Leon Trotsky, then Lev Davidovich Bronstein, a one-time inability to circumvent the quota system amounted to his only significant brush with official anti-Semitism.

In some respects, the Jews of late-nineteenth-century Russia could be likened to the blacks of the Jim Crow South. The comparison is facile, but useful. Like American blacks in Dixie, Jews in the Russian empire had unpredictable and unreliable protection under the law and, too often, from the law. Jews were not entitled to schooling, and they were banned from all sorts of trades or employment. As with African Americans, a burst of progress—the Emancipation Proclamation, the defeat of the Confederacy, and the Thirteenth, Fourteenth, and Fifteenth civil rights amendments to the Constitution—was followed by regression and racial segregation enforced by law and violence.

Jews, too, went reeling backward. Not only were their rights taken from them, but so too was the faith that things would get better. The slaves had been freed, the serfs had been freed, but for Jews, time's arrow was hurtling backward. Conditions were getting worse. Life was harder. Is it any wonder that America beckoned? And if not America, then Palestine, the idealized homeland. To these Russian and Polish Jews, Herzl's pamphlet was a road map: this way out.

In the Russian Empire, the document Herzl produced had an electrifying effect. He was not just another rabbi or dreamer, delirious on the vapors of religion, but a secular western Jew, a proper gentleman with a top hat and servants. He had come via Budapest and Vienna, resplendent cities both, and even from Paris, and in all these places, he knew prominent, powerful people—the fabled rich Jews of the West and government leaders as well. He therefore had standing. Just as important, he had timing.

For a thousand years, Jews at the Passover Seder had recited "*L'shana ha'ba-ah b'Yerushalayim*": "Next year in Jerusalem." And while probably few considered "next year" to be anything other than a euphemism for the unreachable future, the fact remained that Jerusalem was a real place, and someday "next year" would arrive. A return to Zion was improbable but not impossible.

Now, though, Zionism was in the air. Herzl published *Der Judenstaat* in 1896, but three years earlier the term *Zionism* had been coined by Nathan Birnbaum, an Austrian publisher. Nearly a half century before that, Benjamin Disraeli, in his novel *Contarini Fleming*, had envisioned a Jewish state, and about three hundred years earlier, Joseph Nasi, a so-called court Jew of the sixteenth-century Ottoman Empire, had come up with a scheme to resettle the Palestinian towns of Safad and Tiberias with Jews from the Diaspora. Like Herzl, Nasi was not waiting for the coming of the Messiah.

In Herzl's era, much of Europe was being roiled by nascent nationalisms of which Zionism was but one example—although, for many reasons, a very odd example. (For one thing, its "nationals" were scattered all over the globe, and for another, they lacked a unifying language.) But the concept of creating a nation of like-minded people out of like-minded people was certainly in the air. If the Greeks could do it, if the Bulgarians could do it, if, indeed, the Germans and the Italians could do it, then certainly the Jews could do it, too. It's true, they did not have a land of their own, but as every Bible reader knew, they once did.

So it was that Herzl's little pamphlet, written in German, hit with concussive force when it arrived in the Pale of Settlement. David Ben-Gurion, Israel's first prime minister, was ten years old when news of Herzl's words reached his shtetl (Płońsk in Poland), but many years later, he could still recall the excitement it produced.

In a way, this little book caused the same sort of excitement as did Sabbatai Zevi (1626–1676), the so-called false Messiah, and for similar reasons. Zevi's rise corresponded with the massacres of Jews under Bohdan Khmelnytsky (1595–1657), considered the father of the Ukrainian nation. Vast numbers of Jews were killed, ostensibly because they were rent collectors and estate agents for Polish landowners, but also because, in the case of women, children, and others, they were just Jews. As it happened, Khmelnytsky killed more Poles than he did Jews, but there were far more of them to start with. In any case, the mass murders pitched the Jews of the area (present-day Poland, Ukraine, Lithuania) into despondency. Zevi, a charismatic charmer and eccentric who claimed to be the Messiah, later converted to Islam and, after assembling a healthy following, died in obscurity, probably in the Balkans.

Nothing quite as awful as the Khmelnytsky pogrom was happening at the dawn of the twentieth century, but for Jews, the times were nevertheless hardly propitious. Not only were they still confined to the Pale and still living in squalid poverty, but the modest reforms of the liberal czar, Alexander II, were being reversed. For Russian Jews, the new restrictions were the last straw. They immigrated—most to America, some to Argentina, and some to Palestine. For those who remained—at least another three million—Herzl's scheme was a Jewish solution to the Jewish problem.

The kaiser may have been perplexed. Who was this Herzl who was representing the Jews and, on that basis, was granted an audience? The answer was plain, if not particularly flattering. He was a high-strung Viennese writer, an assimilated Jew with conventional views about unassimilated Jews, an apparent neurotic (my diagnosis) with an astonishing capacity for work. Had he ambled out of his Vienna residence at 6 Berggasse and knocked on the door of 19, he might very well have been told by his neighbor, a certain Dr. Freud, that he had delusions of grandeur and other psychic ills to boot. Yet this pitiful Jew, this feverishly neurotic and deluded man, was pulling off one of the great con jobs of history. His power lay solely in the mind's eye of the kaiser. It was not who Herzl was that mattered; it was who the kaiser thought he was.

Whatever the case, nothing stopped Herzl. He found it perfectly reasonable that he should be meeting with the emperor of Germany, the king of Prussia, this prince of the House of Hohenzollern, because he knew that while the kaiser's empire was huge and powerful, the Jewish empire was even greater—as limitless as the prejudiced mind could imagine. It stretched forever, around the globe and from deepest antiquity, and it was endowed, as the kaiser himself had just said, with money galore.

This was the magical wealth of the Jews. This was the vast riches of the tribe. It was immeasurable because it was far too big to occupy a mere physical space. It filled the vast vault of the anti-Semite's imagination: gold or jewels or whatever piled as high as the sky and reaching back one thousand years or so. This was wealth that could not be seen or measured or touched, and it was not used, for mysteriously devious reasons, to alleviate the dreadful poverty of the eastern European shtetl or of urban slums such as Berlin's or London's East End. As if to deepen the mystery, it could not be used, either, to protect eastern European Jews from the occasional pogrom—rapes and murders and such—but it existed nonetheless.

Herzl's unseen entourage was called, is still called, International Jewry. It was a prolific check writer, a force of incalculable political influence. It controlled international banking, also international communism—just about international anything, including at one time (or so the Nation of Islam leader Louis Farrakhan often said) the international slave trade. As recently as 2009, the then Iranian president, Mahmoud Ahmadinejad, referred in a speech to the United Nations General Assembly to Jewish control of international finance. "It is unacceptable that a small minority should dominate the politics, economy, and culture of vast parts of the world through a complicated network, and establish a new form, in fact, of slavery, and harm the reputation of other nations, even European nations and the United States, to attain its racist ambitions," he told the UN.

International Jewry, aka the International Jewish Conspiracy, has always worked in mysterious ways—sometimes in tandem with the forces of international finance, sometimes in tandem with its foe, international communism, sometimes in league with international Masonry—but always for its own peculiar and selfish interests. It had vast powers, including the power to obliterate contradictions.

The kaiser was hardly alone in his conviction that somewhere in Jewland was an immense amount of money. The Ottoman sultan had received Herzl for the same reason. Herzl wanted to buy Palestine outright, and the sultan, hardly an idiot—he had traveled abroad, and his favorite books were the Sherlock Holmes mysteries—nevertheless thought that Herzl had the means to do it. In fact, Abdul Hamid had other territories to sell. How about Syria? How about Sinai? The two men negotiated, Herzl having already smoothed his path with ample amounts of baksheesh. The British had bought Cyprus from Turkey in 1878 and in so doing had established a principle. The hard-up Ottomans were willing to sell some of what they had. Why not Palestine?

In the end, nothing came of Herzl's unlikely meetings with the kaiser or the sultan—or any of the myriad titled or untitled eminences he met with. In the meantime, a relatively few Jews in the Russian Empire were not waiting for permission from either the kaiser or the sultan—or, for that matter, anyone else—to emigrate to that contentious corner of the Ottoman Empire called Southern Syria. By 1882, what later became known as the first aliya was under way. A trickle of Russian Jews established four settlements (one as early as 1878), and at about the same time a little-known emigration from Yemen was trudging north toward Jerusalem. The total number of Jewish settlers was small but hardly insignificant, and they added to the numbers of Jews already living in what became Israel. For more than a thousand years, Jews had been "returning" to Israel, moving to a land they had never seen but which lived, with bubbling streams, milk, and, of course, honey, in their vivid imaginations. For some, the Bible beckoned. For others, anti-Semitism compelled.

It might be useful here to disinter my great-grandparents Mendel and Elke Kohn. Mendel was born in 1850, about ten years before Dreyfus, and way to the east in Poland. On January 14, 1871, he married Elke Wajnbrun, the daughter of Rabbi Joseph Wajnbrun. The couple lived in Ostrów Mazowiecka, which is east and north of Warsaw, about an hour and a half's drive nowadays. The Kohns had been in Ostrów Mazowiecka since at least 1842, when the death of Szulim Kohn was recorded, but the births of his six children were not registered—suggesting that they had been born elsewhere. The Kohns were, in their way, an old Polish family.

In Ostrów Mazowiecka, Mendel Kohn soon established himself as a supplier to a nearby Russian military garrison. He did well. The census showed the Kohns living in a spacious apartment, with one room reserved for a Polish servant. In 1876 the couple's first child was born. He was Rueben, and twenty-three years later, he married Judith Golombeck of the nearby hamlet of Guty. A year later, their first child was born. She was Rebecca, who died, eighty-two years later, a woman of some means, in New York City. It was from her that I get the little knowledge that I have of my paternal grandfather. Of his three children, she knew him best.

The twenty-six-year-old Rueben Kohn joined the mass exodus to America. Why he did so, I can only guess. Maybe his father's business was failing, or maybe it merely was not prosperous enough to support more than one generation of Kohns. America had to be a different story. There the streets were supposedly paved with gold, and while probably few took that literally, it was abundantly clear that in the Polish shtetl, the streets were hardly paved at all. The great Jewish immigration was already under way, and when it was over, almost as many Jews had left the Pale of Settlement as remained. Rueben Kohn of Ostrów Mazowiecka was one of those who left. In 1902 he became Rudolph Cohen of New York City.

Judith and Rebecca stayed behind. It was a common enough arrangement, but one that must have been stressful for the women. They were alone in a land where the authorities could not be relied on for protection. That may be why my grandmother concealed that her husband was no longer in the home—and why she delayed registering the birth of their child, Rebecca, until she needed papers for emigration. In 1904 a man posing as my grandfather told the town clerk that a child had been born. When the clerk asked why it had taken him so long to register the birth, the man said he had been ill (all this was inscribed by hand in the records) and then improbably signed with an *X*.

A diligent town clerk—or one who had not been bribed—might have wondered how the eldest son of a merchant could have been illiterate or, for that matter, why all Jews could write their name in Hebrew, but not this particular one. Whatever the case, the clerk clearly blew no whistle, and passage was secured for America. Maybe when she got to Ellis Island, maybe before, Judith Kohn was told that she had become Judith Cohen, a name only for official and other papers. In Hebrew, her and her husband's names remained unchanged.

They were an odd couple, this Rudolph and Judith. She was a beautiful woman, lovely in her only existing picture, but neither one could have brought much on the marriage market. Judith, artfully posed in that lone photograph, had a hunchback. Rudolph could not provide for his family. He was aimless, maybe a dreamer, a bit of a drifter—to Detroit to see family and look for work, and then back to New York and then off to Detroit again. Rebecca, his daughter, spoke of him with contempt. Once a year, or so my father told me, the couple would take their children—Rebecca and their two American-born sons—to a photo studio on the Lower East Side of Manhattan. There they posed for pictures to send back to relatives in Poland. If only in the picture, the Golden Land was good to them. In reality, their fine clothes had been rented for the occasion.

As with so many immigrants, the New World—a new language, a new culture, a new freedom—overwhelmed and defeated Rudolph. His Old World status was gone. No longer the son of a successful merchant, he worked in the needle trades; a "shirt operator," his death certificate stated. I envision him at his sewing machine, mindlessly running material through the device with a robotic push of his arm—one of three or four dozen occasionally bathed men in a hot, crowded room. I forgive him his peripatetic ways, and I forgive, too, his running after women because his prospects were nil and the work was mindless and the sweatshop was a furnace in the summer. And at night, when he went home, it was to a tenement where the air did not move and the toilet was down the hall and the bathtub was in the kitchen and the noise from the street kept him up, damp from his own sweat. The apartment in Ostrów Mazowiecka, with its high ceilings and the room for the Polish maid, was in his past, and his future was nothing but uncertainty. The promise of the Promised Land was turning out be a curse.

In 1914 Judith succumbed to some disease of the tenements, leaving my grandfather to raise his three children alone. For whatever reason, this proved impossible, and Rebecca, fourteen, was sent to live with relatives, while the two boys, Sam, eight, and my father, Harry, four, were placed in the Hebrew Orphan Asylum, then on the Lower East Side. "The home," as it was called, relocated to Mount Vernon in nearby Westchester County, and my father and Sam went with it. They were both what was called half-orphans. Usually that meant that the father had deserted the family. In this case, though, the father came around from time to time. When he did, my father confronted a man who was virtually a stranger to him. Rudolph spoke only Yiddish. Harry spoke only English. Sam translated.

In the very Russian Empire that the Kohns had just left, something both dramatic and important was about to happen in the exotically and mysteriously named region called Bessarabia (now Moldova). A year after Rudolph Cohen arrived in New York, a fourteen-year-old boy named Mikhail Rybachenko was found murdered outside the city of Kishinev. Word spread quickly that he had been killed by Jews and his blood drained for use in the preparation of Passover matzo. It was said that the boy's main arteries had been precisely punctured. The medical examiner said this was not the case, but the medical examiner was a Jew and could not be trusted.

Rybachenko's body was found on February 13, but it was hardly an explosive discovery. It took months and quite a bit of work for it to produce a pogrom, time for rumor and myth to lethally combine—time for the local newspaper to build circulation in a time-tested fashion.

In his account of the Kishinev pogrom, *Easter in Kishinev*, Edward H. Judge goes into the remarkable history of the blood libel, a tenacious myth that neither truth nor facts nor common sense could eradicate. Readers of Geoffrey Chaucer's *The Canterbury Tales* may recall *The Prioress's Tale*, with its account of the murder of a boy by Jews. Chaucer wrote some one hundred years after Jews were banished from England, so it's clear the myth was well established.

Chaucer lived in the late Middle Ages, but the murder of Rybachenko took place at the beginning of the twentieth century, in 1903. Cars were on the streets, telephones in homes, and patients on the couch at 19 Berggasse. Little of this applied to Russia and still less of it to Bessarabia, one of those ethnic mosh pits where Russians, Romanians, Bulgarians, Ukrainians, and Moldavians came together, rarely happily. As Judge suggests, about their only point of agreement was the depravity of the Jews, who made up approximately 12 percent of the province. True to the stereotype, that 12 percent constituted 80 percent of Kishinev's merchants and almost all of the local revolutionaries.

In Kishinev, the local paper, the *Bessarabian*, continued to run Jew-baiting stories. Some were so preposterous that they seemed designed to test the credulity of its readers. One reported a development sure to ruin local vintners: that Jews had developed an amazing process for making wine without grapes. The newspaper published any rumor it could find or invent about the murder of poor Rybachenko, who, as the authorities knew, had been done away with by his uncle. It said that the boy's body had been found without any marks or bruises, that his mouth had been sewn shut, and he had those telltale puncture wounds. It also reported that the boy had visited the shop of a Jewish tobacconist just before disappearing.

From February to April, the rumors festered. In their own diffident way, the authorities did what they could do to combat them. Nonetheless, it was widely understood that a pogrom would be condoned, and that Christians could enrich themselves at the expense of Jews and even murder them without legal consequence.

On Easter Sunday, the pogrom commenced. It lasted two days and claimed the lives of 51 people, 49 of them Jews. An additional 424 Jews were injured, 700 homes were damaged, and 600 shops were looted. More than a quarter of Kishinev's buildings were damaged.

The pogrom had a worldwide impact. By 1903, there were considerable Jewish communities in some of the world's major cities. Just as the *Bessarabian* catered to its own readers, so did the papers of New York and London cater to theirs. In New York, the newspapers of William Randolph Hearst, the *Evening Journal* and the *American*, dispatched an odd but inspired choice to go to Kishinev and report on what had happened: Michael Davitt. The Irish nationalist Davitt turned his dispatches into a book, *Within the Pale,* which was published later that year. In it, Davitt uncovered little that was not already known, but he was a forceful, appalled outsider, unbiased except for a celebrated commitment to social justice.

Davitt attributed the riots to "the horrible influence of the ritual murder propaganda upon untutored minds possessed of ignorance and fanatical conception of religion." He warned Russia to justly deal with its Jews—its "Semitic malady," as one official put it to him—or risk radicalizing its four million Jewish subjects.

Too late. Many Jews were already radicalized. (Indeed, one of them was soon to organize the assassination of Vyacheslav Konstantinovich Von Plehve, the interior minister and a vigorous anti-Semite.) Others took another lesson from the pogroms—one that did not apply to Russia or Russian authorities, but instead to Jews: they needed to defend themselves. The gravamen of the charge was contained in Chaim Nahman Bialik's poem "In the City of Slaughter." Bialik, who would go on to become Israel's national poet, had been sent to Kishinev by an Odessa-based Jewish organization to see for himself what had happened. What he found clearly both appalled and disgusted him: timidity, cowardice, an abject failure to mount any effort at self-defense. He wrote about how the heirs . . .

> *Of Hasmoneans (Maccabee warriors) lay, with trembling knees,*
> *Concealed and cowering—the sons of the Maccabees!*
> *The seed of saints, the scions of the lions!*
> *Who, crammed by scores in all the sanctuaries of their shame,*
> *So sanctified My name!*

It was tough stuff. It was also, according to Judge, unfair. The Jews had organized a self-defense force, but with uncharacteristic alacrity, the authorities disarmed it. After the pogrom, the Jewish Bund, a labor organization, gathered still more self-defense forces. In a pogrom later that year in the town of Gomel, Jews already had a defense organization in place. These became the prototype for the Jewish fighting forces that would emerge in Palestine, and they changed a mind-set. No longer would the bedraggled Jews of the Pale look to the czar for protection—"If only the czar knew what was happening," was the supposed lament—but to themselves.

In some sense, Kishinev was the last straw, although hardly the last pogrom. Things were not getting better for Jews; they were getting worse. Immigration, mostly to America, accelerated. But by now, the arguments of the Zionists in favor of Palestine were beginning to resonate even more. Maybe the streets in America were indeed paved with gold, but those streets still belonged to Christians. What they could give, they could take away—like the epaulets on Dreyfus's shoulder or the rights that one czar had granted and another had rescinded. For Jews, progress seemed always to be attached to a rubber band: it could only go so far before it was snapped back.

4

Yiddishe Kops
Everywhere You Look

In the fall of 1743, a fourteen-year-old boy entered Berlin at the *Rosenthaler Tor*, the only gate in the city wall through which Jews (and cattle) were allowed to pass." Thus begins Amos Elon's almost unbearably sad book, *The Pity of It All: A Portrait of the German-Jewish Epoch 1743–1933*.

The boy was Moses Mendelssohn, the future philosopher. He was poor, possibly shoeless and certainly penniless, and was entering a city that not only had few Jews but wanted it kept that way. Yet within two generations, the boy's grandson, the musical prodigy Felix Mendelssohn, was the toast of Berlin and so rich that he did not really have to work for a living. He and many other Jews (or former Jews) occupied the very center of Berlin's cultural and commercial life, so much so that thirty of Berlin's fifty-two private banks were owned by Jews, and the greatest of all German banks, Deutsche Bank and Dresdner Bank, were founded with Jewish participation.

Things were hardly different in that other great German-speaking city, Vienna. There, 40 percent of the directors of public banks were Jews or of Jewish descent. In Budapest, Yuri Slezkine, author of *The Jewish Century*, tells us, by 1921, nearly 90 percent of the stock exchange members were Jews. Before

World War I, Jews made up about 5 percent of Hungary's population, yet it is no anti-Semitic exaggeration (or nightmare) to say that they controlled many of the nation's banks and much of its industrial sector.

In central and eastern Europe, rich Jews, very rich Jews, accomplished Jews, very accomplished Jews, famous and celebrated Jews, creative and lauded Jews, present and future Nobel laureates, filmmakers and actors and poets and writers and socialists and communists had seemingly materialized out of nowhere—or, almost magically, out of the wood and mud of the shtetl. Jews were suddenly everywhere, seemingly controlling everything, and if you had just come to town from provincial Austria, from Linz to Vienna for instance, and you were a sixteen-year-old kid, impoverished and living on an orphan's pension, you would hear of the Jews, of their wealth and their power. And, of course, of the nefarious ways they got that wealth and power. And you would notice their banks and their homes and their department store (Gerngross, the largest in town) or if they had come from the east and were pious, you would notice their beards and forelocks and weird manner of dress. Adolf Hitler would have noticed.

There was a reality to the Jews and an unreality to the Jews—a myth and a lore, a past and a present, a sameness and a difference, and then something unaccountable: this achievement, this brilliance, this infuriating success. Who were these people? They were no different from other people. They were the same as other people. You could recognize some of them; they looked Jewish. You could not recognize others of them. They didn't look Jewish.

As is often the case with "the other," the women were more exotic, erotic, sexier. But none of that was true, or necessarily true. Their religion was odd. That was true, but so what? Their language was odd too. But again, so what? They used the blood of murdered gentiles for some of their traditional foods. But they didn't. That was a myth for peasants who lived in the forest and walked in the mud.

But they were smarter. True, they were also more devious. They were clannish, too, and dishonest, and they would cheat. They were lousy horsemen and rotten soldiers, and a youth could drink them under the table, but they were smarter. That was the long and short of it. Look around. Look at the proud houses on the placid shores of the Wannsee, in Berlin, the ones set back from the street, a long driveway, stables, a boathouse, and servants scurrying in and out the side doors. Look at the homes in Grünewald, also in Berlin, or in Budapest, up the hill in Pest and later even in Buda, and everywhere in Vienna: Jews. Jews, Jews. The myths about Jews were false, totally false, libelously false, the bilious rantings of demagogues—and yet there was a hard, irrefutable truth about those grand homes. Jews lived in them.

Three things were happening. First, Jews were becoming rapidly urbanized and, in the process, acquiring the street smarts of city people. In 1860 Berlin had a Jewish population of 19,000; by 1925, the figure was 173,000. In 1860 there were about 41,000 Jews in Warsaw; by 1930, the number was over 350,000.

The trend was repeated in many of the major cities of Europe: Vienna and Budapest, of course, but also Paris and London. Jews were not abandoning the land (they were usually forbidden from owning any) but were moving instead from town, village, and shtetl to city and also moving from east to west, away from the repressive lands of the Russian Empire to the more progressive countries to the west.

At the same time, Jews were capitalizing on the skills they had been forced to acquire as toilers on the margins of society. Moneylenders became bankers, and shopkeepers became merchants. My great-grandfather Mendel Kohn, of the Polish town of Ostrów-Mazowiecka, was in this way typical. He went from being a peddler, to a carter, to a merchant engaged in the apparently lucrative business of provisioning a nearby Russian army garrison.

These traits, what is known in Yiddish as having *Yiddishe kop* (a Jewish head), were not the end of the story. Jews had something else going for them as well: a hunger for education. Maybe this could be attributed to the need to be literate in Hebrew so that the Bible and its myriad commentaries could be studied. (Didn't Christians also need to read the Bible?) Or maybe it had something to do with the urgent need to keep books and records, for how else could one be a merchant or moneylender? Or maybe it just was some sort of peculiarly Jewish lust for learning. Whatever the case, in Berlin around 1900, approximately 5 percent of the eligible general population attended high school. The figure for Jews was about 65 percent.

About the same sort of statistics applied to all the major cities of eastern and central Europe, and even in Russia, where about 15 percent of Jewish youths were gaining, against formidable barriers, entrance into a university, and others were being sent abroad to study. (Weizmann relates how affluent Russian Jews got around the quota for high school admission, about 10 percent within the Pale, 5 percent outside it and just 3 percent in Moscow and Saint Petersburg, by paying gentile youths to take the entrance exam, thus enlarging the pool and making room for more Jews.)

These phenomenal education statistics applied to females as well as males. In Prussia, 42 percent of Jewish girls attended high school. The figure for the general population was 2.7 percent. It's possible that the occasional Jewish girl was being prepared for business, but most of them were being educated just for the sake of learning. (The great salons of Berlin were originally the creation of wealthy Jewish women.) It would take years for the general population to catch up.

All this education, all these financial and commercial skills, all this drive and determination—and these *Yiddishe kops*—had to lead somewhere, and it did. It produced vast wealth—not the sort of wealth Kaiser Wilhelm II envisioned, but a remarkable affluence and prosperity nonetheless. The meticulous Germans knew, for instance, that in Frankfurt am Main in 1900, Catholics paid an average of 59.40 marks per year in taxes; the Protestants, 121 marks; and the Jews, an incredible 427.50. The extent of Jewish affluence was simply astounding.

But the depth probably got more attention. The Rothschilds had already set the standard for unimaginable wealth. It was the English branch that famously loaned the government of Benjamin Disraeli the funds to purchase a controlling interest in the Suez Canal Co.—a deal between old Jewish money, Lionel de Rothschild, and newer Jewish money, the D'Israelis, a family of Sephardic Jews that in two generations and a fortuitous conversion (Disraeli's father, Isaac D'Israeli, had his son baptized at age twelve) had elevated the grandson to the premiership of England. Having lost an apostrophe but gained an empire, Benjamin Disraeli could only have agreed with Heinrich Heine: conversion was indeed "the ticket of admission to European culture."

Beyond the Rothschilds, however, was a level of Jewish wealth that, while somewhat less glittering, was nearly as impressive. In England, where Jews before 1914 were only 0.3 percent of the population, 20 percent of the millionaires were Jewish. In Germany in 1908, Jews accounted for 31 percent of the richest families. Jews then were about 1 percent of the population.

In Hungary, Jews went from not being able to own land before emancipation (1792) to owning vast estates by the end of the nineteenth century (20 percent of large acreage properties by 1910). With all that came a bundle of aristocratic titles: 20 percent of them, in fact. T. D. Kramer, whose history of Hungary's Jews (*From Emancipation to Catastrophe*) tells this utterly amazing story, says that one in every five hundred Jews had a title. Jews, hungry to prove their Hungarian bona fides, were much more likely to speak Hungarian than other ethnic groups in the polyglot nation and helped establish it as the national language.

All this wealth was both notable and noticeable. All those rich Jews, all those fancy carriages and mansions in choice neighborhoods, could not help but attract attention. Still, the Jewish populations everywhere outside of the old Russian Empire were small, and it is doubtful, for instance, that your average Berliner would have been all that aware of the homes going up on the Wannsee and, more to the point, that some of them were owned by Jews.

It was harder to miss, though, what was happening in music and art, in literature, in law, in medicine, in painting, in science, and in journalism: Jews, Jews, and more Jews. In the cities of Warsaw, Budapest, and Vienna, half of all doctors were Jews. In Vienna, about half of all lawyers were Jewish, and in all those cities and others as well, so many journalists were Jews that the term *journalist* was synonymous with *Jew*.

Jews arose seemingly out of nowhere to constitute the new European middle class. They not only were consumers of culture but also were the creators of it. They made up nearly the whole of the central European middle class, an astounding achievement for a people that, just a tick of history's clock earlier, had existed on society's periphery, often considered subhuman.

There was no denying Jewish accomplishment. There was widespread agreement that something stunning had happened. The only disagreement was about how it happened. What, exactly, explained how in Hungary, for example, this particular minority group—not the Romanians nor the Ruthenians nor the Ukrainians and not the more numerous Germans nor even the Magyars themselves—had gone from penury to prosperity? What was it about these Jews? What made them, well, smarter?

That question was commonly asked in the nineteenth and twentieth centuries, which, for better, but more often for worse, assigned all sorts of attributes to ethnic groups, many of them invidious. That sort of inquisitiveness has since been largely suppressed. At the core of the Holocaust, after all, were some malevolent and loony genetic theories so that now, in reaction, we are all enjoined from speaking of Jews in a way that suggests a genetic difference or, if you will, advantage.

Indeed, there are numerous sociological and cultural explanations for Jewish achievement, and we can watch some of them being validated by a reassuring reversion to the mean: the grandson of the Jewish capitalist becoming a used car dealer and then marrying another dealer's daughter. Their progeny will not be Talmudic scholars.

What's more, we need only look at the amazing accomplishment of

Asians—both in Asia and elsewhere—to see that other peoples can do as well. Asian Americans are routinely referred to as latter-day Jews, which, in the sense that the term is meant, they very well may be. (Asians, while only about 5 percent of the American population, compose about 15 percent of Harvard University's undergraduate enrollment, down from a peak of about 20 percent, suggesting to some that a quota has been imposed.) Like Jews, they are widely seen as not only intrinsically smart but smarter still for assimilating so effortlessly into the larger American culture.

Even so, none of these Asians had quite the imagined attributes of the Jews, if only because none of them had quite the storied history, mythology, and religious opprobrium. Idi Amin, the brutal ruler of Uganda, foolishly kicked out his Indians for a whole lot of real or imagined reasons, but not for the death of Christ. To Europeans, Jews were in a class of their own. Say what you would about them, they were not a people to be trifled with.

The kaiser himself was convinced of that. Later in life, he waxed anti-Semitic, attributing Germany's World War I defeat and his own abdication and exile to the Jews. "The tribe of Judah," he wrote, had stabbed him in the back.

"Let no German ever forget this, nor rest until these parasites have been destroyed and exterminated from German soil!" He suggested a "regular international all-worlds pogrom à la Russe" as "the best cure" and opined that Jews were a "nuisance that humanity must get rid of some way or other. I believe the best would be gas!" Here was a man truly ahead of his time.

That future "enemy," the one that had purportedly done the vanquishing, the one whose power was as immense as it was invisible, was standing right before the kaiser in the person of Theodor Herzl. The very fact that this Viennese scribbler, this stuffy bourgeois in his black coat, hat, vest, and beard, had even gained entry into the kaiser's tent was testimony to the enormous power of anti-Semitism. The man himself, to conjure the plaintive words of the pathetic Shylock, did bleed if pricked, did laugh if tickled, and would die if poisoned, but beyond what made him an ordinary man were aspects that made him powerful. He was, in short, partially a figment of anti-Semitic fantasy, a preposterous concoction of the anti-Semitic mind. But without it, Israel would not have been necessary—or possible.

5

Thirty-Nine Steps
Toward World Domination

Israel's founding document was the Balfour Declaration of 1917, issued in the name of Sir Arthur James Balfour, the British foreign secretary. It informed Lord Rothschild, titular head of England's Jewish community, that "His Majesty's Government view[s] with favour the establishment in Palestine of a National Home for the Jewish people," and it was issued not just because the Englishmen of those times were kindly disposed to the plight of the Hebrews—they were all nurtured on the Old Testament, after all—but also out of a prudent respect for the uncontested power of the Jews. For the kaiser, and for so many Europeans of that time, Jewish power, Jewish wealth, Jewish organizational acumen, Jewish brilliance, and, of course, Jewish evil were givens—truths, uncontested yet invisible. Proof of it all could be seen and not seen—felt, admired, and feared.

The Balfour Declaration is often said to have been a form of payback to Chaim Weizmann, the Russian-born Zionist leader, for the contributions he made as a chemist to Britain's World War I effort. It was, really, nothing of the sort. Instead, it was a genuine expression of pro-Zionist sentiment by important members of Britain's political class. Steeped in the philosemitic traditions of English Protestantism, they dearly wanted to see the return of the Jews to the Holy Land. Some of them simply felt that Jews belonged where they had been in their Sunday school Bible tales. Others believed that the return of the Jews was a prerequisite to the end days and the second coming of Christ. In either case, this particular brand of British Zionism was based on sometimes sentimental, sometimes standard, but always genuine religious belief and not some IOU due the astonishingly accomplished Weizmann.

Balfour himself personified what could be called Christian Zionism. He told Weizmann that he was more familiar with the place-names of Palestine than he was with the more relevant names of French towns where, in appalling numbers, British troops were then being slaughtered. At the same time, when Weizmann expressed his antipathy toward czarist Russia, Balfour was perplexed. But Russia was an ally of England's, he said, to which Weizmann responded with a brief tutorial on Russia-Jewish relations. It was all news to Balfour.

For all his infatuation with Zionism, Balfour was nonetheless infected with a mild case of anti-Semitism. This seeming contradiction was, in fact, quite common, especially among Britain's upper classes, and in no way suggested anything approaching what the century would see later. It was not even really Jew hatred, since that entails a certain passion, and these Englishmen were coolly indifferent to Jews and their mad scramble toward equality. The aristocracy and the gentry feared no one and no thing. They had succeeded splendidly at birth. They were what they were, and no one could take that away from them.

These Englishmen knew that Jews were not Englishmen, not in the same way that they were. Jews were a people apart. They had a different religion, of course, and they were invariably of recent or relatively recent arrival in Britain, and if they came from elsewhere—as the D'Israelis did, from either Spain or Italy—they did not look as Englishmen did or Englishmen should. One glance at Benjamin Disraeli revealed that something was dreadfully wrong. If he was not quite the "black, Portuguese nameless Jew" that Anthony Trollope created in his novel *The Prime Minister*—no doubt with Disraeli in mind—he was no stereotypical foxhunter, either.

Despite their snobbishness, despite their emphasis on ancestry and pedigree, the English ruling classes presented the Jew with the happiest, most liberal place in Europe. All institutions were open to him—even the army—and while it is true that it took Lionel de Rothschild ten years to be seated in the House of Commons, this was not because the oath ending "upon the true faith of a Christian" was expressly anti-Semitic but rather because it was an anachronistic holdover from previous religious wars that had nothing to do with Jews. When the oath was abandoned, de Rothschild took his seat.

Coming from the dark, Jew-hating lands of the czars, Weizmann was delightfully surprised to find a British upper class that tended to support his cause. "We had discovered, in the English political world, a heavy preponderance of opinion in our favor," Weizmann wrote in his 1949 memoir, *Trial and Error*.

Weizmann was not so foolish as to believe that this "heavy preponderance of opinion" was based entirely on religious sentiment or an infatuation with Jews themselves. As with the kaiser, as with the sultan, these important Englishmen—and that very important Welshman, the future prime minister, David Lloyd George—also believed in the immense but invisible power of the Jews and the need to get them on Britain's side in World War I. For much of the war, Britain had two overriding goals. The first was to keep its ally Russia in the war and the second was to draw its friend the United States into it.

Both nations had substantial Jewish populations and, in the case of the United States, some Jews of considerable influence—the publisher of the *New York Times*, for instance; the owners of Sears, Macy's, and other department stores; and, of course, the "Our Crowd" set: Schiff, Warburg, Goldman, Guggenheim, Sachs, and Seligman. They represented immense wealth, but not—not yet, anyway—immense political power.

The Jewish vote was not only limited to a few congressional districts, but the Jewish voter was also hardly inclined to support the anti-Semitic czar in his war with the kaiser. The socialist congressman Meyer London, representing New York's Lower East Side, even voted against Woodrow Wilson's proposed declaration of war. London was so anti-Zionist that a year later he gruffly declined to introduce a resolution in support of the Balfour Declaration. "Let us stop pretending about the Jewish past and let us stop making fools of ourselves about the Jewish future," he said. These blunt positions cost him. In 1914 he had defeated Henry M. Goldfogle. In 1918 Goldfogle defeated him.

Russia presented Britain and its allies with an even more challenging case. The Balfour Declaration was issued November 2, 1917, just a week before the Bolshevik Revolution changed Russia, the war, and the world.

To many in the British government, including Balfour and Winston Churchill, the revolution seemed the work of Jews. Churchill was particularly alarmed. He saw Jews everywhere, especially in radical movements, and it hardly mattered to him (or to most anyone else, actually) that some of his Jews were no longer Jews: lapsed, converted, renounced, or even anti-Semitic. Despite any protestations these Jews might offer, they were nonetheless seen as Jews who were acting as Jews and, given all that, had a proclivity for radicalism, particularly communism. They would, if they could, yank Russia out of the war. As for the average Russian Jew who was not a radical, a communist, or even a socialist, the regime he was being asked to support, sometimes to fight for, was the very same regime that either condoned pogroms or did little to stop them. The czar was king of the Russians but definitely not of the Jews.

It is difficult at this remove to understand what the Englishmen of the late nineteenth and early twentieth centuries meant when they referred to the power of the Jews. The most celebrated, if not perplexing, of these figures was Churchill. His philosemitism was genuine, or at least it seemed so, and he persisted in his support of a Jewish homeland long after it could be defended on grounds of practicality or British self-interest. Moreover, Jews were not some distant ethnic group, a mere rumor of a people where fantasy could substitute for reality.

Churchill had firsthand knowledge. He had been the champion of Jews and their aspirations since early in his career when he represented a Manchester district that was one third Jewish. He *knew* Jews. The average Englishman, especially one of Churchill's social class, simply did not. The Jew was a stranger. The Jew was exotic. The Jew, therefore, was capable of anything. It was not all that shocking when in 1920, Wilfred Steed, the editor of the London *Times*, hailed *The Protocols of the Learned Elders of Zion* as an authentic document although it was actually a forgery concocted by the czarist police and published in 1903. It supposedly revealed a Jewish plan for world domination. Not surprisingly, Steed also blamed the Jews for World War I and the Russian Revolution. To his credit, he later retracted his endorsement but not, probably, his feelings about Jews. *The Protocols* might be a forgery, but for him they almost certainly reflected a reality.

Churchill, too, bought into that reality. His feelings about a Jewish homeland were well known, but he insisted they were not based on juvenile Bible lessons but on the overriding need to keep Russia in the war and to induce the United States to enter it. The Balfour Declaration, he said, was "more than some sort of sentimental aspiration." It was nothing less than diplomatic pragmatism, an obligation made in wartime to "enlist the aid of Jews all over the world."

Churchill did not limit his support for a Jewish national home to Jewish audiences or to the *après-dîner* parlors of great British homes. In his important and riveting account of the creation of the modern Middle East, *A Peace to End All Peace*, David Fromkin quotes what Churchill told a delegation of Palestinians in Palestine itself: "It is manifestly right that the scattered Jews should have a national centre and a national home to be reunited and where else but Palestine with which for three thousand years they have been intimately and profoundly associated?

"We think it will be good for the world and good for the Jews, good for the British Empire, but also good for the Arabs who dwell in Palestine, and we intend it to be so."

This was March 1921, and a clearer statement of support no Zionist could have wished. It not only made Churchill's intentions clear and forcefully stated the government's policy but also stood in stark contrast to the usual diplomatic mumblings of British officials before Arab audiences. By that time, the Arabs were both restive and embittered, and British officialdom, especially the military, was looking upon the Balfour Declaration with horror—a kind of diplomatic blunder that could not be justified or explained. Churchill was having none of it.

Churchill never forsook Balfour. To him, it was a matter of honor, a promise tendered, a promise to be kept. He adamantly demanded that Britain continue to honor the declaration's intent, which he kept insisting was not some woolly expression of sentiment. "It was considered that the support which the Jews could give us all over the world, and particularly in the United States and also in Russia, would be a definite, palpable advantage," he said.

Was Churchill being frank? Did he believe what he was saying, or was he using the myth of Jewish power to advance a sentimental or religious aim under cover of prejudice? One would think that, Churchill being Churchill, he was a friend of the Jews, and that's all there was to it. "Personally, my heart is full of sympathy for Zionism," he said.

But the record is muddled. Like many others in his time, Churchill had no compunction against describing Jews as enormously gifted and, by implication, enormously dangerous. "Some people like Jews and some do not, but no thoughtful man can doubt the fact that they are beyond all question the most formidable and the most remarkable race which has ever appeared in the world," he once said.

It had not escaped Churchill's attention that the Jews of Europe had become the embodiment of modernity. They were disproportionally represented in the sciences—physical as well as medical—and the arts and music and, of course, the new, exotic, and erotic sciences of the brain. More importantly—and, to some, more ominously—Jews were disproportionally involved in the new political parties of the left, including the communists. Yuri Slezkine quotes Istvan Deak, the Columbia University scholar of central Europe: left-wing intellectuals did not simply "happen to be mostly Jews, as some pious historiography would have us believe, but Jews created the left-wing intellectual movement in Germany."

The most frightening of these left-wing parties was, of course, the communists, and here the proportion of Jews (or non-Jews of Jewish ancestry) was simply astounding. The indefatigable Slezkine tells us, for instance, that more than 60 percent of the exiles who returned to Russia in trains like the famous sealed one that brought Lenin home were Jews. The train that took Lenin to the Finland Station contained twenty-eight others, more than half of them Jews—and the train itself was financed by yet another Jew, the mysterious and mysteriously rich Alexander Helphand.

As for Lenin, his Jewish ancestry was well known (or suspected) among his colleagues but later suppressed by Stalin. By then, the early 1930s, the preponderance of Jews in the communist hierarchy had gone from being an awkward fact to an embarrassment. Twice in that decade, Stalin thwarted attempts by Lenin's sister Anna to reveal that their mother was descended from Moshe Itzkovich Blank, a tavern keeper from the shtetl of Starokonstantinov in what is now Ukraine. (Lenin himself, perhaps acknowledging his little secret, once told Maksim Gorky, "A smart Russian is almost always a Jew or somebody with an admixture of Jewish blood.") Stalin had the information declared "inappropriate for publication."

The astounding number of Jews associated with radicalism, and particularly with communism, has its appropriate sociological and historical explanations—not the least of them being that Bolshevism was initially substantially free of anti-Semitism, while the monarchists and other right-wing parties most definitely were not. But all this was much too rational for an age that believed fervently in racial and ethnic differences, particularly when it came to Jews. The evidence, after all, was all around them: the stunning achievements in finance and science, literature and medicine, and, above all, the disproportionate presence in radical movements. So the answer had to be what it had always been: Jews were Jews, and that was all there was to it.

This view was shared by demagogue and democrat alike, by raw anti-Semite and sophisticated philosemite. Churchill was in the latter group. From everything he said and wrote, he believed—as anti-Semites did and do—in the stark duality of the Jew: weak yet strong, intellectually vigorous yet physically pathetic, invisibly rich yet visibly poor, good and evil. Churchill put it this way: "The conflict between good and evil which proceeds increasingly in the breast of man nowhere reaches such intensity as in the Jewish race." He was referring to the Jewish proclivity to be both democrats and communists, and he noted that all but one of the early Soviet leaders were Jews or of Jewish ancestry. Churchill, of course, excluded Lenin.

Churchill saw things in operatic, apocalyptic terms, and his view of Jews was in that context. Here, though, was a man in full possession of extraordinary intellectual powers who nonetheless believed in this Jewish duality—not that every Jew possessed this quality, but that many did. "It would almost seem as if the gospel of Christ and the gospel of the Antichrist were destined to originate among the same people," he said.

That remarkable observation earned Churchill a rebuke from the British newspaper the *Jewish Chronicle*, but he was only finishing what he had started. Earlier, he had said of Jews, "It may well be that this astounding race may at the present time be in the actual process of producing another system of morals and philosophy, as malevolent as Christianity was benevolent, which, if not arrested, would shatter irretrievably all that Christianity has rendered possible." And because Churchill apparently was never content to make things easy for the historian, he prudently qualified his generalizations and stereotypes. Martin Gilbert, in his book *Churchill and the Jews: A Lifelong Friendship*, quotes him as saying there could be "no greater mistake, than to attribute to each individual a recognizable share in the qualities which make up the national character. There are all sorts of men—good, bad and, for the most, indifferent—in every country, and in every race. Nothing is more wrong than to deny to an individual, on account of race of origin, his right to be judged on his personal merits and conduct. In people of peculiar genius, like the Jews, contrasts are more vivid, the extremes more widely separated, the resulting consequences more decisive."

One of those consequences, for sure, made Churchill see Bolshevism as a "Jewish movement."

Churchill's views, if uttered today, would no doubt be denounced as anti-Semitic. Yet the correlation between Jews and communism, Jews and radicalism of all sorts, was both real and stunning. Churchill was right about

Jews—Jews and communism and Jews and achievement. Something was going on. Something odd and exciting and dangerous was happening.

All this sounds silly or disturbing to our ears, but it was common in Churchill's time, and if you add to these strictly secular beliefs about Jews (nothing here about Christ killers) an overlay of crackpot Darwinism about Jews and their wayward genes, and then mix in the usual conspiracy theories (Jews in league with Masons, and so forth), you had manufactured a Unified Theory that could account for practically anything. There was simply nothing the Jews could not do.

Fromkin directs us to the extremely odd person of Gerald Fitzmaurice, a friend of the far more influential (and rich) English diplomat Sir Mark Sykes. Fitzmaurice cultivated what we would now consider a cinematic persona, living in hotels and playing a shadowy role in British-Turkish relations. He was the first dragoman (guide, interpreter) at the British embassy in Constantinople, where he detected that the Young Turks, who had seized effective control of the Ottoman government, had themselves fallen into the clutches of Jews.

Fitzmaurice was one of those keen observers who saw Jews everywhere, and he had no trouble seeing them in Salonika, the northern Greek city that was then about half Jewish. Salonika was where a spontaneous Young Turk insurrection had occurred in 1908 and where, coincidentally, the ancestors of Sabbatai Zevi's followers had settled and thrived. These were called *Donmeh* (converts), and they were neither Muslim nor Jewish—although they were later expelled from Greece as Muslims. Whatever their religion, some of them were active in the Young Turk movement.

The British embassy in Constantinople became alarmed. Its sympathies were with the government it knew rather than the one it didn't—predictability, above all. Fitzmaurice offered ample reason for concern. He realized that the Jews were in control, and the Jews, both for obscure reasons of their own and an understandable hatred of czarist Russia, were in league with Germany. Fitzmaurice was not to be easily dismissed. He was amply credentialed. He spoke Turkish. He knew the country.

In the end, which was to occur six years later, Turkey did indeed come into the First World War on the side of Germany. It did so, though, because it had age-old differences with Russia and newer ones with Britain. The English, no longer coaling their fleet, were coveting the oil of Mosul in what is now Iraq. Not only did Jews have nothing to do with any of it, but to the extent that they participated in the war as a people, they did so in Palestine by fighting the Turks.

Fitzmaurice, though, was hardly disgraced. When he reported his astonishing discovery, he was not reprimanded or summoned to England for observation. On the contrary, others either seconded his judgment or found it riveting. One of those was Hugh O'Beirne of the Foreign Office, who hit upon an idea: "If we could offer the Jews an arrangement as to Palestine which would strongly appeal to them, we might conceivably be able to strike a bargain with them as to withdrawing their support from the Young Turk government which would then automatically collapse." He, too, was not summoned for observation.

It took a novelist to tie up a whole lot of loose strings. He was John Buchan, formerly Lloyd George's director of information services, who, after the war, turned his hand to fiction. In the most famous of his novels, *The Thirty-Nine Steps* (later turned into a classic Alfred Hitchcock movie), Buchan set out his explanation for just about everything:

> Away behind all the governments and the armies there was a big subterranean movement going on, engineered by very dangerous people. He had come on it by accident: . . . Things that happened in the Balkan War, how one state suddenly came out on top, why alliances were made and broken, why certain men disappeared, and where the sinews of war came from. The aim of the whole conspiracy was to get Russia and Germany at loggerheads. . . .
>
> The Jew was behind it, and the Jew hated Russia worse than hell. . . . This is the return match for the pogroms. The Jew is everywhere . . . with an eye like a rattlesnake. He is the man who is ruling the world just now, and he has the knife in the empire of the Tsar.

Buchan might have seen Jews everywhere, but his weird notions hardly harmed his career or besmirched his literary reputation. In fact, he was just a man of his times, in all likelihood a good fellow, swell company, a talented chap who might have taken this Jew thing a bit too far, but, well, he seemed to be on to something. The evidence was pretty clear, pretty startling—pretty frightening. In truth, he did not see Jews that differently than did other Europeans (or Americans).

On the question of the Jews, there was not all that much separating Buchan from either the kaiser in Berlin or, to a lesser degree, the much more benign Churchill in London. These men thought they were on to something, and it had little to do with religion. Yes, the Jews were not Christians, and in the east of Europe, they were often culturally (and physically) distinct, but their salient difference apparently had to do with intellect . . . something like that. These people, the Jews, were doing extraordinary things, becoming rich and accomplished in such a stunning fashion that it could not be ignored. It had to be acknowledged—and fought. The daring would do something. The daring would recognize reality, disregard social niceties, brush away liberal pieties, and do whatever had to be done. After all, what Europeans were doing in Asia and Africa, the Jews were doing in Europe itself. They were colonizing it.

6

Rudolph the Shirtmaker
Dies in the Bronx

The blow that killed Rudolph Cohen in the Bronx was struck years earlier and thousands of miles away in Poland. He died February 18, 1921, when a truck he could not hear bore down on him. But the cause of death, the death certificate notwithstanding, was the wallop administered years before by a Polish policeman who came upon young Rudolph rifling through his father's cart. Suspecting a thief, the cop deafened the kid with a hard cuff to the ear.

Meanwhile, what of Rudolph's parents, Mendel and Elke Kohn? They remained in Ostrów Mazowiecka. At Rueben's death, Mendel was seventy-one and his wife, two years younger. The old man lived until 1931; Elke died four years later. By then, none of their children was still in Ostrów Mazowiecka or, probably, Poland. The youngest, Leo, had first gone off to Warsaw, where he and a sister operated a photo studio, and then in 1921—just ahead of a new, restrictive immigration policy in the United States—took off for America. He opened a dress shop in Detroit.

What life was like for the old couple, I cannot say. Did their children in America send them money? Again, I cannot say. My father never said a word about his grandparents—not, mind you, because he chose not to, but because the death of both his parents had severed him from all who went before. His sister and brother were likewise silent about their family back in Ostrów

Mazowiecka. But Leo, the child who was the last to leave Poland, was apparently troubled about having emigrated before his parents died. In 1976, when I interviewed him, he produced a picture of his father's tombstone and read off the date of death, which had been rendered in Hebrew. He shorted the old man by three years, making it appear that he had left Poland only after his father had died. Actually, he was already in America.

The old couple lived in an apartment on the second floor of a large house in the middle of town. They were not alone. I found other Kohns in the census and other records, and I assumed some of them were relatives. I assume also that my great-grandparents were getting increasingly poorer, and while that worried them (I suppose), what worried them as much or maybe more (I suppose) was the way that Poland was changing.

The newly independent and newly aggressive nation had fought a brief but ferocious war against the equally new Soviet Union. My mother was living in the nearby Polish city of Ostroleka and remembered Bolsheviks coming into town and throwing open the grain storehouses. She and her sister and brother made off with a loaf of bread, but retribution for such acts was harsh and swift. The anticommunist troops of the new Polish republic retook the town, and the storehouse looters were shot.

Many of those executed were Jews. I can say that with some certainty, since Jews made up a disproportionate share of Poland's communists. This made a whole lot of sense. Communism was hostile to religion, and the religion of Poland was Roman Catholicism, which, like its many communicants, was significantly anti-Semitic. (In Russia and the Ukraine, the Orthodox churches were similarly tainted.) Communism eschewed nationalism, and nationalism and anti-Semitism were often linked. For communists, the primary allegiance was to class or ideology, not to nationality or *Volk*, a German term for peoplehood often redolent of a kind of mystical, virtually tribal, sense of identity. This appealed to Jews, since no matter how hard they tried, they usually could not be accepted as Poles or Russians. In due course, the communists would come to see Jews the same way. In this, the revolution was not all that revolutionary.

Little wonder, then, that so many Christian Poles found the Jewish affinity for communism both frightening and loathsome. Jews were not only *not* genuine Poles—not Polish, anyway—but they were often enemies of the state, in league with next-door Russia (now doing business as the Soviet Union) and allied with the forces of secularism, progressivism, and all the repugnant isms of the time.

For Jews, the promise of the republic became a curse. Poland's postwar government—the government of the Church and the army—became more and more anti-Semitic. All sorts of restrictions were imposed on Jews. The country's domestic politics were taking a nasty turn.

Poland was hardly an anomalous state. Throughout eastern Europe, the Jews lived in a paradox. The better things got in general, the worse they got for them. The republics that had come spilling out of the Austro-Hungarian and Russian horns of plenty were not merely the products of the disintegration of empire but also the rise of nationalism.

Joseph Roth, the Galician-born Jewish writer of the interwar years, described in his novels the allegiance that Austro-Hungarians felt to the emperor. Roth felt himself stateless after 1918 and the collapse of the Austro-Hungarian monarchy. Even as a Jew, he could somehow connect to the emperor in Vienna, as could the railway stationmaster whose uniform mimicked the one that Franz Joseph always wore. But once Galicia collapsed into its ethnically constituent parts—Polish, Ukrainian, and so forth—there was no room for the Jew, even though Roth himself was not much of one. In reality, no Jew, no matter how secular, could be an authentic Pole or Russian or Ukrainian. The Jew was indelibly an "other." He was now being defined by language or religion, and his uniform, no matter how impressive, was totally beside the point. Anyone could put on a uniform. Not anyone could be a Pole.

The new republics of Europe were creations of peoples. Poland was the land of the Poles. It was where people spoke Polish and were Roman Catholics. They were no longer part of the Russian or German or Austro-Hungarian empires. The Poles fought almost everyone: Russians, Ukrainians, and also took lands that had traditionally been German. These were vicious wars relegated now to footnotes, but they were part of a great cataclysm; the population transfers and ethnic cleansings that preoccupied Europe for so long and continued in the Balkans until the end of the twentieth century.

Jews were not Poles. In this, both sides for once were in agreement. For about 80 percent of Polish Jews, Yiddish was their first language. My grandparents were typical. All four of them came from Poland, yet I know not one word of Polish but plenty of words of Yiddish. Polish cuisine was unknown in our house, and when, as a boy of six or seven or eight, I went down the street in Passaic, New Jersey, to visit my friend Johnny, the food his mother Mitzie served—How delicious was her kielbasa!—was not only exotic but also virtually pornographic.

Their apartment was a different world—the next village, really—where the food was different and the language coarse and the religion with its looming crucifix a bit scary. Johnny's family lived above the grandiloquently named Passaic Athletic Club, a sporting facility consisting of some club chairs and the earliest of early television sets.

Johnny's father, also Johnny, was a sporting type, and he thought it was great entertainment to put boxing gloves on me and his son and have us fight it out in the kitchen. I hated these fights. I sensed that I was supposed to lose because I was not Johnny's son and because Jews, despite the occasional professional boxing figure, were not supposed to be fighters.

For Big Johnny, I was something other than his son's friend. I was also a Jew, an oddity. He would examine the reddish hair on my arms and wonder if that was characteristic of all Jews. I couldn't help him there. He would ask me about the fighting between Jews and what he called *Ay-rabs*, and I really couldn't help him there, either. Still, I had the feeling that I was supposed to know such things; that I was supposed to possess inside information of some sort.

One day Big Johnny took out the gloves, laced us up, and put us in the middle. I always fought with my eyes closed. This time I blindly powered an uppercut into Johnny's jaw, dropping him to the linoleum like the proverbial sack of potatoes. I was ecstatic. I had knocked him out! To my surprise and fright, Big Johnny chewed me out. I became confused and angry.

The Poland of Johnny's family and the Poland of my family were two different countries. There was just nothing about me that was Polish, and I could watch the annual Kościuszko Day Parade in New York with no more sense of identity than if it were the Irish on Saint Patrick's Day. The contingents from Saint This or Saint That—the church, the academy, the society—had absolutely nothing to do with me. The food was not mine, and the costumes were not mine, and even the people, with their Slavic features, were not mine: not my people. Johnny and I boxed not because his mother and my mother were Poles and this was something that Poles did but because his mother was Polish and mine was not, and this, symbolically, is what Poles once did to Jews.

For Jews, the Nazi occupation of Poland was a calamity beyond words; an era for which there was no precedent. But there was a foreshadowing. There was a premonition. Life for the Jews of Poland was getting increasingly difficult. For Mendel and Elke Kohn, things were turning more and more rotten. The world's economy was in a depression; anti-Semitism had gone from de facto to de jure, and in 1924 America had closed its doors. The days of unrestricted immigration were over.

America was fed up with its large alien population: so many Italians, so many Greeks, so many Slavs, and, of course, so many Jews. Immigration quotas were based on the census of 1882, when the United States had few Jews, and among those, very few from eastern Europe and southern Europe. The Johnson-Reed Act of 1924 attempted to ensure that the United States would remain ethnically what it had been in the nineteenth century. This was done not just because many people felt that America should have a certain, northern European look, but because some exceedingly scientific studies had concluded that the people of eastern and southern Europe were morally and intellectually inferior—although not quite as degenerate as blacks or Asians.

Later on, the machinery of immigration fell into the hands of a coterie of State Department officials whose anti-Semitism was both ill disguised and, after the advent of Hitler, increasingly lethal. Some of these officials felt that although Hitler was a brute, he had nevertheless been provoked by the Jews. This was precisely the naïve view of William E. Dodd, a historian posted to Berlin in 1933 as the American ambassador. Jews "held a great many more of the key positions in Germany than their numbers or talents entitled them to," he said. Dodd, the protagonist of Erik Larson's *In the Garden of Beasts: Love, Terror, and an American Family in Hitler's Berlin,* came to change his mind.

Mendel died about a year before Adolf Hitler was made chancellor of Germany. For the Jews of Ostrów Mazowiecka, a trap was being closed. To the west, a hideously anti-Semitic regime had been installed. To the east was the repressive Soviet Union. Elke was still alive (she would live until 1935) and so, too, were Ostrów Mazowiecka's other Kohns. They wanted to get out. With America no longer a viable choice for emigration, where could they have gone? South Africa or Argentina, both of which had Jewish communities? Or Cuba or Mexico, where Jews were going as well? But for most, these were not palatable choices. If they left the country of their birth, they'd prefer one where they had relatives and the chance of establishing themselves. One good option remained: Palestine.

In 1938, representatives of thirty-two countries met in Évian-les-Bains, France, to discuss the plight of Jewish refugees. The situation was dire. Three years earlier, Hitler had promulgated the Nuremberg Laws, which deprived Jews of citizenship and prohibited marriage between Jews and other Germans. Early in 1938, he annexed Austria, and an additional 200,000 Jews fell into his hands. By July, when the Évian conference convened, it was clear that Hitler would soon be on the march again. He already had his eye on Czechoslovakia, which had as many as 350,000 Jews.

The Évian conference lasted nine days and did incalculable damage. Franklin D. Roosevelt, who had, in fact, conceived of the conference, sent as the United States representative the industrialist Myron C. Taylor, a former CEO of US Steel. Taylor went off to Évian, possibly aware that he was participating in a sham.

The choice of Taylor was a typical Roosevelt ploy. In Taylor, he got a figure of immense prestige, but whatever his standing in society, he was not a government official, and saving refugees was, inescapably, government business. As was so often the case with Roosevelt when it came to Jewish matters, he was having it both ways: showing concern, but not too much.

In briefing his new ambassador William Dodd before he left for Berlin, FDR distinguished between sentiment and statecraft. The Nazis' treatment of the Jews was shameful, he said, "But this is not a government affair."

Roosevelt was articulating what much of America felt. It did not have much of a beef with Hitler's insistence that Jews had too much power, and that they were disproportionately present in important areas of the culture, the economy, and science. Although the Nazis were on their way toward implementing policies that would later earn the umbrella term *Holocaust*, that was not yet the case. They had proved themselves to be brutal, even murderers, but it was still inconceivable to most observers—although not to all—that they would attempt to murder every Jew they could. Still, official Washington, with its wishy-washy policies and its casual anti-Semitism, assured Hitler that the world was supremely indifferent to his barbaric policies.

Most of the major countries represented at the Évian conference pleaded refugee fatigue; they were full up, thank you. The French delegate said his country had reached "the extreme point of saturation as regards admission of refugees," and the Australian delegate, commendably frank, said simply, "As we have no real racial problem, we are not desirous of importing one."

Hitler could hardly contain his glee: no one wanted the damned Jews. Of the 600,000 Jews in Germany when the Nazis took power, about 150,000 had already fled. They included some of the more celebrated names—Albert Einstein, Hannah Arendt, Billy Wilder, Peter Lorre—establishing beachheads of the gifted in New York and Los Angeles, in particular, but also stocking the faculties of black colleges in the South. Ordinary German Jews, especially those who had migrated from the east, found that the United States, with its pathetically small immigration quota—and the nasty hurdles erected by anti-Semitic State Department officials—was out of the question. They went instead to Palestine, which, until 1939 and a British reversal on Jewish immigration, had been both welcoming and simpatico. By then, a flood of immigrants had fled the rise of Nazism. Some 174,000 Jews arrived in Palestine in the years 1933 to 1936, most of them from eastern Europe but with a considerable—and potent—admixture from Germany. The latter were often professionals, and among their accomplishments was the transformation of Tel Aviv into the "White City," with its collection of Bauhaus architecture. By 1940, 450,000 Jews lived in Palestine. The Germany-in-exile that Herzl had envisioned was on its way to fruition.

For the desperate Jews of Germany, and for the even more desperate ones to come, Palestine was not some Zionist dream, not some attempt to graft Judaism or European-Jewish culture onto a hostile Middle East, not some attempt at colonialism, but a life preserver. They grabbed onto it for dear life. It's not that they had nowhere else to go—the Dominican Republic offered to take as many Jewish refugees as possible—it was just that they had *virtually* nowhere to go.

The Évian conference was a dud, one big shrug of the shoulders. With the exception of nongovernmental actors—particularly representatives of Jewish organizations—it consisted of a gathering of the coolly indifferent or the totally hamstrung. Golda Meyerson, the former Milwaukee schoolteacher who had moved to Palestine and become Golda Meir, represented the Palestinian Jewish community. She was denied permission to sit with the other delegates but was, as she later recounted, inundated with expressions of sympathy. She reacted with characteristic pithiness. "There is only one thing I hope to see before I die, and that is that my people should not need expressions of sympathy anymore." If later, as the prime minister of Israel, she evinced a toughness and a certain contempt for the solicitous opinions of goodwilled others, it was because of experiences like Évian. Millions of Jews were about to be murdered, and the world could not be bothered to do anything about it.

The Évian Conference ended July 15, 1938. By November of that year, Sendel and Rivka Grynszpan were trapped in a no-man's-land between Germany and Poland. They were both Polish Jews but had long lived in Germany. Along with about twelve thousand other Polish Jews, the Gestapo had collected them and dumped them over Germany's eastern border. Poland took them in only reluctantly, and Germany, with no reluctance whatsoever, would not take them back. The plight of these semistateless Jews was detailed in the major newspapers, and although Germany insisted it was handling the situation as humanely as possible, few in France, of all places, believed anything other than the worst.

In the fall, Rivka Grynszpan wrote a postcard to her son, Herschel, who was living aimlessly in Paris. She described their plight and asked him, pitifully and totally unrealistically, to arrange for their emigration to America. The postcard was dated October 31.

On November 7 an overwrought Herschel Grynszpan went to the German embassy and announced that he was a German and needed to show an important embassy official a certain document. Ernst vom Rath, a junior embassy officer and indifferent Nazi, was summoned. He took Grynszpan into his office, offered him a seat, and asked him his business. Grynszpan said, " 'You are a filthy kraut, and now I will give you the document in the name of twelve thousand persecuted Jews!'" With that, Grynszpan pulled out a revolver purchased that very morning (the price tag was still on it) and fired five times, hitting vom Rath twice.

Vom Rath, who had possibly sought a foreign posting to escape the ideological claustrophobia of Nazi Germany, died the following afternoon. It was enough time for the industrious regime in Berlin to mount an enormous propaganda effort that featured a fast train to whisk the body out of France, but one that moved at a purposeful, funereal pace in Germany so that it could be viewed by the multitudes on its way to Düsseldorf. Vom Rath, unknown in life, got a state funeral of Wagnerian proportions. Hitler himself attended.

For the Nazis, the murder proved providential. They announced that the Jews had declared war on Germany and had fired the first shot, and Germany would not shy from the test. "We understand the challenge, and we accept it," the foreign minister, Joachim von Ribbentrop, vowed in his funeral oration. Just as vom Rath had gone from obscurity to the very personification of an entire nation, so had the seventeen-year-old Grynszpan become a hit man for an entire people. Kristallnacht, the government-authorized pogrom, followed. It consisted of two days of arson, vandalism, and murder, and it erased any doubt about the nature of the Nazi regime.

Grynszpan was still in a French jail when the Germans invaded France in 1940. He was seized by the Nazis but not, as you might imagine, executed after the customary torture. Instead, he was taken to Berlin, where he was to be the defendant in a show trial to prove to a skeptical world that he was indeed the agent of International Jewry.

In the end, the trial never came off. Grynszpan was transferred from one concentration camp to another, apparently kept alive at the behest of important Nazis in the event he could someday prove useful. He died sometime before the end of the war, probably executed.

His parents wound up in Israel.

7

Jew, Jew, Who's a Jew?

In 1960, at the age of nineteen, I went to work for a Midwest-based insurance company. Its New York office was located in the Empire State Building, then the tallest building in the world. I had just flunked out of college, having left home a year before, taken an apartment in New York with some high school friends, and let my schoolwork and much of the rest of my life go to hell.

My sorry academic record did not seem to matter much to the branch manager of the New York bureau. He had the commanding corner office with a massive desk and a home in suburban Short Hills, New Jersey, a place I had never heard of but which I was reliably informed was restricted: no Jews. That seemed to fit, because the manager was a "restricted" sort of guy: white haired, impeccably groomed, a former master salesman who responded to every query with agreement: sure, right, I can see your point. He was gracious, ingratiating, inoffensive, and so politically cautious that he eschewed the *New York Times* and instead read the *Herald Tribune*, which had once been the house organ of the New York business community but had since become the vehicle for the so-called New Journalism of Tom Wolfe and Jimmy Breslin—rectitude having been replaced by galloping sentences punctuated by exploding exclamation points. He noticed none of it.

He was a deeply exotic person to me. Since I was the junior of the two mail boys, it was my job to make the rounds several times a day, dropping off mail, picking it up, merrily spreading office gossip as I went, and always looking forward to my moment or two with the branch manager with the impeccably combed hair.

It turned out that he was as fascinated with me as I was with him. Whereas he was a High Goy (although possibly Catholic), I was one of only three Jews in the branch office. The other two were of no interest because neither had gone to college and therefore was not management material.

I, on the other hand, was still going to college—at night, as it happened, but college nonetheless. Maybe for this reason, he and I used to chat. He occasionally asked me about things Jewish. For some reason, B'nai B'rith, the Jewish fraternal organization, fascinated him. He spoke of it as if it were the Jewish version of the Masons, membership in which, office rumor had it, was required for promotion to the higher echelons of Hardware Mutual. It was the utter Jewishness of me that had him in thrall. He lived in his own ghetto, as I did in mine, and he wanted to know more, get outside the walls. One day he said he knew I'd do well in the company.

Why?

Because Jews are good in business.

Bingo! There it was, a blurt of bigotry. But it was one so flattering, so useful, so possibly true (it was much too early to tell) that I said nothing. I wasn't appalled by what he said. I just thought it was somewhat funny, since being good in business was not something I cared about—I wanted to be a writer—and besides, I suspected it was not true. The insurance business was about numbers, actuaries, underwriters, and such, and I was hopeless in math. I'd already run up a string of failures (algebra, geometry) and was facing the prospect of trigonometry, knowing it was a suicide mission.

The branch manager knew none of that, and so if he liked me for all the wrong reasons, it was all right with me. We got along well until one day he asked me to send some books and stuff to his daughter, a college student in Virginia. I did what I was told—and inserted a note asking her to lunch next time she was in New York. In about a week or so, his demeanor changed. I had gone from promising Jew to threatening or insolent Jew. If he could like me because I was Jewish, he could hate me because I was Jewish.

It figured also that he was right. My colleague in the mail room, the other Jew, was an exception (indeed, he was) who sought no college education.

And the other, who was in workers' comp, I could not understand because he seemed smart. But he was already trapped with a wife and kids and stuck behind a pauper's desk, processing claims—maybe another Kafka, I could have supposed, if I had only known then that Kafka had also been in workers' comp.

In this redoubt of bigotry, the ninth floor of the Empire State Building, which we shared with DuPont, there were no blacks and no Asians and no Hispanics, and this was because blacks smelled funny, as the branch manager himself told me, and Asians were unacceptable: one showed up as a temp and had the temerity to use the universal ladies' room. She was discharged the next day upon the complaints of the many women of DuPont. And there were no Hispanics because there were no Hispanics in the City of New York—the term was unknown. There were, however, Puerto Ricans aplenty, but they were porters and such, and they wore work clothes and not snap-brimmed fedoras.

As for the Jews, we were the exotics, sharp as Eversharp, sharp as a whip, sharp as a razor—not just smart, but canny and also unscrupulous. Someone like me could help the company. But I had to be watched. I could go far, but not too far. I was good in business, but not at the country club in Short Hills, wherever the hell that was, and certainly not at the Midwestern headquarters of the insurance company, where it snowed so much that tunnels connected the various buildings, a Siberia of the accommodating, the genial, the unironic, the boring—men who knew the secret rituals of the Masons and did not, for some reason, consider any of that funny.

The snowbound Home Office, a location that rewarded success as if it were failure, was no place for Jews. This was the Golden Age of Bigotry, where every ethnic group had its presumed culture—some of it behavioral, some of it physical—and the recent Holocaust was not a lesson, but a mere overseas event. Jews were still assigned their place: if not a ghetto, then a middle-management neighborhood where they could be contained. They were smart—smart in business, not so smart at the ninth hole—and the one thing about smart was that it was both useful and dangerous. By the middle of the twentieth century in Europe, it was only dangerous.

It is a commonplace to say that the creation of Israel was an understandable, if misguided, response to anti-Semitism, particularly—and above all—the Holocaust. It also can be said—in fact, it *needs* to be said—that Israel was created not just in reaction to anti-Semitism but *by* anti-Semitism. Consider the ridiculous figure of the kaiser, overdressed in the desert heat. He was childish in some ways and narrowly educated, but he was no imbecile. Yet, we know from letters he wrote from exile in Holland that he believed that a handful of his fellow Germans, the *1 percent* of them who were Jews, somehow brought down his empire and landed him across the border, where he was to spend his last days.

The stab-in-the-back formulation was hardly original with the kaiser. It had actually originated with one of his most important commanders, General Erich Ludendorff, later a right-wing politician. In no time, the usual suspects were identified, the most prominent being Jews and communists—a redundancy as far as many Germans were concerned. When Bavaria itself briefly became a Soviet republic, an exercise in chaos that lasted a bit more than a year, it turned out that Jews were indeed prominent in the new government—additional proof, if any had been needed, of the stab in the back. For the kaiser as well as many others, the dagger that stabbed Germany in the back had a Star of David etched into the hilt.

This conviction now seems preposterous. But at the time, not only did many Germans (and others) believe that Jews had such fiendish power, but the purported role the Jews played in Germany's defeat explained so many things, not the least of them being the defeat itself. After all, Germany had not been invaded; incontrovertible proof of defeat on the battlefield was sorely lacking. It's not as if the war did not take its toll. Toward its end, the civilian population suffered; food was in short supply or not available at all. But these were the sorts of things that clever and unscrupulous middlemen could manipulate.

Where, though, were the gutted buildings, the bombed-out cathedrals, women fleeing with their appalling tales of rape? Where was the pillage, the cataclysmic final battle? Not only were these lacking, but important German politicians very quickly treated the defeat as if were a mere technical matter— something relating to some obscure document. In Berlin, the kaiser's defeated troops marched proudly through the Brandenburg Gate as if they were the victors, and the provisional president, Friedrich Ebert, his finger clearly held up to the coming political wind, treated them as such. "No enemy has vanquished you," he declared.

Germany, indeed much of Europe, was having a recognition problem. The stereotypical Jew of yesteryear was now dressed in a cutaway and spats, not in the costume of the ghetto. He had cut or trimmed his beard and, increasingly, he knew not a word of Yiddish. Not only were Jews converting by the droves, but even those who remained true to the religion were attending temples, not *shuls*, where a Bachian organ and a choir sent music into the rafters, and the men congregated around the *bimah*, where the Torah was kept, wearing a felt homburg and not the traditional *kippah*, or skullcap. This sartorial, ideological, and theological assimilation produced a dilemma: What do you do with a Jew who is no longer a Jew?

This might sound like an absurdity, but a glance at the Spanish Inquisition proves otherwise. In 1492 King Ferdinand II and Queen Isabella I announced their "decision to banish all Jews of both sexes forever from the precincts of our realm." Up to 400,000 Jews emigrated, leaving behind much of their considerable wealth (this was a prosperous community), but an estimated 50,000 Jews instead chose baptism to avoid expulsion.

Up to this point, there is nothing particularly novel about this story. Jews were forever being expelled from this or that country (England, parts of Italy, parts of Poland, and so on), but where Spain departed from the script was to encourage conversion and allow the converted to remain. These former Jews were called *conversos*, or, if they continued to secretly practice Judaism, *Marranos*. Within a century or so, there were possibly 100,000 *conversos*, and they had emerged, as had the Jews before them, as a force in finance, trade, law, commerce—the usual stuff—and even the church, which was not the usual stuff at all. In other words, here were Jews who were not Jews. These were Christians—at least they proclaimed themselves to be that—who were acting as Jews. The conclusion was obvious: what made a Jew a Jew was not religious belief at all. It was something else: something in the blood.

Germany was Spain all over again. By the end of the nineteenth century, Germany's Jewish community was both affluent and influential but, as in Spain in the fifteenth century, its influence was proscribed both by law and custom. The highest level of German society was, of course, the royal family—or families, since until the unification forged by Otto von Bismarck, Germany consisted of twenty-seven constituent states. In 1871 the king of Prussia also became the German kaiser, and whatever that kaiser was, his grandson, as we have seen, was an anti-Semite.

The anti-Semitism of the Prussian court was a far different matter from the anti-Semitism of the Nazis, which was to follow. Kaiser Wilhelm II had his *Kaiserjuden*, Jews with whom he occasionally associated. He could not overlook some very important Jews, such as Bismarck's banker, Gerson Bleichroeder; or Albert Ballin, the head of the Hamburg-America Line; or Walther Rathenau, the Prussian industrialist who became the foreign minister in the Weimar era. (Rathenau was assassinated in 1922.) But they could not make a dent in the officer corps, which in Prussia and much of Germany represented the very soul of the nation. (Wilhelm II invariably wore a uniform.) In 1909 the *Frankfurter Allgemeine Zeitung* reported that between 25,000 and 30,000 Jews had served in the army since 1880, and not one had been promoted to officer. On the other hand, about three hundred converts had been given a commission—yet another example of how right Heine had been.

Keeping the regular army's officer corps *Judenfrei* meant something more than what we now might call occupational discrimination. The army was the ne plus ultra of German society. In Prussia, the army was the state's highest calling. A Jew could be rich, could be influential, could be important, but he would be outranked by a lieutenant just out of cadet school.

Into the twentieth century, these and other restrictions remained enforced. It took the abdication of the kaiser and the declaration of the republic for them to fall—and then, sometimes, only in name. Before that, though, there had been countless other restrictions and taxes on Jews and the occasional and inexplicable outburst of anti-Semitic violence, particularly the so-called Hep-Hep riots of 1819. ("Hep! Hep!" was an acronym for the Latin *Hierosolyma est perdita*, "Jerusalem is lost.") It seemed that for every step forward, German society would rebel, stiffen, and throw down yet another gauntlet for the Jew to pick up. Edicts of emancipation were followed by their repeal; Jewish salons, presided over by the wives and daughters of prominent Jews, were attractive to non-Jews and then, suddenly, not. Non-Jews formed their own—and barred Jews from membership.

For many Jews, there was but one thing to do: convert. At times, the rates were astounding; at other times, they were merely high. The rate of baptism among Jewish men peaked at 21 percent in 1918, and in certain cities—Breslau, for instance—it exceeded 50 percent. German thoroughness notwithstanding, these figures have to be considered approximations.

Almost all of Berlin's famous salon hostesses converted. Heinrich Heine converted—reluctantly, unhappily, looking immediately afterward sick and pale. Conversion was hardly a rare event; it was common, a switching of labels, a conversion from one nonbelief to another. Karl Marx's father converted in 1824, when Marx was six years old, but the family continued to attend Sabbath meals at an uncle's home.

Inexorably, German-Jewish society was merging into the larger German society—not, mind you, the German-Christian society, because that was a redundancy. As in Spain, the Jews were no longer Jews. In some cases, they had become sincerely devout Christians. In most other cases, though, they had merely ceased to be Jewish—although not Jews.

It's hard to estimate how much of German-Jewish society became just plain German society and whether the figure approached the 60 percent probable for pre-Inquisition Spain. The figure, in any case, was high, especially among the middle and upper classes—higher, it seems, than the society could tolerate. What could it do—what would it do—if Jews were no longer Jewish? What could it do if the Jews no longer kept kosher or attended synagogue or kept any of the holidays? To a religious Christian, it might be enough that a Jew had accepted Christ. But to the more secular minded, that was beside the point. He or she was already thinking of Jews as a race, as a people, as a tribe with common characteristics and, shall we say, talents.

The plain fact was that something was going on with the Jews. Anyone could see it. They were dominant, if not dominating, in so many occupations. They were prominent in so many fields. They were such a minuscule slice of the population, a soupçon of a people, and yet they seemed to be everywhere, doing everything and doing it very well. They were clearly, if not peculiarly, different, and attempts were made to find out how. In his book *Smart Jews,* Sander L. Gilman of the University of Chicago chronicles some of them. A Yale sociologist argued in the 1920s that the Romans, in the first century, "had weeded out" the most rebellious and violent of the Jews, leaving a population somewhat docile but also, we may infer, somewhat wiser.

An Oxford University professor of botany theorized that, actually, the selection took place somewhat earlier, during the Babylonian captivity (sixth century BC) to be (more or less) precise. Still others thought that the Jewish secret of success stemmed from some intrinsic physical characteristic, such as brain weight or brain size. Jewish brains were weighed and measured and sometimes, as luck would have it, differences were discerned, only later, as luck would also have it, to be disproved by scientists merely looking for the truth.

Gilman's approach to all of this is as an impatient scold. He is skeptical of all explanations or, even, that any explanation is needed. He recounts the cautionary tale of how Jews and Italians once performed so poorly on intelligence tests that they were both adjudged a collection of imbeciles. But testing has been improved since then (the World War I era), and more recent tests do not suggest that either Jews or Italians are in the least way dim. On the contrary, they show Jews in America and Britain having a higher than average IQ.

Gilman reminds us that in the popular imagination, genius and madness are closely linked, so that a people who were smarter than most were also madder than most—and more dangerous to boot. But this madness was not of the type that saw deranged figures running through the streets, a dagger aloft, a bloodcurdling yell in their throats. This madness was more silent, more subtle, and far more dangerous. It involved cunning, and, what's more, it was not isolated in this or that individual. The Jews were a people of madmen, or geniuses—"a nation of deceivers," in Immanuel Kant's charming phrase.

It sometimes seems as if everyone had a crack at divining the reasons for Jewish achievement—their presumed brilliance or the link between their intelligence and their madness, or the link between their intellectual proclivities and their puny athleticism. Thorstein Veblen had something to say about their "intellectual preeminence," and Wagner about the sort of music they composed, and Mark Twain about their superior cunning, and, of course, Nazi after Nazi about their innate corruption, their vileness, and how it hardly mattered if these people were formed by the banks of the Tigris River in Babylon or by the ruthless Romans or by a millennium of European restrictions and oppression. What mattered was that they needed to be exterminated.

As in Spain, the society rebelled. With the dawn of the Nazi era, Jewishness finally got legally defined in an apparently logical way: blood. Jews were Jews. They could not be anything else, just as a parrot, taught many words and even some logic, can't be anything other than a parrot. It could take three or four generations before Jewishness was sufficiently diluted so that it no longer mattered. Germany turned on its Jews, dicing them down to "half Jews" and "quarter Jews," and then refining the madness further by factoring in marriage. After a while, it would no longer do to simply expel the loathed Jews. They must be killed.

The final word on this matter must, ironically, belong to the Nazis. Their insistence that the Jews were indeed a people—a people and not a religion; a people and not an ethnic group—and shared some innate (invidious) characteristics, turns out to be right. Ignoring the ugly and totally mad traits that National Socialism attributed to Jews, the fact remains that new genetic testing shows that Ashkenazi Jews share a certain DNA—that they are, in this sense, a people.

This assertion engenders vigorous opposition. Anything that tends, even in a perverted reading of the evidence, to substantiate Nazi dogma or, by extension, contemporary American racism, is bound to be deemed repellent and rejected swiftly. At the same time, all the other explanations for Jewish cultural, scientific, and mathematical achievement seem like well-intentioned but wholly unconvincing attempts to avoid the obvious: Jews are different. In his book *Legacy,* Harry Ostrer, professor of pathology and genetics at New York's Albert Einstein College of Medicine, marshals all the *new* evidence and concludes that Ashkenazi Jews do indeed share certain genetic qualities that make them, as the word is customarily used, a people: "The evidence for biological Jewishness had become incontrovertible," he wrote.

Once he consolidated power, Hitler's first war was against the Jews. So was his last. He struck first, and he struck early, because he knew that if he did not, the Jews would strike at him. "The struggle for world domination will be fought entirely between us, between Germans and Jews. All else is facade and illusion. Behind England stands Israel, and behind France, and behind the United States. Even when we have driven the Jew out of Germany, he remains our world enemy."

Hitler reportedly made these statements to Hermann Rauschning, an archconservative politician from Danzig, whose book, *Hitler Speaks,* was later attacked as largely an invention. Whatever the case, this quote has an authentic ring since Hitler said this or something similar many times over.

It is likely that many Germans scoffed at the assertion that they were at war with the Jews or that the Jews were so powerful as to be considered dangerous and accorded the backhanded honor of being labeled an enemy. Still, it is just as likely that many others believed him or thought maybe he was on to something. Hitler was a clever propagandist, and while the force of his madness concerning Jews was probably not shared by the bulk of the German population, neither was it robustly rejected. Hitler was saying things that others might either agree with or, at least, consider in the realm of the possible. It started with nodding agreement. Jews *were* too powerful, and they *were* too rich, and they *were* overrepresented in various fields. Good people could agree on that. FDR would have nodded his head, and so, for that matter, would have his new man in Germany, Professor Dodd of the University of Chicago. Dodd had just the proper amount of anti-Semitism to represent Washington in Berlin.

Whatever the case, Hitler was in earnest. He characterized Jews as a disease. In his book *The Coming of the Third Reich*, the Cambridge University historian Richard Evans harvests some of Hitler's more pestilential remarks about Jews into one bundle: "The Jews were indeed a 'pestilence,' 'worse than the Black Death,' 'a maggot in the decomposing body of Germany'"—altogether worthy of eradication.

Adolf Hitler said he made war against the Jews only because the Jews had made war against him. Jews were about 1 percent of the German population, and while they were certainly a talented bunch, they were unarmed and hardly known for running amok in the streets. On that basis alone, it is tempting to dismiss Hitler's statement as hyperbolic propaganda. Any man clever enough to take over Germany, who had an appreciation of opera and the music of Wagner, who had set out early in life to be an artist, could not possibly be so dumb as to think that World War II was forced upon him as a defensive action against the Jews.

The record, though, argues otherwise. Hitler did consider the Poles and other Slavs to be subhuman, and he was determined to eventually enslave those populations and use them more or less as beasts of burden. Still, he harbored a special and intense antipathy for Jews—an antipathy tinged with admiration and a certain amount of fear. His fear-respect for Jews was such that he even attributed the Red Army's fierce fighting qualities to Jewish influence. Similarly, the Polish resistance movement, by far the most formidable in Nazi-occupied Europe, had to be the product of Jewish organization or Jewish leadership— Jewish *something*—if only because Nazi dogma insisted that the Poles were incapable of such bravery and organization. The Jews, on the other hand—well, the Jews were capable of anything.

Everything Hitler said about Jews has to be accepted at face value. There is no doubt that he considered Jews to be his enemy and an enemy of considerable potency with an astounding reach. It was not enough merely to exterminate them in Germany and, later, elsewhere in the ever-expanding German empire, but also in countries that were thousands of miles away. To that end, Hitler kept a wary eye on the American Jewish community, attributing its influence to the clear intention of Franklin Roosevelt to enter the war on the side of Britain. And it was the Jews, too, who somehow kept Britain in the war, fighting a losing battle, when it could have reached an accommodation with Germany—a racially compatible nation, after all.

Zealous Nazis saw themselves as dedicated public health officials. They were on a worldwide and urgent hunt for a particular microbe: the Jew. If it existed anywhere in the world, it could propagate and launch another attack. At the famous January 1942 conference in a stately villa on the shore of the Wannsee, the convener of the meeting, Reinhard Heydrich, chief of the security service of the Reichfürer-SS, made clear just how obsessed he and his associates were with Jews. He came not only with a list of the Jewish population of the countries Germany then occupied, but also the Jewish populations of countries that, it seems to us now, the Nazis could never occupy: Ireland, Portugal, Sweden, Switzerland, even England. Richard Evans, in *The Third Reich at War*, concludes that the Nazis wanted to pressure these countries into surrendering their Jews—turning them over to be murdered. Later that year, in fact, Heinrich Himmler went to Helsinki to ask Finland—an ally of Germany—to return about two hundred German Jews who had sought asylum in that country. He did not demand the two thousand or so Finnish Jews, just the ones who had fled Germany. They were his, and he needed to kill them.

The trip is almost incomprehensible: the second or third most important official in a country then at war on two fronts venturing to a nearby country in order to arrange the murder of a handful of Jews. (In the end, four families were turned over to the Nazis and sent to Auschwitz.) Himmler would not have made the trip if he had not known with certainty how much his boss was obsessed with Jews and the supposed danger that even a handful could pose. All of this was insane, preposterous, ludicrous, and hard to understand—so much so that it runs the danger of veering into the literally unbelievable. The Nazi hierarchy, from Hitler on down, was convinced that it was engaged in a fight to the death with International Jewry, a figment of its own imagination. Germany had guns and planes and ships, but the Jews—ah, the Jews!—had their devious brains. It was, somehow, an even match.

Hitler was in deadly earnest about Jews—what they were and what he would do to them. His private statements were no different from his public ones. We have no record of him admitting to a confidant that he knew he was exaggerating the importance and threat of the Jews because he needed a bogey-man. On the contrary, in those intimate moments when he might have leaned over to confess—or boast of—his artifice, he said just the opposite. At a private dinner with the fanatical Himmler and Heydrich, he said, "In the Reichstag, I prophesied to Jewry, the Jew will disappear from Europe if war is not avoided. This race of criminals has two million dead of the [First World] War on its conscience, and now hundreds of thousands again. Nobody can tell me: But we can't send them into the morass! For who bothers about our people? It's good if the terror that we are exterminating Jewry goes before us."

On another occasion in 1942, Hitler told both Himmler and Hans Hein-rich Lammers, for a time among the half dozen most powerful Nazis, that if the Jews did not leave, he would have no choice but to seek "total extermination." "Why should I regard a Jew as any different from a Russian prisoner? Many are dying in the prison camps because we have been driven into this situation by the Jews. But what can I do about that? Why then did the Jews provoke the war?" Nothing for public consumption here.

Hitler's statements were preposterous on their face. If Jews were so power-ful, why was he able to kill them by the millions with so very little opposition? If they had such wealth, why were German troops in the east encountering such poverty in the ghettos and shtetlach of Poland and Russia? If they were, as anyone could see, *Untermenschen*—lice ridden, emaciated, dressed in rags, and hideously diseased—how could they also be *Übermenschen*, possibly capable of defeating Germany?

Probably older Germans appreciated the lunacy of what Hitler was saying. But a younger generation had grown up with anti-Semitic propaganda and had undoubtedly learned its lessons well. (By 1944, a twenty-year-old infantryman had spent almost all his school years being indoctrinated by the Nazis.) The Jews had become the universal explanation, the cause of anything that went wrong. In the hands of Nazi propagandists, the Jews had great plasticity. They could be rich and poor, strong and weak, and even though, as the end of the war approached, they had been almost annihilated, they still retained an im-mense power and would, without a doubt, seek vengeance. A soldier, fretting about what would happen if Germany lost the war, said in a letter home quoted by Evans, "The Jews will then fall on us and exterminate everything that is German, there will be a cruel and terrible slaughter."

Historians may still quibble about what the average German knew about what had happened to the average Jew. Still, while the Final Solution had been devised in secret, it had been executed in public. Hundreds of thousands had participated in, witnessed, or otherwise knew of the killings. The German-Jewish community had evaporated, and although the absence of Jews might have seemed normal to younger Germans, their elders knew better. They knew who had once owned that store or this building or taught at that school or run that shop. Jews had never made up more than about 1 percent of the German population in general and were only 4 percent of Berlin's, but there had been more than a half million of them, and in the small towns, where they were shopkeepers, physicians, and such, they had been highly visible. Jews continued to exist in whispers and rumor and the furtive hints to others of another time—a tilt of the head, a look—Here, at one time: Jews.

So the Germans knew what had been done to the Jews—what *they* had done to the Jews—and whether they had participated in the killing was almost beside the point. They had been complicit in the murder of Jews in the way they had not been in the murder of the insane or the chronically ill—euthanasia programs that had to be halted due to public unease.

The Nazis early on forbade Jews to have pets. A Holocaust memorialist explained this policy this way in a *New York Review of Books* article: "The reason for that is that first the animals had to go and then the owners could be removed. Because if animals would stay in an apartment, they wouldn't get food, they'd make noise, this would cause a commotion. Maybe the Aryan neighbors wouldn't care about the Jewish neighbor being deported, but they would truly care about a little cat meowing."

As the plotters against Hitler realized almost a year before the end of the war, and as many a German military man had feared even before the 1939 invasion of Poland that started the war, the war was lost—the war against Russia, against France, against Britain, and against the United States of America. The irony is that the plotters, led by Colonel Count Claus Schenk von Stauffenberg, a Bavarian nobleman and professional soldier, precipitated a furious purge of dissidents in the military and may have prolonged the war.

Following the July 20, 1944, attempt to kill Hitler by placing a bomb in his East Prussia field headquarters, the Wolf's Lair, various organs of the Nazi Party and its security apparatus (the SS and so on) grew in importance and power. Three days after the plot, the Nazi salute—Heil Hitler!—replaced the standard military one, and officers throughout the armed forces, or *Wehrmacht,* outdid one another in expressing and exhibiting their loyalty to and adoration of Hitler. Much of this was genuine—an appalled reaction to what had, after all, been a treasonous attempt to kill the head of state—and some was an understandable effort merely to stay alive. (About twenty thousand Germans were executed in the months following the attempted coup.) In the general population, Ian Kershaw writes in *The End,* his account of why Germany held out for so long, there was an eruption of indignation and sympathy—hardly the stirrings of revolt. In Germany today, Stauffenberg is the most popular street name (Beethoven is second), and he has become a national hero—proof, as he insisted at the time, that not all Germans were in thrall to the führer. True enough. But although Stauffenberg himself had once been appalled at the slaughter of the Jews, he'd agreed that the Poles deserved colonization and, until the reversal at Stalingrad, that Hitler was a military genius.

If anything, the plot confirmed Hitler's belief both in his own destiny and that the professional officer corps, much of it of aristocratic pedigree, was a bunch of dolts. He continued the war, a monumental exercise of demonic willpower and diabolical charisma that ended only when Hitler chose to take his own life. By then, a war of stark aggression had been transformed, both in reality and in the pronouncements of the propaganda ministry, into one of desperate defense—a last-ditch attempt to turn back the rapacious Russians, a seething horde that had invaded from the east. There was yet another reason to continue the war: the revenge that Jews would surely exact. The difference between the Russians and the Jews was that the former could be seen everywhere, while the latter had all but been exterminated. Still, the war against both went on.

Troops and material that were needed at the western or eastern fronts instead were used up to the last moment in the killing of Jews. Trains that could have been useful in the war effort were instead diverted—no, not diverted, since killing Jews had primacy—*retained* for the task of murder. Hitler was in a desperate war against a formidable enemy. Time was running out. This was a fight to the death between Nazi Germany and the Mind of the Jews.

8

Democracy:
Is It Good for the Jews?

Sometime in the winter of 1938, the foreign correspondent G. E. R. Gedye, of Britain's *New Statesman and Nation* magazine, met at night with two young women he described as "Jewesses." One was twenty-three years old, "plump, thick-set, rather Nordic-German looking with short-cropped hair." The other, twenty-two, was "slightly built, pretty, vivacious, and self-assured." Gedye called her Miss A; he called the other Miss B. They were both medical students, and both were caught in a volcanic upsurge of anti-Semitism, some of it remarkably petty, some of it astonishingly violent.

Jews were segregated from Christians in the medical school's lecture hall. In the surgical labs, they were forbidden to dissect Christian corpses and were forced to secure Jewish ones, no easy task given religious strictures regarding the sanctity of the dead. This was degrading, possibly futile as well, but a mere nuisance compared with the rest of what the two women related. They were both routinely beaten by their Christian schoolmates. Miss B told Gedye of the time she was accosted, smacked around, and then, when it was clear that no one would intervene, bent over a chair and held down by four students.

"'Another flung my dress up over my shoulders, and the sixth began to bash me with all his strength across the buttocks with a police truncheon. How many strokes I got I cannot tell you—the pain of the first five was excruciating, and then I lost count. They didn't seem to hurt so much anymore—I only heard the excited shouts of the thirty students or so who were looking on.'"

Miss B dropped out of medical school.

"'I am finished. The Christians have got their way. I have wasted three years of my life studying the healing profession, which seemed to be the only worthwhile one in the world, but I dare not go back. I would rather go as a servant in the wildest colony and never touch a book again in life, than face such torture again."

Miss A's experiences were no different. Still, she was determined to tough it out. "They pounded my face to a jelly," she told Gedye. "My upper lip was cut open, also my forehead, which streamed with blood."

A hard punch over her left breast knocked her out. When she awoke, "a Christian attendant . . . helped me onto a chair and pushed me through a window, saying anxiously, 'Be quick, for heaven's sake, or they'll beat me for helping you.'"

The two were among 20 Jewish students out of 160 in the medical school. Most of the other Jews were men, and they, too, were harassed and beaten. Sometimes Miss A or Miss B would come across pools of fresh blood in the hallways and realize that yet another of their number had been beaten up. Soon there would be no Jewish medical students at all.

After interviewing the medical students, Gedye went to the Central Criminal Court in hope of seeing for himself "the beating-up of Jewish lawyers." This had been so frequent an occurrence that not a single one of the area's "couple of hundred" Jewish lawyers showed up that day. Nonetheless, Gedye got the lay of the land:

"Some sixty or so anti-Semitic lawyers would collect in the advocate's refectory and make their plans. The guardians of law and order in the corridor would be withdrawn by arrangement, after which the Christian lawyers would post sentinels at all exits and then in bands of twenty would scour the corridors for Jewish barristers. . . . On catching sight of a Jew, the twenty set on him with the utmost violence, hitting him with sticks and fists until bleeding and half-conscious, they have hunted him to the exits where the sentinels finish the job and fling him into the streets."

Gedye got this information from a Jewish lawyer he had interviewed. The lawyer told him how the gang of anti-Semites would even invade courtrooms while trials were in session. When that happened, the anti-Semites would silently wait while the judge, with a knowing nod of the head, would quickly wrap things up and leave the courtroom.

"As he withdraws, the assault and battery on the Jewish pleaders begins. I asked him [the lawyer], as I had asked the girl students, pro forma—I knew the answer—whether there was no protection to be had from the police or the courts and was met by the same bitter laughter and the query, 'But I thought you knew this country?'"

This country?

Germany?

No, Romania.

Gedye was in Bucharest, a city of about 40,000 Jews (out of 728,000 countrywide) and the capital of a nation that was something of an ethnic mess. All sorts of neighboring territories had been awarded Romania at the end of World War I, and with them had come an ethnologist's feast of Ukrainians, Bessarabians, Bulgarians, and Russian Jews. Romania had turned bitterly anti-Semitic— not because of German intimidation or even out of envy, but of its own accord. Romanian anti-Semitism was a bottom-up phenomenon, neither imposed nor imported from abroad. German anti-Semitism did not instigate Romanian anti-Semitism. It merely validated it.

Romanian fascism was a particularly nasty variant of a particularly nasty ideology. Its anti-Semitism was no different. Romania had the same passion and determination as Germany, but lacked its Teutonic know-how and organizational acumen. Still, the Romanians did their level best. They killed at least 280,000 and possibly as many 469,000 Jews, figures all the more astounding for Romania's refusal or inability to adopt a plan of methodical murder. No Final Solution for Romania. No extermination camps. Romanian murder was haphazard and often extemporaneous—a pogrom in one town but not the next; an order issued for mass murder on one day and then not the next.

The Romanian army was, in effect, the state's murder weapon. But the bulk of the murders took place outside the borders of Old Romania itself on lands the army had seized from the Soviet Union following World War I. In the next war, Romania joined Germany in attacking the Soviet Union. Wherever its troops went, they killed Jews and Gypsies with great zest. For the most part, though, the Jews of Old Romania were spared.

Romanian anti-Semitism was extremely convoluted, complicated, and, when it came to murder, inconsistent. In this regard, it matched Romanian politics with its coups, putsches, and extraordinary numbers of political assassinations. The country was at times a democracy, a monarchy, a democratic monarchy, a dictatorship, and a near-absolute monarchy. Its rulers were men who imposed or tolerated harsh, homicidal laws and regulations on Jews and then, often based on personal relationships or love affairs, would spare the occasional life. Jew hatred was not a matter of racist ideology. This was, in a sense, personal—very personal.

Romanian anti-Semitism was not produced by the country's transition to democracy and not something created out of whole cloth by an agitator. On the contrary, it had always been an indelible part of Romania's national character. But it took the dynamics of democracy to poke it with a stick, to waken the beast and make it roar. The Jews of Romania suffered greatly, not because one man—a monarch or a dictator—insisted on it, but because of what the people wanted. To this day, anti-Semitism remains so unremarkable, so much in the fabric of the society, that the Romanian banknote, the leu, features the picture of Nicolae Iorga—poet, playwright, and prime minister (1931–32), as well as anti-Semitic pamphleteer and hideous Jew hater.

Romania is an interesting and ominous case study. Its Jew hatred was extraneous to any large German minority parroting a Nazi party line. It consisted of the usual stuff about Jews being greedy, too rich, too cheap, too powerful—too much of everything. It had the usual religious component as well, only in Romania it was not the Roman Catholic Church but the Orthodox Church that sanctified the hate, and it embraced the standard paranoiac anticommunism, a fear heightened by a border with the Soviet Union. It also had the approval of what today might be called the establishment: a thoroughly anti-Semitic intelligentsia. Even when the leader was not himself an anti-Semite, the political climate under the democracy was such that he had to keep his views to himself. King Carol II, the sometime monarch-dictator, had Jewish friends and associates, and a Jewish mistress, but did little to defend Jews in general.

What was true for Romania was more or less true for the rest of eastern Europe. The Poland that emerged from the Russian, Austro-Hungarian, and German empires went from being ruled by a monarch (the czar, the emperor, the kaiser) to being a parliamentary democracy. It was always a shaky democracy—after all, Poland had never been one—but for the first time in its history, an electorate chose its leaders, and those leaders imposed anti-Semitic laws and regulations.

The advent of democracy, of a parliamentary system, was a wonderful, progressive development, but not for the country's minorities, particularly the Jews. Once again, electoral politics meant pandering to a substantial number of anti-Semites. In Romania, as in the rest of eastern Europe, anti-Semitic politicians could exploit existing prejudices and not worry too much about being admonished by either other politicians or the nation's moral leaders. The Orthodox Church was either exuberantly anti-Semitic or indifferent. The army, a supremely important institution, was deeply conservative in both a religious and cultural sense, and it, too, did not have much use for Jews. In Romania, even the urban intelligentsia, much of it French oriented, enthusiastically took up anti-Semitism as a banner of its nationalism. In short, all over central and eastern Europe, the phenomenon first exploited by Vienna's Karl Lueger was becoming an increasingly powerful force.

The importance of anti-Semitism in the electoral politics of the interwar era coincided with the rise of fascism. And while anti-Semitism is often considered an integral part of fascism, that was not always the case. The Italian fascism of Benito Mussolini was initially so free of overt anti-Semitism that a few Italian Jews gladly enlisted. (Mussolini himself was a different matter; he was, it appears, a common anti-Semite.) One of those Jews, Ettore Ovazza of Turin, whose correspondence with Mussolini reeks of sickening praise, founded a fascist newspaper and remained a steadfast, if totally deluded, fascist past 1938 and the institution of Nazi-inspired anti-Semitic legislation. (Ovazza was murdered by the SS in 1943.) Still other Jews cited Mussolini and his movement as an example of the sort of things that Jews could do in Palestine. The pride, the militancy, the concussive chest beating of once-bedraggled Italy, was worth some emulating. By the mid-1930s, however, that had changed. There was no separating anti-Semitism from fascism or, for that matter, from nationalism. To hate Jews was to love one's country. To love one's country was to hate Jews.

Mussolini took power in 1922, Hitler not for another eleven years, and for some time, Mussolini assured Italian Jews that German anti-Semitism would stay in Germany. Indeed, he suggested that Hitler's obsession with Jews was a Teutonic fixation: one of those Germanic things that the Italians, so much more worldly and accommodating, would not only reject but also find downright puzzling. "Race! It is a feeling, not a reality: ninety-five percent, at least, is a feeling. Nothing will ever make me believe that biologically pure races can be shown to exist today," he told a journalist in 1933.

The European country with the most Jews was Poland. This unfortunate land—*God's Playground*, the British historian Norman Davies aptly entitled his history of Poland—has come to have its interwar history defined almost exclusively by the conditions and treatment of just a single minority, the Jews. But Jews, 10 percent of the population, were hardly Poland's only minority and hardly Poland's largest (that was Ukrainians), yet they were different in a significant respect. They were concentrated mostly in cities and towns—less than 5 percent of them were in agriculture—and they were spread across the country. In other words, Jews were everywhere. This was not the case with the Ukrainians (14 percent of the population) or Byelorussians (3 percent), who were concentrated, respectively, near the borders of Soviet Ukraine and Soviet Byelorussia. These minority groups yearned to join their countrymen on the other side of the frontier. The Jews, in contrast, wanted no such thing—if only because there was no such thing. They yearned for a greater acceptance and assimilation in Polish society. Instead, much of Polish Jewry was simply murdered.

Poland's interwar history is both complex and convoluted. Fourteen governments rose and fell between 1918 and 1925. The history is further complicated (or obscured) by context, or lack of it. To most Jews, American Jews in particular and especially those of Polish descent, Poland was one vast charnel house. It was the country where the Nazis located their extermination camps not just because it contained the most Jews but also because the Nazis felt that the local population, thoroughly terrorized, would be either supportive or indifferent. To many American Jews, Poland was one immense and endless pogrom. Nothing good can be said about it.

Not surprisingly, many Poles take umbrage at this telling of their history, and they have a champion in Davies, the British historian. He points out that Polish nationalism was an insecure affair, unsteady on its feet, and wary of the substantial minorities within the country—Jews being just one. There was more concern about Ukrainians and Byelorussians and, consequently, persecution of them both. (As always, bigotry produced amazing distinctions and imaginative terms. Roman Catholic Byelorussians were called White Poles, a relative compliment.) Poland also had over one million Germans as well as a scattering of Czechs, Russians, and Lithuanians. Of the country's seventeen provinces, Poles were a minority in three.

The Jews, too, were a non-Polish-speaking minority. About 80 percent of them claimed Yiddish as their primary language, and in many cases it was their *only* language. They knew more Hebrew, a dead language reserved for the synagogue, than they did Polish. Many small towns were exclusively Jewish and Yiddish-speaking, as were whole neighborhoods of larger cities. The language barrier was not a trifle—not, as American Jews might imagine, a case of Polish being spoken outside the home and Yiddish within. On the contrary, for many Jews, Yiddish was it—the only language they had. This not only made it impossible for these Jews to communicate with non-Jews but even with assimilated Jews.

The bulk of the Jewish community comprised a nation within the nation—although, with accelerated assimilation, that was fast changing. For assimilated Jews, Poland was, for a while, not such a bad place. Davies put it this way: "Most sadly, the destruction of Poland's Jews by the Nazis . . . destroyed the living memories which could put Jewish History into an appropriate context. The many common experiences which the Jews of Poland had shared with the country's other inhabitants were rapidly forgotten."

By this Davies was referring both to the common experience of being a despised minority and the somewhat less common experience of being an assimilated, ordinary Pole. There were many of the latter; many Jews for whom Polish was their preferred language, and many, too, who openly exulted in Yiddish. Warsaw had a vibrant Yiddish theater and press and a substantial number of Polish Jews who saw themselves as both Polish and Jewish—just as, Davies observes, American Jews see themselves as both American and Jewish, nothing oxymoronic there.

"But Polish history was not treated in a similar way. Once historic Poland had been turned into the Babylon of modern Zionist mythology, Poles and Jews had to be treated as two completely separate sets of humanity."

Davies is defending the Poles from the charge of universal anti-Semitism—no exceptions allowed. The many Poles who risked their lives during the Holocaust to save Jews need recognition—they have certainly earned it—and the more numerous Poles who objected to anti-Semitism in the interwar period likewise deserve acknowledgement. Poland was not Nazi Germany.

Still, the record is appalling. As with much of the rest of central, eastern, and southern Europe, democracy hardly thrived in Poland, and the term "minority rights" must have been met with dumb stares, if not outright hostility. In fact, Poland's reputation for intolerance was so well established that World War I's victorious allies made it (and some other emerging nations) sign a treaty guaranteeing minority rights as a condition of its independence. In Poland's case, the minority the Allies had in mind were the Jews—already the victims of over one hundred pogroms in the year following the armistice. Poland was heading into darkness.

By 1926, Marshall Józef Piłsudski had seized power in a coup. Piłsudski was an odd fellow, and his was an odd coup. He was a military man by profession, but not by training, and a man of the moderate left and not of the typical hard right. After seizing power, however, he rectified that and moved right. Pertinently, Piłsudski was not an anti-Semite. Jews liked him for who he was and for his relatively enlightened policies, but some of their affection was a reflection of the fear and hatred they felt for his archrival Roman Dmowski, an uncomplicated anti-Semite. When, for instance, the World War I allies imposed the Minorities Treaty on Poland and set its borders not at all to Dmowski's liking, he blamed the "international Jewish conspiracy" and labeled Lloyd George, the British prime minister, "the agent of the Jews."

Dmowski's anti-Semitism was hardly of the country club variety. His convictions ran deep, and while he had antipathy toward Poland's German minority as well—he felt that they, as well as the Jews, had too much of the country's wealth—he felt a special animus toward the Jews. His solution to the "Jewish problem" stopped short of genocide—he never advocated murder—but included, as a last resort, expulsion. He wanted the Jews gone.

Piłsudski accommodated. Poland became a de facto anti-Semitic state. Unlike in Nazi Germany, Jews never lost their citizenship or had their property confiscated, but over time, life became nearly unbearably harsh. For all of Dmowski's talk about inordinate Jewish wealth, the fact remained that this was a poor, if not impoverished, community, with 80 percent living below what today would be called the poverty line. Many of these poor Jews were shopkeepers or tavern owners, and for them the government had some very special initiatives. It prohibited Sunday sales, meaning that Jews who observed the Sabbath on Saturday (most Jewish shopkeepers did) would lose two days of work. It also nationalized the sale of alcohol, tobacco, and matches—traditional Jewish livelihoods—and it decreed that the name of the shopkeeper be posted for all to see, a clumsy (and probably unnecessary) device to highlight ethnicity.

Poland's university campuses, like those of Romania, offered no respite from anti-Semitism. The intelligentsia of that era, if the term can be applied to brawling youth, were hardly the leftists they would become in the 1950s, the 1960s, and even later. Instead, they were enamored of nationalism and its handmaiden, fascism, and romanticized violence for its supposedly bracing and purifying qualities. It's hard to say how many of the faculty were in agreement and how many were simply cowed, but it is clear that only a minority objected—and they, more often than not, paid dearly for their principles. Students had all the usual religious, nationalistic, or outright crackpot reasons for hating Jews, but they had another reason as well: there were simply too many Jews, especially in the professions of law and medicine.

As early as 1921, Jewish quotas were instituted at the University of Lvov's School of Medicine and the School of Law. The effort was blocked by the minister of religious creeds and public education, who deemed the quotas unconstitutional. His objection is worth noting not because it had a long-term effect—quotas were soon introduced almost everywhere—but because it showed that not all Poles were anti-Semites or would tolerate anti-Semitic measures. Their anti-anti-Semitism was sometimes the product of heartfelt empathy with Jews and sometimes the result of a passionate and deeply conservative attachment to Polish-Christian ideals. Whatever the reason, these anti-anti-Semites were brave people. This was an age infatuated with violence and its presumed cathartic effect. It was a nasty time.

By the late 1930s, the universities had instituted "seating ghettos": the so-called ghetto benches where Jews were required to sit. Once again, some brave faculty members protested. And once again, this appeal to reason or tradition was rebuffed. Jews had to sit where they were told. Only they would not. Instead, they lined up against the wall. This was virtually a call to battle, and hordes of Christian students set on them, while the faculty either joined in or looked the other way.

It did not take long for college life to become intolerable for Jews, and they left. As if in anticipation of the coming German occupation, universities became *Judenfrei*, and not long after that, the Nazis marched in and showed the Poles how to really do anti-Semitism. The process inaugurated by the Poles was finished by the Germans. Over one thousand years of Jewish life in Poland had come to an end.

In her book *On the Edge of Destruction*, Celia S. Heller wrote that the Jews of Poland "came to represent a conquered population." That nation had been in Poland since the first millennium—way before Poland itself became a nation. Successive waves of Jews were invited into the Polish territories by monarchs who valued their commercial abilities and entrusted them with certain tasks, such as collecting rents, managing estates, and lending money. None of these vocations exactly endeared the Jews to the non-Jewish population, and so, in effect, Jewish-Polish relations got off on the wrong foot. Yet even if Jews had become mere farmers or laborers, it is still not likely that they would have been embraced. They were not Christians, hardly an insignificant difference, and they were already freighted with all the myths of anti-Semitism, including the most powerful one about their responsibility for the death of Christ.

Yet once again, the belief that democracy and the passage of time would bring progress proved wrong. For Jews in particular, the creation of the Polish republic made things much more fluid and uncertain. It coincided with the accelerated movement of Jews out of the ghetto or the shtetl, from country to city. Warsaw became 30 percent Jewish.

The observation that democracy was bad for the Jews and could really be bad for mankind in general is not original with me. Hannah Arendt and Theodor Adorno noticed the same phenomenon and came to fear it. The cause of their apprehension was, of course, what had happened to their beloved Weimar Germany—not just a democracy but, in its sheer number of political parties and the virtues of its constitution, an exemplary one. This Germany, *their* Germany, gets the lion's share of attention; it went from so good to so bad so quickly that, as with a reeling drunk, it's hard to take your eyes off it.

But Germany was not the central or eastern European exception. Yes, it had Hitler and the Nazis and started the war and created extermination camps and so much more that is now so familiar and yet, when you think about it, so persistently strange. It was, however, just more determined, more creative, more efficient—more *German*—in its anti-Semitism, of which, probably, it had less than, say, Poland or Romania. They all had the same disease—the one they thought they had, their so-called Jewish problem—and the disease that convinced them they had a problem, anti-Semitism. They all veered to the right, and in doing so fell on their Jewish population with varying intensities of hate and with varying degrees of homicidal fury. The exception was Czechoslovakia, a stolidly middle-class nation led by a rare and courageous statesman, Tomáš Garrigue Masaryk, a man so exceptional and progressive that he took his American wife's maiden name, Garrigue, and made it his own. He was his nation's president from the 1918 armistice to 1935.

As for the others—Austria, Poland, Hungary, Italy, Romania, Greece, Portugal, Spain, the Baltic states, and the Balkans—they all became right-wing dictatorships of one sort or another, with some never even giving democracy a chance to fail. Anti-Semitism did not play a major role in all of them—Italy held out for a while, and, oddly enough, so did Francisco Franco's Spain—but it was present in all of them. What's pertinent is that all these new democracies crashed. Country after country lacked the necessary institutions or traditions to make democracy work, especially respect for minority rights. They had politicians and political parties that either exploited anti-Semitism or lacked the requisite principles to stand up to it. In these respects, they resembled the Middle East.

9

Anti-Semitism
Among the Semites

It was 2007, and I was down at the Dead Sea in Jordan, attending a World
Economic Forum conference on the Middle East, when in the coffee lounge
of the rather posh Jordan Valley Marriott Resort & Spa, I picked up the *Jordan
Times*, an English-language newspaper, and found an explanation for what had
happened on September 11, 2001, at New York City's World Trade Center: the
Jews had done it.

Around me were assembled Arab businessmen and government leaders, the
immensely wealthy and the less immensely wealthy. I looked around, feeling
furtive. This stuff was the rawest anti-Semitism, yet this newspaper was intended not for the man in the street, whose supposed gullibility was storied, but
for the business and governmental elite of Jordan. Did any of them notice what
was in this newspaper? Did any of them care?

I read on. The attack on the World Trade Center was the work of Israel's
feared intelligence agency, the vaunted Mossad. The proof was the fact that of
the Center's precisely 1,478 Jewish employees, not one reported to work that
day. They had all been saved. They had all been forewarned.

What was the editor thinking? Did he think his readership was going to
believe this trash? Was he worried that this account of what allegedly tran-
spired on September 11, 2001, would reflect badly on the paper and its veracity?

And what about the paper's most important reader; the entity known as the palace—in other words, the king?

The *Jordan Times* is sanctioned by the government and owned partially by it. No censors are stationed at the newspaper, but the staff knows what is permitted and what is not and what the consequences could be for offending the palace. So it is reasonable to conclude that whoever authorized the publication of that column thought it was unremarkable; maybe it was something he believed himself, but in any case it was not something the palace would find offensive. After all, the substance of the column was the stuff of everyday speculation—no, not speculation, but conversation. The Jews were behind the September 11 attacks. This was a fact. *It was well known.*

The phrase "It is well known" is itself well known. It is the response to any cynic who might question a universally accepted myth. Some things are so obvious that no proof is ever needed. In fact, the very absence of proof proves (beyond a shadow of a doubt) that no proof is needed. In the case of the September 11 attacks, the outcome proved the theory. The victims, aside from those poor souls who were killed on the spot, were the Arabs themselves. America and the West would blame them. Therefore, the obvious perpetrators, if only because they were the obvious beneficiaries, were the Israelis—in other words, the Jews.

Wait. There was more. The attacks were huge, flamboyant: two skyscrapers were demolished in New York; the Pentagon just outside Washington was also hit. Who was capable of doing such a thing? Not the Arabs. Certainly not the Arabs. Few Arabs believed they had the skills to pull off such a spectacular terrorist attack. This could not be the work of Osama bin Laden and Al Qaeda. This had to be the work of an intelligence service. This had to be the work of the Mossad. It was clear. It was obvious. *It was well known.*

This version of that awful day's events was not just whispered in the coffeehouses or the souks but also published or broadcast in most Arab countries, sometimes in semiofficial newspapers such as Egypt's *Al Ahram Al Masai*. The script was changeable. Sometimes it was the American government that had induced the attack in order to justify the later invasion of Iraq; sometimes it was the United States working in tandem with the Mossad; sometimes it was the Mossad alone. And, almost always, the allegation was buttressed with amazing specificity: the number (60, sometimes 120) of Jews or Israelis who were deported from the United States on account of their involvement in the plot or merely for being part of a vast Israeli espionage ring.

The Middle East Media Research Institute, a Washington-based pro-Israel research organization, compiled these and other examples of how the September 11 attacks were perceived in the Arab world. By monitoring the press, radio, television, and broadcasts of the Friday sermons from various mosques, it provides an impression of the Middle East that is strikingly similar to that of fascist Europe in the 1930s and 1940s—and strikingly different from the image emitted by the region's leaders. The elite of the region talk a different language. They speak the English of globalization; not just the globalization of commerce, but the globalization of political and cultural values, and it is largely these people that Westerners, including journalists, talk to.

But beyond the first-class lounge or the hotel meeting room or the restaurants in Washington or New York where Arabs and Israelis tell the same jokes and laugh at the same punch lines, an anti-Zionism that is indistinguishable from anti-Semitism is commonplace, unexceptional, and unquestioned. It is a widespread belief, uniting Arab and Persian, Sunni and Shiite, explaining so much, if not everything. It is, as it once was in Europe, a widely accepted belief system, and while it may lack the proximate affirmation of a huge department store or an imposing bank or even an obvious and alien effect on the culture, it does provide an answer to so many questions.

These Jews are spoken of no differently from how Hitler once spoke of them. Robert S. Wistrich, in his book *A Lethal Obsession: Anti-Semitism from Antiquity to the Global Jihad*, puts it this way: "The demonic images of Jews presently circulating in much of the Arab world are sufficiently radical in tone and content to constitute a new warrant for genocide." Actually, with some nips and tucks, this was just the familiar "warrant for genocide" updated a bit. The situation in the Arab world approximates what existed in pre-Holocaust Europe: in other words, the preconditions for genocide. Just as in pre-Holocaust Europe not everyone was an anti-Semite, so, too, in the Middle East, anti-Semitism is not the universal secular belief of a whole people. Some Arabs are anti-Zionist without being anti-Semitic, and some are neither, and some simply don't give a damn.

Ever since the Second World War, the region has been saturated with anti-Semitic messages, originally from Germany itself, and now homegrown. As in Europe both before and during the Holocaust, children have been schooled in anti-Semitic doctrine: the blood libel, Jewish control over international finance, and on and on. Meanwhile, the media has originated and spread such pernicious and ludicrous tales as chewing gum altered by the Mossad and sold to Palestinians to make women hypersexual. The vilest anti-Semitic messages have issued from the mosques on Fridays and these sermons have gone unrebutted or, worse, broadcast by a mass media that almost always answers to the government.

The contemporary Middle East is not the Europe of yesteryear, not even when it comes to anti-Semitism. In a certain sense, it's worse. Whereas the anti-Semitism of interwar Europe had a large component of myth—the all-powerful Jews, the International Jew, the Jew as sinister capitalist and sinister communist—the anti-Semitism of today's Middle East rests on a solid foundation of fact. Israel truly is awesomely powerful. Its birth, its victories in war after war, and its ability to dominate a region seem as uncanny and mythical as any tale of Jewish power or evil. The Jews of Europe were a paradox: victim and victimizer. The Jews of the Middle East are unquestionably victimizers—at least, that's how their neighbors see them.

The other salient difference is that the Arab nations, as opposed to the interwar European nations, contain almost no Jews. They are gone. A scattered few remain in Lebanon, Syria, and Iraq and maybe a remnant of one hundred or so are in Egypt, a county where as late as the 1950s there had been eighty thousand. The once-numerous Jews of the Middle East—including those of non-Arab Iran—have mostly dispersed around the globe, a Diaspora of the Diaspora.

Of course, there are still many Jews in the Middle East. They reside in Israel, which to much of the Muslim world is just Palestine by a different name. They have territory that by rights is Arab, and just to make matters worse—much, much worse—they have Jerusalem, the city from which Muhammad ascended to heaven and a Muslim city for over a thousand years. Jewish control is not merely a geopolitical fact. It is an affront to Islam.

To the pious Muslim, the ghetto of Israel, the Jewish quarter of the Middle East, could be eliminated or expunged. A rampage could occur, a pogrom—there were ample precedents in Muslim history—and the Jews could be brought under control. The borders, the squiggles drawn on maps by heathens and fools, could be erased. What was done in a day could be undone in a day. Or a year. Or even ten. There is always time to right a wrong. Muhammad took his time before turning on the perfidious Jewish tribe of Qurayzah, which had sided with his enemies. Negotiations had been conducted. Emissaries went back and forth. In the end, though, all the tribe's men were killed, the women and children sold into slavery. This, too, was precedent.

The annihilation of the Qurayzah was, to paraphrase countless Mafia movies, nothing personal. It had nothing to do with the Qurayzah's Judaism and everything to do with its having chosen the losing side in tribal warfare. It was one of three Jewish tribes in the Medina region, the part of the Arabian Peninsula called the Hejaz. The other two were merely expelled from the area. None of the tribes played any role in the death of Muhammad, which was by natural causes.

Still, the Qur'an mentions Jews more than fifty times and some of these references are distinctly unflattering. There is more than enough there to support a contemporary anti-Semite's insistence that Judaism, like Christianity or Hinduism, is to be loathed because it is not the true belief, but it is to be especially loathed because the Jews have taken Jerusalem, Palestine, and, in the process, the pride of the Arabs. "Allah has cursed them on account of their unbelief," says the Qur'an—sufficient for any anti-Semite right there.

Traditionally, Christians were Islam's archenemy. Not only did the Qu'ran contain the occasional warning about them—"Do not take the Jews and Christians for friends"—but they periodically picked up their shield and lance and set off to liberate the Holy Land from the infamous Saracen and, by way of diversion, to kill as many Jews as possible. ("Leave no single member of the Jewish race alive," ordered Godfrey of Bouillon, the leader of the First Crusade.) For the longest time and, to an extent, to this day, Christians took pride of place in the hierarchy of Muslim enemies. (George W. Bush discovered that when in 2001 he said, "This *crusade*, this war on terrorism is going to take awhile.")

If Jews were not crusaders, they were hardly imperialists or colonialists either. They were distinctly not the men (and the occasional woman) who treated the Muslim world with contempt, appreciating it only for its pornographic charms—all those delicious harems, all those wives—and then locking it up, region by region, as a way of securing the route to India or, in some cases, protecting indigenous Christian communities. Jews might be vile people, but they had the attribute of insignificance.

Some scholars suggest that the Islamic peoples of the Middle East were innocent of European-style anti-Semitism at least until the last part of the nineteenth century. That supposedly changed with the arrival of Zionism and Jewish settlers from Europe. Yet in 1840, way before Herzl had promulgated his call for Jews to return to Zion, the charge of ritual murder was brought against the Jewish community of Damascus. A Catholic priest and his servant were the purported victims.

Still, a distinction has to be made between Muslim anti-Semitism and its more lethal and virulent variant in Europe. This is not to say that up to the modern era, the Muslim lands were some sort of paradise for Jews. They were not, and even the so-called Golden Age in Spain, where under Muslim rulers the Jewish community thrived, was marred by episodic pogroms and forced conversions. It was an order to convert or face death that induced the great theologian, physician, and ethicist Moses Maimonides to abandon Cordoba for southern Spain and ultimately North Africa. (He eventually settled in Egypt.)

Maimonides's peregrinations suggest that the Golden Age had its rough spots. In fact, no single rule applied everywhere, and no single place was the same as another. Maimonides had to leave Cordoba, but he was welcomed in Fez, Morocco (every bit as Muslim as Spain), where he studied at the University of Al-Karaouine. He wound up in Egypt, no less an Islamic land than Moorish Spain, and became both the leader of Cairo's Jewish community and court physician to the Muslim grand vizier al-Fadil and then to Sultan Saladin, the Kurd who established himself in Egypt and to this day is renowned for having liberated Jerusalem from the crusaders.

The one constant in the Arab world for Jews is that they were deemed *dhimmis*. The status varied from place to place and time to time, but the term connoted second-class citizenship and applied to Christians as well as Jews. *Dhimmis* were sometimes barred from holding public office, had to pay higher taxes, often were forced to wear identifiable clothing or insignia, could ride a donkey but not a horse, could not bear witness against a Muslim, could not bear arms, could not proselytize, and, in some places, could not take an Arab name—all in all, a petty-cum-odious set of rules and regulations but, on balance, better than what was often obtained in Europe.

Muslims, too, mounted pogroms and on occasion were as determined as their Christian brethren to murder Jews. But while a robust Muslim-Jewish antipathy is of a much more recent vintage, it has its antecedents and finds its theological justification in the Qur'an. As Wistrich points out, the Prophet's so-called "Jewish wars in Medina and Khaibar were taken as exemplary— ending as they did in the expulsion or extermination of the Jewish tribes in seventh century Arabia." The lesson is clear: what Muhammad had done once, others could do again.

✡   ✡   ✡

Jew hatred had become a notable part of the Middle Eastern political dialogue. Nazi agents took advantage of a rising Arab concern regarding Zionism. To the Nazis and, after a while, the Arabs as well, the Jews settling Palestine were not merely white Europeans—standard-issue colonists who simply worshipped a different God—but the loathsome, extremely dangerous Jew about whom the Nazis were recognized experts. By the late 1930s, German agents were already in the Middle East. They were there for several reasons: to obtain oil, to control the Suez Canal, to thwart Britain, but also to extend the Final Solution to where the Jewish problem had originated.

In World War I, the Middle East had been something of a sideshow, and its oil reserves, while of growing importance, were not yet crucial. (Britain was still importing oil from the United States.) In World War II, the Middle East may not have been quite center stage, but it and its oil had become very important indeed. This time the German threat was not so far removed but as close as the Egypt-Libya border and within striking distance of the Suez Canal. Germany now had friends, if not outright allies, in various Arab states. It pronounced itself, frankly and honestly, willing to do for the Arabs what the Arabs could not do for themselves: kill every last Jew.

Nazi-inspired pogroms erupted in both Iran and Iraq, countries where Britain had maintained a heavy colonialist presence. The region was inundated by Nazi propaganda, much of it as anti-Jewish as it was anti-British or anti-French. Egypt, once something of a refuge for desperate European Jews, turned ugly. The Nazis had operatives all over the region—in Iraq and Iran, in particular— but probably the most important one of all was, by the beginning of the war, no longer in the region at all. He was in Berlin.

Mohammed Amin al-Husseini was the scion of a Palestinian family of great influence. In 1922 he was appointed the grand mufti of Jerusalem by the British high commissioner of Palestine, Sir Herbert Samuel, a Jew. The position of mufti was an old one—usually held by a religious scholar with the authority to issue fatwas, or decrees—but Samuel added to its prestige and power by creating a Supreme Muslim Council and making the mufti its president. The council controlled a considerable amount of money. Husseini had always been dangerous. Samuel made him powerful as well.

In choosing Husseini, Samuel was trying to strike a balance between two powerful Palestinian families—the Husseinis and the Nashashibis—but he made the mistake of focusing on the clan and not on the man. Husseini was a first-class Jew hater who, religious figure notwithstanding, did not shrink from using violence. As early as 1920, he was inspiring attacks on Jewish settlements, and he took a leading role a decade later in the more widespread and somewhat better-organized Arab Revolt of the late 1930s.

Husseini was a genuine Palestinian nationalist and by no means the only important figure behind the various revolts. He was both Samuel's mistake and his gift to Zionism. The mufti soiled the cause he led, polluting Palestinian nationalism with Jew hatred and aligning it with Nazism. He made simplicity possible. The complicated matter of what to do with two peoples who cherished the same piece of real estate was made into a morality play: on one side, good Jews, victims of the Nazis, and on the other Nazi-tinged Palestinians. What could be neater?

By the late 1930s, the mufti was a wanted man. He absconded to Beirut, where the British could not arrest him and the French, ruling under their League of Nations mandate, simply would not. (Maybe it was in this period that Husseini learned how to play one Western power off against the other.)

For the Palestinians, their revolt of the late 1930s was something less than a success but hardly a failure. It did not create a Palestinian state or force the British to steam home, but it did cause Whitehall to do an about-face on the Balfour Declaration, which was beginning to look like a huge mistake. To the British foreign service, the idiocy of taking the side of a reviled minority against an oil-rich majority was becoming plainer and plainer.

With war looming, Britain chose sides. It limited Jewish immigration to just 75,000 over five years and insisted that any immigration after that be at the sufferance of the Arabs—in other words, next to none. As part of its plan, Britain offered Palestine independence within ten years, but under conditions that guaranteed a substantial Arab majority. Britain, in effect, reneged on the promise of Balfour and, in so doing, condemned the promise of Zionism to what Leon Trotsky (and later Ronald Reagan) called the "ash heap of history." Within a decade, however, it was the proposed Palestinian state that had turned to ash.

The long-term ramifications of Husseini's anti-Semitism and penchant for violence were more significant. Jews and Arabs drew away from each other, re-locating to safer areas and segregating themselves. Mostly it was Jews who did the moving, since mostly it was Arabs who were instigating the violence. Jews responded in kind, sometimes not bothering to sort the guilty from the innocent. Indiscriminate reprisals ensued, innocent Arabs suffered, and some in the Palestinian upper class moved out of Palestine entirely. This loss of leadership, repeated over and over again as violence became more and frequent, cost the Palestinians immeasurably.

By the 1930s, the Jews were learning to deal with widespread Arab violence and developing tactics that were used later in the wars of 1947–48. The Jewish community readied its self-defense and political structure. Even the militant revisionists—the movement founded by Ze'ev Jabotinsky and the precursor to the Likud Party—put aside their differences with David Ben-Gurion's mainstream leadership to deal with the common enemy, the Arabs. The Jews planned for a coming war. The Arabs did not. For one, it would be a War of Independence. For the other, it would be a *nakba*. A catastrophe.

In some respects, a Palestinian-German alliance seemed only natural. They had common enemies: Britain, France, and, of course, Jews. So Husseini's attempt to enlist both Hitler and Mussolini in his cause merely adhered to the age-old rule that the enemy of my enemy is my friend. But Husseini went further. By the end of 1941, the mufti was in Berlin, where he met with the top Nazis, including Hitler. There is some dispute about what exactly was discussed and the exact terms used, but there is no dispute that Husseini helped organize Balkan Muslim SS units and blocked the escape of Jewish children from German-occupied Europe, fearing they would wind up in Palestine. They were almost certainly killed.

Husseini's defenders always insisted that he knew nothing about the Holocaust. This is simply not credible. In his meetings with Hitler as well as with Himmler and other top Nazis, it is not likely that they swallowed their pride concerning one of their proudest achievements. Their actual words are unknowable, but not the physical evidence that Husseini was deemed worthy of some expense and thought. He was put up in a villa in the Krumme Lanke section of Berlin and, along with Rashid Ali el Gailani, the former premier of Iraq, received a healthy living allowance. In an essay written for the US National Archives and Records Administration, Richard Breitman and Norman J. W. Goda report that "from spring 1943 to spring 1944, Husseini personally received 50,000 marks monthly and Gailani 65,000 for operational expenses. In addition, they each received living expenses averaging 80,000 marks per month, an absolute fortune. (A German field marshal received a base salary of 26,500 marks per year.) Finally, Husseini and Gailani received substantial foreign currency to support adherents living in countries outside Germany."

The Breitman-Goda essay draws on documents declassified by the CIA in 2010, as well as what was previously reported in some books, notably Jeffrey Herf's *Nazi Propaganda for the Arab World* and the Wistrich volume. The report states that "Hitler himself signaled his intention to eliminate the Jews of Palestine. In a November 28, 1941, conversation in Berlin with the mufti, Hitler said that the outcome of the war in Europe would also decide the fate of the Arab world. German troops intended to break through the Caucasus region and move into the Middle East. This would result in the liberation of Arab peoples. Hitler said that Germany's only objective there would be the destruction of the Jews."

For Hitler and the Nazis, this was not mere talk. Death squads (*Einsatzkommando*) were attached to Field Marshal Erwin Rommel's *Afrika Korps,* although they did not report to him but were, as was the custom in those matters, to operate autonomously. They were to come in right behind Rommel's army as it thrust into Egypt and take "executive measures" against the Jews. The *Einsatzkommandos* would then follow the army up into Palestine and eradicate the Jewish community there as well. As it turned out, Rommel was stopped by the British Eighth Army. The death squads, having been moved to a jumping-off point in Greece, remained there.

On March 1, 1944, Husseini went to the Radio Berlin studios outside the city to broadcast a message to the Middle East: "Arabs, rise as one man and fight for your sacred rights. Kill the Jews wherever you find them. This pleases God, history, and religion. This saves your honor. God is with you."

The shortwave station Husseini used that day was established especially to broadcast propaganda messages to the Arab world. Historian Jeffrey Herf says it began transmitting in Arabic as early as 1939 and pretty soon was a regular presence on the airwaves. Given the literacy rate in the Arab world, radio was not only an effective propaganda tool but also often about the only one available. The Nazi broadcasts were anti-British and anti-French, and explicitly anti-Semitic—about half the content, according to one Allied estimate.

The Nazis presented National Socialist rhetoric and ideals as if they were in harmony with Islamic ones—their "shared goals and shared ideals," Himmler called it. They mined the Qur'an for useful passages: "You will meet no greater enemy of the believers than the Jews" (Sura 5:82). They also turned Hitler into a quasireligious figure; a sort of minor prophet ("By resisting the Jews everywhere, I am fighting for the Lord's work"), and even managed to find in the Qur'an words that Muhammad did not say, such as an order to fight the Jews "until they are extinct." It's impossible now to gauge the impact of this propaganda effort, since, among other things, radios were hardly common in the Arab world at that time. Still, the confluence of anticolonialism, Arab nationalism, Islamism, anti-Zionism, and anti-Semitism must have had an impact.

In much of the world, what the Nazis were doing was considered abhorrent. Not so in the Middle East. There they were seen as anything from admirable to merely useful. At the very least, they had made the right enemies. Not surprisingly, at the end of the war, these enemies of the loathed British or French or Jews were allowed to stay on, especially in Egypt. As for the mufti, once he made his escape from Berlin, he was welcomed back to the Arab Middle East, a popular figure, hardly the anathema he would have been almost anywhere else in the world. He took his place in the newly formed Arab League as leader of the Palestinians. Some Arabs held their noses, but they held their tongues as well.

Germany lost its totally invented war with the Jews, but the Arabs were confident they would easily win the real one for Palestine, which was fast approaching. This is a mistake they made over and over, each time preparing their people for an easy victory that turned out to be a humiliating defeat. This was particularly the case with the 1967 war, which was initiated by Egypt at the very time that about 15 percent of its army was bogged down in Yemen. It resulted in a rout for which the Arab man in the street was totally unprepared. Until the last moment, Gamal Nasser's all-important and highly influential state radio, the Voice of the Arabs, was proclaiming victory.

The Arab armies, especially the Egyptian army, did better in the 1973 war, but in the end, the result was the same: defeat. Over time, these defeats led to a crisis of confidence in Arab culture itself. Something was obviously wrong with the culture or the governance. Arab glory had begun to recede with the Battle of Tours (about 732), which halted the Islamic conquest of Europe. And from there on, it was nothing but downhill. By the end of World War I, the region had been widely colonized by European countries and outposts of Western oil companies. The creation of Israel had added insult to injury, and with each war, some of the more handy excuses vanished.

In the 1973 war, the Arab armies were supplied by the Soviet Union and had launched their attack on Yom Kippur Eve—the holiest day of the Jewish year. They had actually caught the Israelis by surprise. They had actually crossed the Suez Canal in the south and taken the Golan Heights in the north—and yet they lost. What was going on? What could explain it all? Intellectuals supplied credible, reasonable answers: appalling literacy rates, for instance, or removing half the population, women, from the larger economy and dismissing their intellectual contribution. But for the less thoughtful—for those who, like the perplexed Germans, wondered how their country had lost the First War—another answer announced itself: the Jews. Fortunately, there was always anti-Semitism.

Let's go back to the column in the Jordanian newspaper. It said something more than the claim that Jews (or Israel or the Mossad) were actually behind the September 11, 2001, attacks. It said that Jews *were capable* of such an attack, which *was* remotely possible. (After all, a ragtag bunch of Islamic militants had actually pulled it off.) But more than this, it suggested that somehow every Jew who worked in the World Trade Center had been alerted that an attack was coming—and that all these Jews in turn kept the secret, refusing to alert the blind newspaper vendor in the lobby, or the mistress in the typing pool, or the guy in the next pod—the one with three kids who was a best buddy. This was, of course, beyond anyone's organizational abilities, and to believe such a thing is possible takes either heroic credulity or a profound belief in the evil power of Jews. Or both. Either way, it meant the Jews could do it. The Jews could do anything. Among other things, they took the ash of Auschwitz and molded a nation from it.

Wistrich, in his comprehensive survey of contemporary anti-Semitism, begins a chapter by citing the late French philosopher Vladimir Jankelevitch, who recognized the bitter truth in Israeli psychiatrist Zvi Rex's remark that "the Germans will never forgive the Jews for Auschwitz." Jankelevitch observed that the Germans would not be alone in this regard. The Holocaust was an immense crime for which the Germans were chiefly responsible but for which the list of coconspirators is long. There is no need to call the roll here, but only the countries not conquered by Germany had clean hands. As for the rest, most of them were complicit.

For these countries, as well as for Germany, anti-Zionism is a godsend. It is one critical step removed from anti-Semitism, and it is based not on some imagined genetic difference, not on something inherent and immutable, but strictly on behavior or policy. Anti-Zionism is anti-imperialism. Anti-Zionism is anti-colonialism. Anti-Zionism is a protest against the (clearly wrong) occupation of the West Bank. Anti-Zionism is a recognition of and championing of the rights of Arabs and a howl of protest at the wrongs done them. Anti-Zionism rests firmly on the belief, virtually uncontested, that if the Jews of today set out to establish a nation in a place where they were not wanted, the world simply would not permit it. Who could argue with that?

In the Arab world, the word *Zionist* has become synonymous with *Jew*. *Anti-Zionist* is the polite term reserved for swell hotels where forums and meetings are held. *Anti-Zionist* is the term of the educated classes, of the first-class lounge.

But outside the lounge or the meeting hall, where the porters and the waiters can be found, no such sophistry is practiced—or condoned. The Zionist is the Jew, and the Jew is the enemy. He is despicable and malevolent, cunning in his evil and evil in his cunning, and this has all been true since the time of the Prophet.

Out in the halls or in the supply room or on the loading docks or at the end of the laundry chute are people who believe that the Mossad somehow got a shark to attack tourists in the Red Sea, causing one death and adversely affecting Egyptian tourism. "What is being said about the Mossad throwing the deadly shark [into the sea] to hit tourism in Egypt is not out of the question," said the governor of the South Sinai region. These things are believed because they have been broadcast on the radio and written in the newspapers and discussed on the street. It is the truth, sir.

It is well known.

10

A Sensation at Saratoga

Theodor Herzl was a thoroughly European European. In pursuing his dream, he went all over Europe, meeting with important—or merely titled—Europeans, including, of course, the kaiser of Germany. This made sense, since Europe was where the bulk of the world's Jews lived, and Europe was where the Middle East's colonial powers were located. For Herzl to have taken America into consideration would have been sheer folly. The United States had few Jews (250,000) and no empire—indeed, it was still consolidating the one it had forged on the North American continent. Historian Frederick Jackson Turner did not consider the frontier closed and the matter settled until 1890, which was five years before Herzl started to write *The Jewish State*. America did not matter at all.

And yet, in the long run, America not only mattered, it mattered greatly. Around the time that Herzl was writing frenetically, America was beginning to absorb vast numbers of European Jews. From the end of the nineteenth century to 1924, when immigration restrictions were imposed, two million Jews came to the United States. By 1945, with Europe rendered virtually *Judenfrei* by the Holocaust, the United States had the world's largest concentration of Jews. The story of how America dealt with its Jews (and they with it) has a huge bearing on how and why the State of Israel came to be created—and, as it happened, to be recognized instantaneously by the only world power to come out of World War II substantially stronger than when it went in. America put the rest of the world on notice that a new and significant nation had been created—and was being welcomed as a colleague by the most important country in the world.

United States recognition mattered. It mattered greatly. But it was the culmination of a painful and complex process, not just in the somewhat hostile American bureaucracy but in the American Jewish community as well. A process that would now be swift—a demand by a powerful and very rich lobby for justice and recompense—would be almost instantly satisfied. But the American Jewish community of the mid-twentieth century was not nearly as powerful as it is now—and not nearly as powerful as many people, particularly anti-Semites, thought it was back then. In some respects, it was a timorous community, unsure of how to embrace the movement for a Jewish homeland while fervently embracing the American homeland it already had. How would it look to non-Jews? Would Jews somehow be defined by their Zionism? Would this make Jews of those Jews who hardly considered themselves Jews? Many American Jews were not at all sure of what it meant to be a Jew—an American Jew, a Christmas-celebrating Jew, a Jew with a non-Jewish spouse, a Jew for bar mitzvahs only, a Jew considered a Jew only by non-Jews, but not necessarily, or maybe reluctantly, by other Jews. The legendary pot had not melted all Jews. Some were deracinated instead.

For a time, it seemed that the United States would be no exception to Herzl's dictum that the greater the number of Jews, the greater the amount of anti-Semitism. Early on, there were so few Jews in the country—of the 38.6 million Americans counted by the 1870 census, only 200,000 were Jews—that they were hardly even noticed. Over in the vast Russian Empire, however, a great stirring was under way. Pioneers were sending back word of America. Strange place-names were being mentioned; not only New York but also Baltimore, Chicago, San Antonio, and San Francisco. An immense immigration was proceeding, propelled by the pogroms of the Russian Empire. By 1900, one million Russian Jews had made the trek—and then, in almost no time, another million were added. As Herzl might have guessed, anti-Semitism took off.

It took time to prove Herzl right—and even then he was not right for very long. But for a while, American anti-Semitism surged, and it did so at a time when it could do the most damage: the 1930s and 1940s, when European anti-Semitism turned homicidal. It was then that Europe's Jews needed, first, defenders elsewhere in the world and, second, a refuge. They were failed on both counts—not entirely, not absolutely—but so much so that Hitler was able to murder 70 percent of Europe's Jews, and the world did little about it. When America did get around to aiding Europe's Jews, it was only as part of its war effort (and incidental to it)—and even then America went to war against Germany because Germany first went to war against it.

The Jews, the powerful Jews of anti-Semitic fantasy and just a bit of reality, were powerless to save their coreligionists—even their relatives—across the sea. By the 1960s, however, the situation had righted itself. Jews had the power they'd needed twenty years earlier. They were now in a position to insist that America help Israel—an alliance that was worth far more than trees planted or donations made. America's ugly infatuation with anti-Semitism was resoundingly over. In the nation's entire history, maybe only six Jews were killed on account of being Jewish: the provocative Denver radio host Alan Berg in 1984; the Australian Talmudic scholar Yankel Rosenbaum, a victim of the Crown Heights, Brooklyn, riots of 1991; Aaron Halberstam, shot in 1994 when a gunman opened fire on a van carrying religious students; and the falsely accused Leo Frank in 1915. Arguably, the civil rights workers James Goodman and Michael Schwerner, murdered in Mississippi in 1964 along with the African American James Chaney, can be included, since they were both identifiably Jewish. (Schwerner was known as "the bearded Jew.") By way of comparison, the Tuskegee Institute estimates that 3,446 blacks were lynched from 1882 to 1968.

Judged by violence and compared with Europe, American anti-Semitism seemed to be an irrelevance. For the longest time, there was very little of it, but as Herzl might have noted, there were very few Jews as well. It's hard to say when that changed, but by the 1860s, something was happening. The great Jewish immigration from eastern Europe was in the future, but here and there Jews were becoming prominent and rich. One of those—both very prominent and very rich—was Joseph Seligman. A German-born banker and the very personification of New York's Jewish wealth, he went to register at a hotel in the tony resort town of Saratoga Springs, New York, confident, we can be sure, that he was in his element. It was June 1877, and Seligman, to his absolute mortification, was rudely turned away. America had entered a new era.

Seligman, a charter member of what came to be called "Our Crowd," had once been offered the US Treasury Department by the very man who during the Civil War had tried to bar Jews from parts of the South, President Ulysses S. Grant. (President Lincoln had overruled him.) At Saratoga, Seligman had intended to stay, as he had before, at the sumptuous Grand Union Hotel, supposedly the largest in the world.

The Seligmans were barred without the usual euphemistic excuse ("We are overbooked, sir"), but explicitly because they were Jews. The hotel's manager, Henry Hilton, was adamant. The Grand Union was being overrun by Jews. Christians were avoiding the place, and business, which then as now was business, was none too good. Hilton stated his reasons in a letter to a friend: "As [yet] the law . . . permits a man to use his property as he pleases, and I propose exercising that blessed privilege, notwithstanding Moses and all his entire descendants object."

"A Sensation at Saratoga / New Rules for the Grand Union. No Jews to Be Admitted," headlined the *New York Times*. The paper played the story on page one. Important people took sides. Henry Ward Beecher, the prominent Brooklyn clergyman, brother of the *Uncle Tom's Cabin* author Harriet Beecher Stowe and, like her a prominent abolitionist, sided with Seligman, whom he knew. The *Brooklyn Daily Eagle* sided with the hotel. From a strictly business point of view, Hilton had done the right thing, the paper said. Jews were clannish and stuck to themselves, and that, as anyone could see, did not make for compatible hotel guests.

The Grand Union slammed the door on the indignant Seligman some seventeen years before the French military framed Captain Alfred Dreyfus. But the incident at Saratoga, thousands of miles away and a triviality compared with a four-year ordeal on Devil's Island, was nevertheless a product of the same forces that Herzl later identified and that Hilton, in his letter to a friend, so frankly revealed: too many Jews. Too many Jews produced a reaction. Herzl was right about that. Christians recoiled and then pushed back.

In 1889 another Seligman was snubbed on account of his religion. This was Seligman's nephew, Theodore, who was blackballed from New York's Union League Club explicitly because he was, as it was put at the time, a "Hebrew." What's noteworthy is that his father, Jesse, was both a member of the club and had been its vice president. None of that mattered. Younger members of the club were insistent on applying new standards for membership: no more Jews.

As it was with Joseph Seligman, the snub was nothing personal. It was just the strong feeling of the younger members, one older member told the *New York Times*, that "men of the Jewish race and religion do not readily affiliate in the social way with persons not of their own persuasion." They quite openly owned up to their prejudice, which the *Times*, using the new term, called anti-Semitism.

No doubt Henry Adams thought the younger members of the Union League Club were exactly right. The impeccably credentialed Adams was the grandson of one president (John Quincy Adams) and the great-grandson of another (John Adams), and until he wrote his classic *The Education of Henry Adams* to great, if posthumous, acclaim, something of an underachiever by his family's standards. Nevertheless, he was always an accomplished bigot, yet another area where posterity has recognized him.

Possibly the older members of the Union League Club, having come of age when Jews were a rarity, could not appreciate how much things had changed. Adams, though, was keenly on top of the situation. "God tried drowning out the world once," he wrote in a 1906 letter, "but it did no kind of good, and there are said to be 450,000 Jews now doing Kosher in New York alone. God himself owned failure."

"The Jew has got into the soul," he wrote in another letter. "I see him—or her—now everywhere, and wherever he—or she—goes, there must remain a taint in the blood forever." He proposed a solution to the Jewish problem: "I want to see all the lenders at interest taken out and executed."

Surely Adams was not being wholly serious, but his sentiments would not have shocked that great social reformer Jacob Riis. In his 1890 book *How the Other Half Lives*, an exposé of the horrid living conditions in New York's tenements, he had a chapter called "Jewtown," in which he had this to say about its residents: "Money is their God. Life itself is of little value compared with even the leanest bank account."

To some non-Jews, the Grand Union served as an analogy for why Jews had to be limited, whether it was from a resort or a university. "The summer hotel that is ruined by admitting Jews, meets its fate not because the Jews it admits are of bad character," wrote one Ivy League president, "but because they drive away the Gentiles, and then after the Gentiles have left, they leave also." The writer was Lawrence Lowell, president of Harvard and an important figure in the movement to keep Jews from overwhelming quality universities. He had his work cut out for him.

As the number of Jews increased, they became neither exotic nor rare, and barriers went up. As first these Jews were an unassimilated mess—often bearded and oddly dressed men emitting a guttural din—but their American-born children were a different matter. Unaccented and clean shaven, these men (and some women) came knocking on the doors of the great WASP institutions, the Ivy League colleges, and as they had in Europe, they were demanding entry on the basis of merit.

The ivory tower was quickly surrounded by a moat of quotas and discriminatory requirements. The situation was particularly dire in New York City. There, Columbia University was besieged by Jews. By 1920, about half the students at its College of Physicians and Surgeons were Jews. Up in Cambridge, Massachusetts, Harvard's Lowell took note and moved to protect his own institution from the Jewish onslaught. There the proportion of Jews had gone from a tolerable 6 percent in 1908 to 22 percent in 1922—nearly one quarter of the class.

Lowell moved to limit Jews to 15 percent of the student body. He did this, he argued, to control a surging anti-Semitism and to keep Harvard the Harvard it had always been. Lowell was rebuffed twice by the university's board of overseers, but he persisted. Finally, he was allowed to use interviews and letters of recommendation to access an applicant's "aptitude and character"—and that did it. By 1933, when Lowell retired, Jews were a tolerable 10 percent of the student body.

Where Harvard went, others followed. By 1938, Columbia's medical school was down to 5 percent Jews. Three years earlier, Yale's medical school accepted 76 applicants from a pool of 501, David M. Oshinsky tells us in his story of the fight against polio (*Polio: An American Story*)—"About 200 of those applicants were Jewish, and only five got in." He quotes the dean's instructions: "Never admit more than five Jews, take only two Italian Catholics, and take no blacks at all." As a result, Jonas Salk, the developer of the first effective polio vaccine, was rejected by Yale. He went instead to New York University's College of Medicine, then an institution of little prestige but no quotas.

Quotas and outright restrictions might have been reactions to the Jewish onslaught by what were WASP institutions, but they were also consistent with what was going on in the country. America was turning nastily xenophobic, not for the first time—the mid-nineteenth century Know-Nothing movement, which was nativist and explicitly anti-Catholic, was an earlier example—but this time "Rum and Romanism" were replaced by communism and socialism. These newest of Americans not only talked funny, they thought funny. There were, in fact, quite enough of them in the United States. By congressional edict, the Statue of Liberty executed an about-face, and Emma Lazarus's wretched refuse were told to buzz off.

By the 1930s, American anti-Semitism had become pretty much institutionalized. The easy entry into fine hotels that Joseph Seligman had once taken for granted had become a thing of the past. My own parents chose their resorts by samizdat, the newsletters of the synagogue, or fraternal organizations such as B'nai B'rith or the Knights of Pythias, or by a careful scrutiny of newspaper ads. The phrase "Walk to Church" meant that Jews were not welcome. As a kid, I was instructed not to seek work at certain Long Island beach clubs because of their rumored anti-Semitic policies. Looking back now, I wonder if the rumors, supported by the irrefutable phrase "everybody knows," had any basis in fact.

Leonard Dinnerstein, in his essay "Antisemitism in Crisis Times in the United States," wrote that the high-water mark for American anti-Semitism was the period between the two world wars. The United States was then in the throes of great social change—not only the vast immigration from eastern and southern Europe but also blacks from the South to the North and everyone from the country to the city. The Protestant culture, once unassailably dominant, was taking a battering. Music was changing, literature was changing, fashion was changing, the permissible was changing, and from newly communist Russia was coming an ideology that was threatening to change everything.

Jews were conspicuous in these movements and, as they had been in Europe, avatars of modernity—sometimes, as with George Gershwin and Irving Berlin, combining (or exploiting) black music (jazz, blues, ragtime) with standard Tin Pan Alley fare to produce songs like 1911's "Alexander's Ragtime Band." The song not only had lyrics evocative of stereotypical black speech ("That's just the best-est band what am, oh, ma hon-ey lamb"), but also it was popularized by Al Jolson, the Lithuanian-born son of a rabbi. He sang it in blackface.

By the end of the 1930s, it seemed to some that American popular culture was largely a Jewish affair. Around the time that Berlin was writing "Alexander's

Ragtime Band," other Jews were creating the movie business. Still other Jews were entering radio, a mass medium even newer than the movies. Taken together, movies and radio seemed to be Jewish enterprises—a long way from railroads or steel, and therefore, one might think, of no concern whatsoever. On the contrary, William S. Paley, the founder of the CBS radio network, and David Sarnoff, who ran both RCA and the NBC network, as well as the film studio bosses Samuel Goldwyn, William Fox, Carl Laemmle, Adolph Zukor, Louis B. Mayer, and the four Warner brothers (Harry, Albert, Samuel, and Jack), controlled industries that were both ubiquitous and invisible—who could see radio transmissions? Movies came in a can, and yet, when projected on a screen thirty feet tall by seventy feet wide, could bring a tough man to tears or, worse, to the edge of sexual excitement. This mass media was, therefore, all that myth and legend said of Jews: invisibly powerful, subversively sexual, and threateningly modern.

A singular and extraordinary example of the power and reach of the new media was the transformation of the itinerant flier Charles A. Lindbergh from unknown to worldwide celebrity in—from takeoff to landing—less than two days. From Long Island's Roosevelt Field to Paris's Le Bourget Field, everything that could be observed was chronicled by newsreels. Lindbergh was shown at Roosevelt Field getting a send-off from his mother and then arriving in France to a rapturous greeting—and from there going to Belgium and then London. At each stop, he was cheered as a combination of royalty and war hero—indeed, he was awarded the Congressional Medal of Honor—with huge, ecstatic throngs both saluting the young man and swooning over him. Lindbergh's arrival in America was no less extraordinary. In triumphalist style, the USS *Memphis* carried him up the Potomac River to a reception at the Washington Monument, where President Calvin Coolidge awarded him the Distinguished Flying Cross. Newsreels got it all.

In the thirty-three and a half hours it took to fly to Paris, Lindbergh earned his fame. He was brave, resourceful, determined, self-effacing, consistently polite, thoughtful (he paid his respects in Paris to the widow of the French pilot who had died trying for a transatlantic flight), and, above all, photogenic. He had a killer smile.

By 1935, Lindbergh and his wife, the former Anne Morrow, were fed up with America and its unrelenting press. Three years earlier, their infant son, Charles Jr., had been kidnapped and murdered; the "Crime of the Century," the tabloids called it. The subsequent discovery of the dead child and the arrest of Bruno Hauptmann, a German immigrant with a criminal past, and his trial (at which Lindbergh testified) brought down a torrent of painfully intrusive publicity on Lindbergh and his wife. The couple sneaked off to Europe. But in 1939, with war approaching, they relocated to the North Shore of Long Island. The normally reclusive Lindbergh had come home to wage a war of his own: he was determined to keep the United States out of the one in Europe.

On September 11, 1941, Lindbergh spoke to the noninterventionist America First Committee rally in Des Moines, Iowa. It was a bit less than three months before the Japanese attack on Pearl Harbor, and so all debate on whether the United States should enter the European war was about to become moot. At the time, though, Lindbergh was the most famous advocate of isolationism, and so his speech was a major event. He did not disappoint.

Lindbergh said that three "important groups" were agitating for the United States to go to war against Germany: "the British, the Jewish, and the Roosevelt administration." Lindbergh was right. All three wanted the United States to fight Hitler, and all three had their reasons. Britain was already at war with Germany and was pleading for America to jump in. FDR would have loved to comply, but the country was in no mood for yet another foreign war. As for the Jews, they yearned for the United States to stop Hitler. By 1941, the Holocaust was under way.

Lindbergh understood. He confessed himself appalled by Germany's excesses, but not, it appears, to the extent that he rejected the occasional honor from the Nazi hierarchy. (In 1938 Hermann Göring, a Hitler intimate and air force commander, presented him with the Commander Cross of the Order of the German Eagle.)

Still, what Germany was doing to its Jews—not entirely undeserved, in Lindbergh's private opinion—was hardly America's concern. The Jews had to understand that. They had to know their place. They had to appreciate that the war most of them wanted would hardly redound to their benefit.

"Tolerance is a virtue that depends upon peace and strength," Lindbergh told that Des Moines audience. "History shows that it cannot survive war and devastations. A few far-sighted Jewish people realize this and stand opposed to intervention. But the majority still do not."

Why even bother with the Jews? Lindbergh supplied an answer: "Their greatest danger to this country lies in their large ownership and influence in our motion pictures, our press, our radio, and our government."

Lindbergh alarmed both the Jewish community and the Roosevelt administration. It was not just the hero's sheer popularity that so intimidated; it was also the extent to which he embodied the zeitgeist. (America First was hardly a standard right-wing organization; one of its supporters was the socialist leader Norman Thomas.) The belief that Jews were "too powerful," in the wording of countless public opinion polls, was widespread, held by at least 40 percent of Americans—and was on the rise. By the end of World War II, with much of world Jewry pulverized, the figure had somehow managed to rise to 55 percent.

Had Jews been asked the same question, they would have responded by saying they had very little power at all. This, of course, was not the case, but what power the community had was severely limited. The 1915 lynching of Leo Frank seemed to prove that. Frank, southern born but northern raised, had come down from New York to run a relative's pencil factory in Atlanta. In 1913, he was accused of the rape and murder of one of his employees, thirteen-year-old Mary Phagan. He was tried in an emotional atmosphere fraught with anti-Semitism, swiftly convicted, and sentenced to death. Governor John M. Slaton, clearly doubting Frank's guilt, commuted the sentence. In August 1915, a group of men—some of them quite prominent—seized Frank from the state penitentiary and lynched him.

The Jewish community had rallied to Frank's cause, and even the *New York Times*, under its then publisher, Adolph Ochs, had thrown itself into the fight. Not only was the *Times* ignored, but Ochs himself—a Tennessean and therefore a fellow southerner—was personally rebuffed when he asked Georgia newspapers to join the *Times* in asking that Frank be posthumously exonerated. Not only did the Georgia papers refuse, but Susan Tifft and Alex S. Jones, in their book *The Trust*, tell us that the *Macon Telegraph* sent Ochs an "angry wire contending that it was the 'outside interference of the Jews,' especially the 'offensive propaganda' printed in the *New York Times*, that had made it necessary to lynch Frank." That was the last time the *Times* stuck its neck out for a Jewish cause.

After that, things got even worse for America's Jews. Their civil rights were not abridged, but anti-Semitism increased, and Jews were feeling the heat. Henry Ford was pouring his money into the *Dearborn Independent*, a vile anti-Semitic rag; and Charles E. Coughlin, a Roman Catholic priest, took to the radio to deliver anti-Jewish diatribes. Throughout the country, organizations that were nativist—and often anti-Semitic as well—sprang up. The most famous and notorious of these was the Ku Klux Klan, which managed to marshal about fifty thousand supporters for a 1925 Washington, DC, march down Pennsylvania Avenue. (As if to prove the power of the new media, the D. W. Griffith film *The Birth of a Nation* helped revive the moribund KKK, which took its regalia from that movie.)

Ford might have been an uneducated tinkerer and Coughlin a maniacal religious zealot, but they had great authority, and their messages were not viewed as repugnant. An open, noncontroversial, and totally shameless anti-Semitism had saturated America. It could be found in the writings of H. L. Mencken and even in the poetry of T. S. Eliot. (In his 1930 *Treatise on the Gods*, Mencken wrote: "The Jews could be put down very plausibly as the most unpleasant race ever heard of." He later recanted and ordered this passage stricken from later editions. As for Eliot, not even the Holocaust dissuaded him; he stuck to his anti-Semitism.)

Most Jews took anti-Semitism for granted. It was a fact of life, something like the weather—and just as unpredictable. It lurked everywhere, and where it could not be seen, it was just under the surface or around the corner. The belief in the universality of anti-Semitism was sometimes as irrational as anti-Semitism itself. Every gentile was an anti-Semite: maybe a smiling, charming one, but an anti-Semite nonetheless. But in mid-twentieth-century America, anti-Semitism did not need to be inferred. It was blatant, aboveboard, undisguised, as plain as newspaper advertisements for resorts that said "Walk to Church."

But anti-Semitism was on its last legs. The space between the genteel dislike of Jews and their mass murder had collapsed, not suddenly with the liberation of the death camps but slowly, inexorably, as if Americans could not process all that had happened after 1941: war with Japan; war with Germany; the atomic bombs; the rise of Soviet Russia; the threat of the Russian A-bomb; the fear of domestic communism; and the immense changes in American society. It took time for the Holocaust to assert itself, to come out from behind more immediate concerns such as winning the war, and for anti-Semitism to be silenced. America had seen the consequence.

All the same, American Jews and their organizations kept looking over their shoulders, expecting the reemergence of anti-Semitism. They had their fund-raising needs, of course, but more than a millennium of Jew hatred had accustomed them to expect a resurgence of anti-Semitism. A well-honed paranoia, a thousand ears to the ground, and yet only the faintest of movements were detected. The Anti-Defamation League turned its attention mostly to championing Israel. Anti-Semitism had faded away, and the ADL was left, like a boathouse on a dried-up lake, a bit forlorn. (By 2013, the ADL was condemning the locker-room bullying of Jonathan Martin, the non-Jewish offensive lineman for the Miami Dolphins.)

Even the oil shock of 1973 failed to produce an uptick in anti-Semitism. This was truly a case of cause without effect. The embargo was imposed by the Arab oil-producing nations and was in direct response to the military aid the United States had provided Israel that year for the so-called Yom Kippur War.

Long lines of cars formed at gas stations. There were endless waits. Americans were mightily inconvenienced, and all on account of the Jews and their insistence on clinging to part of the Middle East. The average American had absolutely no stake in the conflict and a huge stake in both the price of gas and its availability. Yet hardly a peep. Polling showed no real increase in anti-Semitism. It was not Jews who were blamed for the price and scarcity of oil but, first, the Arabs and, second, the oil companies.

The price of gas, the collapse of banks, the depredations of speculators, the prestidigitations of money managers, the rush to unnecessary wars, the conviction of the American Jonathan Pollard for spying for Israel—none of this produced the eruption of anti-Semitic fury that so many Jews feared was coming, always coming. Even when the occasional anti-Semitic publication or web page made a stab at establishing the usual links—photos of Jewish financiers linked to Jewish politicians linked to Israeli figures and then linked to bankruptcies, unemployment, and mortgage failures—nothing happened. Nothing! Two heads of the Federal Reserve in a row—Arthur Greenspan and Ben S. (for *Shalom*!) Bernanke—could both be Jews and their ethnicity was hardly ever mentioned. And when Bernanke's successor, Janet Yellen, was announced, it did not matter at all that she, too, was a Jew.

America, a land that Herzl never considered for his Jewish state (although others had), had turned out to be pretty much what Herzl wanted for Jews: a country where a Jew could be safe, where a Jew could prosper; a country without formal restrictions, discriminatory laws, or religious tests for citizenship or public office; a country where a Jew could even chose not to be a Jew—and not a Christian, either. In America an observant Jew, Senator Joseph Lieberman, could run as the Democratic vice presidential candidate in 2000, and not a pejorative voice was raised. Sixty years earlier, America couldn't rouse itself to rescue German Jewish children whom Hitler desperately wanted to kill.

11

Twenty Thousand
Charming Children,
Twenty Thousand Ugly Adults

In 1940 a Lithuanian Jew named Hillel Kook arrived in America from Palestine. Kook was the son of one prominent rabbi and the younger brother of another, but the rabbinate was clearly not for him. His family had moved to Palestine in 1924, when he was nine, and by the age of fifteen, he had joined the Haganah, the Jewish paramilitary force and predecessor of the Israel Defense Force. Within a year, he had moved to the right, helping to establish the Irgun. The Irgun was implicated in two infamous acts of terrorism: the bombing of the King David Hotel in 1946 and the Dar Yassin massacre of 1948. By 1936, Kook was one of its leaders, and when he came to America, it was as the assistant to Ze'ev Jabotinsky, the militant Jewish nationalist. Within a certain circle, Kook was famous. He soon made himself disappear.

Hillel Kook became Peter Bergson. Soon there were Bergsonites and a Bergson Group, consisting of hard-core Revisionists such as himself and a widening, but still limited, circle of people whose passion was the plight of Europe's Jews, but not necessarily Zionism. Among them was the incredibly prolific screenwriter, author, and playwright Ben Hecht (*Scarface*, *The Front Page*, *Twentieth Century*, *Gunga Din*, *Wuthering Heights*, and *His Girl Friday*, among others). In 1941 Hecht left Hollywood and set up an office at the storied Algonquin Hotel in Manhattan. He also returned to newspaper writing, this time not as a scrappy street reporter, as he had been in his youthful Chicago days, but as a columnist for the left-leaning New York tabloid *PM*. Hecht, by then, was a very angry man, and he had a vast new subject to write about: Jews.

"A people to whom I belonged, who had produced my mother, father and all the relatives I had loved, was being turned into an exterminator's quarry, and there was no outcry against the deed," he wrote in his autobiography *A Child of the Century*. "No statesmen or journalists spoke out. Art was silent. Was the Jew so despised that he could be murdered en masse without protest from on-lookers, or was humanity so despicable that it could witness the German crime without a moral wince?"

In his newspaper columns, Hecht proclaimed his hatred for the Germans, but he soon learned to hate the British too, although for a different reason: the lid they had placed on Jewish immigration to Palestine. He even permitted himself a little hate for his fellow Jews as well: not "the unassimilated Jews—the Yiddish Jews—(who) were speaking their horror in the Jewish newspapers . . . in the syna-gogues where Jews were weeping and praying." He called these "the locked-away Jews who had only the useless ear of other Jews and, possibly, of God."

It was "the Americanized Jews" he despised. The Jews "who ran newspapers and movie studios, who wrote plays and novels, who were high in the govern-ment and powerful in the financial, industrial, and even social life of the nation were silent."

Hecht knew these Jews. He was a court Jew of the Jews, the studio moguls and other show business impresarios. They were a powerful lot of egomaniacs, men who lived large, who owned racehorses and walked in jodhpurs, who made careers and broke careers and who controlled not just the movie studios but also the movie houses. Inside, though, they were hollow, tremulous Jews, acting like anxious weekend guests in some grand home. But when it came to the nation's culture, they were human tuning forks. They did not need Mr. Gallup and his new polls (he had predicted FDR's triumph over Alf Landon in the 1936 presidential election) to tell them what Americans liked, what they would accept on the screen. Americans did not like Jews, that they knew, but Americans did not know that their movies were made by Jews. This was a good thing, and it should be kept that way.

When Hecht briefly returned to Hollywood, the moguls, whom he identi-fied as "nearly all Jews," took issue with his newspaper columns. They told him about a secret meeting of important studio executives and major producers that had been convened by Joseph P. Kennedy, fresh from England, where he was the American ambassador. (Actually, Kennedy had been asked to speak.) Kennedy had a warning for them: "He had told them sternly that they must not protest as Jews, and they must keep their Jewish rage against the Germans out of print," Hecht wrote in his memoir.

"Any Jewish outcries, Kennedy explained, would impede victory against the Germans. It would make the world feel that a 'Jewish War' was going on."

Hecht was recklessly promiscuous with his quotation marks, and he provided neither names for the people who supposedly attended the meeting nor the date it was held. But he essentially got it right. Kennedy, by then, had become persona non grata at the Court of St. James's and was on his way out as ambassador. He had already gotten himself into hot water by telling the *Boston Daily Globe* that "democracy is all done" in England, and that America would follow if it too went to war against Germany.

In his meeting with the studio bosses, Kennedy was equally blunt. The forum for his talk was a luncheon at Warner Bros., where, according to an account in David Nasaw's *The Patriarch,* he said pretty much what Hecht had recorded. Douglas Fairbanks Jr., the actor who would go on to become a war hero, provided Roosevelt with a written account of the lunch the day after it happened. "He apparently threw the fear of God into many of our producers and executives," he told the president.

The speech—actually a three-hour harangue—was a reprise of Lindbergh: the Jews were using their influence in the media (in this case, film) to nudge the country into war. Like Lindbergh, Kennedy was warning the Jews for their own good. This is the way Fairbanks put it to Roosevelt: "He continued to underline the fact that the film business was using its power to influence the public dangerously and that we all, and the Jews in particular, would be in jeopardy if they continued to abuse their power."

A name Hecht does mention is that of the storied producer (*Gone with the Wind*) David O. Selznick. Hecht had compiled a list of twenty studio heads and major producers, and was hitting them up to support the creation by Britain of a Jewish army to fight the Nazis. He was getting nowhere ("My twenty moguls were men loud in ego, but the Jew in them was a cringing fellow almost as frightened of the world as the Jews in a German-policed ghetto") when he was advised by the director Ernst Lubitsch to call on Selznick.

Selznick would have been a big catch. He was not only a renowned producer but was also married to Irene Mayer, the daughter of L. B. Mayer, whose name was affixed to a major studio, Metro-Goldwyn-Mayer. Selznick turned him down flat.

"I'm an American and not a Jew," Selznick told Hecht.

"If I can prove you are a Jew, David, will you sign the telegram as a cosponsor with me?"

Selznick accepted the challenge. Hecht then telephoned three persons of Selznick's choosing and asked them what they would call Selznick: a Jew or an American. Selznick's first call was to Martin Quigley, the publisher of a movie industry trade publication. With Selznick eavesdropping on an extension, Quigley answered Hecht's question: Selznick was a Jew.

Next up was Nunnally Johnson, the producer-director-writer. He too said Selznick was a Jew.

Last came Leland Hayward, the theatrical agent turned film and theater producer. "For God's sake, what's the matter with David?" Hayward exclaimed. "He's a Jew, and he knows it."

Selznick enlisted in the cause.

The dichotomy between Jew and American, the insistence that one had to be one or the other, provides a sense of how insecure even the most secure of American Jews were until relatively recently. The tendency is to dismiss them as both timid and paranoid, of not so much being afraid of anti-Semitism as they were ashamed of their own Jewishness. That was sometimes the case. But these Jews were at most one generation out of the shtetl. Many of them had little religious conviction, and yet they thought they were being asked to suffer the penalty of the pious. And all of them, regardless of their conviction, were living in a maelstrom of Jew hatred, a world that was ridding itself of Jews at a horrendous pace.

There was the sense—there *had* to be the sense—that whatever was happening in Europe could, under the right circumstances, happen in America as well. After all, what was Germany but a sort of Teutonic America? Never mind all the facile references to Bach, Beethoven, and Brahms, and never mind, too, references to Goethe and Hegel and, if you like, Moses Mendelssohn. The present counted, and it was just as impressive as the past. Germany was the land of science. It had collected thirty-seven Nobels between the inauguration of the prizes in 1901 and the installation of Hitler as chancellor in 1933. By comparison, Americans had won only thirteen in that period. The United States picked up the pace afterward—helped by refugees from Germany and other European countries.

But Germany was more than a vast laboratory. Along with Austria, it was the heartland of both traditional and modern classical music as well as the songs of the café. In film, it was dominant in Europe and as important a center as Hollywood would become. It had a vibrant theater, huge ocean liners, and dirigibles that—until the *Hindenburg* exploded in 1937—were the envy of the world. Its capital, Berlin, was every bit as modern as New York, and while Potsdamer Platz might not have been quite the equal of Times Square, as early as 1924 it required one of the world's first traffic lights.

At the time, a specter haunted many thoughtful Americans. In 1935 the first American to win a Nobel Prize in literature, Sinclair Lewis, published a novel entitled *It Can't Happen Here*. Should there be any doubt about the book's message, the cover line cleared things up: "What Will Happen When America Has a Dictator?"

Lewis was no East Coast lefty but a genuine Midwesterner who had made his reputation writing on American themes. His book resonated, not only because of the seemingly sudden and inexplicable triumph of fascism in Europe, but also the simultaneous rise in America of Huey Long, the demagogic governor of Louisiana. The Kingfish, as he was called, had become the virtual dictator of the state and had a considerable national following as well. By 1935, he was in the United States Senate—running his state from a distance—and preparing to challenge Roosevelt in 1936. His following was immense, and he was perceived as so dangerous that in *The Conquerors,* historian Michael Beschloss quotes Roosevelt as telling Joseph Kennedy, "If there was a demagogue around here of the type of Huey Long to take up anti-Semitism, there could be more blood running in the streets of New York than in Berlin."

But Long, who was assassinated before he could launch a presidential campaign, was hardly anti-Semitic; indeed, two of his closest associates, Seymour Weiss and Abraham Shushan, were Jews. Long had turned on Roosevelt and was propounding a populism that, in both rhetoric and style, sounded similar to what was being heard in Europe. He had the bombastic flair of a European dictator of the sort that filled Jews with dread, and he was, moreover, a Southern populist, part of a movement that had been blackened by the racism and anti-Semitism of Tom Watson, a Georgia newspaper editor (and eventual US senator) who had inveighed against Leo Frank. Long kept the wrong company. It seemed that Sinclair Lewis had a point: it *could* happen here.

✡ ✡ ✡

Hecht and Kook met initially at New York's Stork Club and then later at the Algonquin. It was 1941, and America was not yet in the war. Their meetings were at first somewhat awkward. Hecht had not given much thought to Palestine and was as ignorant as an informed man could be about the situation there. His sole concern was Europe's Jews and his effort to get the United States into the war. He had to shame two different parties: the Roosevelt administration and the American Jewish community. For somewhat the same reason—a quite rational fear that Jewishness and Americanism would be perceived as incompatible—they both shied away from raising a din about the ongoing murder of Jews in Europe.

Kook/Bergson looms large over the question of whether American Jews did all they could on behalf of Europe's Jews, or whether they did far too little. The Bergson Group would argue the latter, and from its perspective, it would be dead right. The proof was that America stayed out of the war and refused to provide a sanctuary for Jews who were being murdered by the hundreds of thousands. What brought America into the war was not moral outrage or a desire to save Britain from Nazism, but Hitler's inexplicable decision to start a fight with the United States.

All during the 1930s, as Jews in Germany, Austria, and the Sudetenland became increasingly desperate to find a nation that would take them in, America remained parsimonious with its emigration quotas. It stuck to those based on the country's ethnic composition in 1890, a period before the great immigrations from eastern and southern Europe. Thus, Austria and Germany together were awarded 23,370 places and Poland a mere 6,542. Poland alone had over three million Jews, most of them desperate to emigrate, most of them destined for the death camps.

Complicating matters, and leaving an indelible moral stain on America's generally admirable record of tolerance, Roosevelt allowed the implementation of this stingy immigration policy to remain in the hands of a personal friend from his days as assistant secretary of the navy, Breckinridge Long. The Breckinridges were an old and distinguished family, providing more than their share of military men, congressmen, and other public figures to the nation. Long, though, was a virtual parody of the foxhunting snob and icy anti-Semite who, as the State Department official in charge of immigration, applied himself to limiting Jewish immigration to even less than what the stingy quotas permitted. In a 1940 directive, Long put his policy down on paper:

"We can delay and effectively stop for a temporary period of indefinite length the number of immigrants into the United States. We could do this by simply advising our consuls to put every obstacle in the way and to require additional evidence and to resort to various administrative devices which would postpone and postpone and postpone the granting of the visas."

The delay strategy was effective. The vast majority of quotas from territories controlled by Nazi Germany went unfilled, and some 190,000 persons, who might have been admitted to the United States, were turned away.

This is what Bergson was up against: a heartless State Department, cruelly paltry quotas, and, not least, an American Jewish community that was pathetically fragmented, feeble, and unsteady on its American sea legs. The Jewish community was stymied by what, after all, was really, the simplest of tasks: to pressure the Roosevelt administration into denouncing Germany for killing Jews. The administration had no trouble railing against Nazi depredations in the occupied countries, but this was always done in general terms, as if the French and the Jews were suffering equally. Bergson and like-minded Jews wanted the White House to do as Hitler had done, single out Jews and not envelop them in hazy terms such as *victim* or *refugee*, or subsume them in the larger population of Poles or Russians. They were *Jews* and they were being killed for that reason.

This task was made ever harder by factional schisms within the Jewish community: the usual division between Orthodox, Conservative, and Reform. At bottom, this was about belief and practices, but that, really, was the least of the matter. The Reform Judaism movement had originated in Germany among assimilated Jews. They had preceded their eastern coreligionists to America and, until the great immigration from the Pale of Settlement, represented the bulk of American Jewry. Reformed Jews were by and large wealthier, were more assimilated, and, significantly, did not appear stereotypically Jewish: no beards, no distinctive garments, and, by the 1940s, no Jewish (or foreign) accent.

The clash between Reform and Orthodox came to a head October 6, 1943. Bergson had organized a march in Washington of between four hundred and five hundred rabbis, many of them Orthodox, some bearded, some in traditional Jewish garb. The march was bitterly opposed by more progressive elements in the community, who either thought it would do no good or it would just plain look bad.

Among the more vociferous opponents of the march were Rabbi Stephen Wise, the head of the Reform movement, and Samuel Rosenman, a White House aide.

Wise was a complex figure: as an ardent Zionist, he was a relative rarity among the Reform, but was strangely passive when it came to denouncing the Holocaust. (He believed, logically enough, that only the defeat of Germany could save Europe's Jews.) He had been born in Budapest, the son of a rabbi, and had come to America at a very young age. Wise was a thoroughly assimilated Jew who had little in common with the rabbis who marched that day in Washington. Among other things, he had access to the White House and the ear of the president.

Rosenman had even less in common with the rabbis. He had been born in San Antonio, Texas, served in the army during World War I, and made his way to New York and Columbia University Law School. He stayed in New York, becoming active in Democratic Party politics, and, predictably, he met Franklin Roosevelt. By 1943, he was a White House aide and the one FDR turned to on matters concerning the Jewish community. When it came to the rabbis' march, Rosenman and Wise were of one mind: the rabbis represented the past, not the present, and certainly not the future. They were not representative of the Jewish community—in fact, in the words of a New York Democratic congressman, the rabbis were an embarrassment. Rosenman suggested that if they came to the White House door, Roosevelt should simply not see them. They did, and he didn't.

But the rabbis' march accomplished some of what Bergson wanted. Bergson wanted a din, a great lament from American Jews: save our brethren. He got that out of the march and a subsequent Madison Square Garden extravaganza called "We Will Never Die." The pageant was produced by the ultimate showman, Billy Rose, along with the famed film director Ernst Lubitsch, and it ran for two nights before going on tour.

All this time, Hecht kept pounding out articles and essays about the plight of the Jews. In 1943 he wrote that of the "6,000,000 Jews [of Europe], almost a third have already been massacred by Germans, Romanians and Hungarians, and the most conservative of scorekeepers estimate that before the war ends at least another third will have been done to death." A version of the article appeared in the *Reader's Digest*, an immensely popular publication targeted for the average American reader. Still, none of this altered administration policy.

Clearly, the ongoing Holocaust was not, as some maintain, unknown to Americans at the time. United States and European newspapers published accounts of massacres, and Bergson took out full-page ads in the *New York Times* lamenting the fate of Europe's Jews. His efforts had almost no effect. The Roosevelt administration would not budge.

During much of the war, Roosevelt avoided mentioning the Holocaust even though he knew about it and had, indeed, been briefed on it by an eyewitness, the Pole Jan Karski, a lieutenant in the underground Home Army. Karski had been smuggled into the Warsaw ghetto and into transit points for the extermination camps. Nonetheless, Roosevelt remained mum on the subject, saying nothing specific until March 24, 1944, when he issued a statement to the press. Until then, he rebuffed efforts by Jewish leaders who wanted him to warn the Germans that they would have to pay for their crimes after the war. The record here is both troubling and ugly.

Roosevelt may have had a touch of country club anti-Semitism. He told Treasury Secretary Henry Morgenthau and another man, a Catholic, "You know this is a Protestant country, and the Catholics and the Jews are here under sufferance"—but his actions probably had nothing to do with personal prejudice and everything to do with American politics. The country remained generally anti-Semitic and xenophobic as well. A country of immigrants was pulling up the gangplanks, alarmed at the religion, complexion, and ideologies of the newcomers. In the case of Jews, they were not welcome allegedly because ideologically they could never be real Americans. Some suspected that embedded in the throngs banging on the doors of the United States were countless communist spies, and before that—as illogical as it may seem—German spies. There was simply no accounting for the duplicity of the Jews—or, as it happened, the paranoid fantasies of anti-Semites.

As for the Jews already in the country, those who were actively seeking the emigration of their brethren were at their wit's end to make a case that both then and now seems so appallingly obvious: Jews were being killed, and no one was doing anything about it, least of all the United States of America. The world, including most Americans, didn't give a damn, and the American president, while confessing himself anguished, was inert.

In *The Accomplices*, Bernard Weinraub's play about Bergstrom, there is a scene in which FDR's cousin, Laura Delano Houghteling, is ushered into the Oval Office and expresses her opposition to a 1939 bill that would have given sanctuary to twenty thousand German Jewish children.

"Twenty thousand charming children would all too soon grow into twenty thousand ugly adults," she tells FDR.

The remark—so cold, so ugly, so patently dramatic—has all the hallmarks of a theatrical invention, but it is that only as regards venue. Houghteling actually made her remark—an attempted bon mot, no doubt—to an important State Department official named Jay Pierrepont Moffat. He noted it in his diary, which his father-in-law, the ambassador Joseph Grew, donated to Harvard. The Holocaust historian Rafael Medoff discovered it there.

The children's bill was sponsored by Senator Robert Wagner, a Democrat of New York, and Representative Edith Rogers, a Republican of Massachusetts. It was supported by, among others, former president Herbert Hoover and former First Lady Grace Coolidge. They were marquee names, but they were easily outgunned by the opposition. America was in no mood to save Jews.

A coalition of patriotic and veterans' groups came out against the bill. One of them was the Allied Patriotic Societies of New York. It sent Francis H. Kinnicutt down to Washington to tell the Senate Immigration Committee why it opposed granting twenty thousand children, all under the age of fourteen, refuge in the United States.

Kinnicutt argued that the bill authorized "separating children from their parents," and that this would be wrong. It would result in them growing up to "begin competing with Americans for jobs." The kids would sooner or later have their parents join them, and that would lead to a further breakdown of the quota system. The kids might themselves become public wards, and if all of that wasn't enough, the bill was in flagrant violation of the quota system.

"We are trying to be reasonable about this matter," the *New York Times* quoted Kinnicutt as saying. "But we must recognize that this is just part of a drive to break down the whole quota system—to go back to the condition when we were flooded with foreigners who tried to run the country on different lines from those laid down by the old stock. There is no logical reason, if this bill passes, why we should not admit twenty thousand children from Spain or wherever else trouble arises."

Kinnicutt had a point. It was echoed later in the hearing by Colonel John Thomas Taylor of the American Legion. "If this bill passes, there is no reason why we should not also bring in twenty thousand Chinese children," he said.

But Kinnicutt's real point came a bit later in his testimony: the bill was not really about twenty thousand *German* children; it was about twenty thousand *Jewish* children. "Strictly speaking, it is not a refugee bill at all, for by the nature of the case, most of those to be admitted would be of the Jewish race."

In the White House, FDR took note. His own wife had urged him to support the bill, but Rosenman strongly felt otherwise. "It would create a Jewish problem in the US," he told the president. Roosevelt demurred.

The 20,000 children were just a small portion of a frantic mass of European Jews clamoring to get to America. The year before, 1938, approximately 125,000 Jews had lined up at various US consulates seeking the 27,000 visas authorized under the US quotas.

The next year, there were 300,000 applicants, one them being Otto Frank, whose daughter Anne would keep a diary when the family went into hiding in Holland.

Jews went wherever they could: some to Bolivia and some to the Dominican Republic and some to Shanghai, where they sat out the war. They were not welcome, though, in the two places they most wanted to go: the United States and Palestine. Each had their quotas.

That same year, 1939, the passenger ship *St. Louis* sailed from Hamburg to Cuba. On board were 930 Jewish refugees who expected to disembark in Havana. The Cuban authorities, after extorting money from those on board, shut them out. The ship then steamed to Florida and lingered off the coast. The United States would not admit the refugees, either. The *St. Louis* pushed on to Halifax, Canada, where again the refugees were denied asylum. The *St. Louis* then returned to Europe, where Britain, France, the Netherlands, and Belgium each accepted some of the passengers as refugees. France, the Netherlands, and Belgium were soon overrun by Germany. It is estimated that about 254 of the *St. Louis*'s passengers perished in the Holocaust.

A version of the Rogers-Wagner bill was approved by the Senate Immigration Committee. However, as amended, it required that the twenty thousand children be deducted from that year's quota. Senator Wagner balked. The bill died.

So, we may presume, did some of the children.

12

You Can't Go Home Again

In the winter of 1945, a Jew from the Polish city of Ostroleka came home from the camps. He had owned a house there and a sawmill nearby, but when he tried to reclaim them, this man who had survived the Holocaust found he could not survive its aftermath. He was murdered on the spot.

This story was told to me in 1976 when I visited Ostroleka, the town where my mother was born and where my grandmother had once run a modest store that sold dairy products. The teller of the tale was a woman known in those parts as "the Jew." As it turned out, she had converted to Catholicism many years before—way before the Second World War and the invasion of Poland by the Germans. Probably, her conversion had saved her life. When I went to see her, she was pushing old age—old enough to think she remembered my grandmother's store (my mother's family had left by the end of 1920)—and she had been a Catholic for a very long time. Nevertheless, she was considered the last Jew in town.

It was dark when my interpreter and I got to the old woman's house, a solid brick structure in a row of them. Her husband let us in and asked us to wait. The Jew was in church. The husband made us tea. By then, I had spent a couple of days in the town, conducting interviews and sightseeing. I had not gone to Poland naively. I was well aware of the country's reputation for anti-Semitism, but in Warsaw I had spent time with intellectuals and dissidents—Poland was still a communist state—and had found not a single Holocaust denier or apologist in the bunch. These were not the anti-Semites of lore, and when I spoke to them of the Holocaust, there was—with one notable exception—not a Pole I met whose views and sentiments did not correspond to my own.

Ostroleka was different. The city, about seventy miles from Warsaw, once had a substantial Jewish community. It was gone, of course. So it was not people I was looking for but places—the synagogue, for instance, or the cemetery. I had done a pretty thorough job of interviewing, calling on the mayor, the head of the local Communist Party, and the town historian. Everyone agreed: the Germans had used the synagogue as a motor pool and blew it up when they retreated. As for the cemetery, it had been paved over and a housing block erected on it. All this made sense. The cemetery no longer had a constituency; many buildings were demolished by the retreating German army.

Toward the end of my visit, I chanced upon a bookstore and on a whim went inside. I found a history of the town, and in the back was a map: Ostroleka as it had been. Little crosses signified the cemeteries; a Star of David marked the single Jewish one. I started off in search of it: past this street and that street and then through some backyards. Ostroleka had been through three wars in the twentieth century alone: the First World War, the Second World War, and, in between, the obscure but ferocious Polish-Soviet war that followed the collapse of the Russian Empire. Wars tend to jumble things a bit, and so the map did not always correspond to contemporary conditions.

I passed through the promised housing block. Just beyond it, the asphalt gave out, and the land began to roll—hillocks, evenly spaced. It took a moment for me to realize where I was. The cemetery! It was not gone. Instead, it had been pillaged and abandoned. The graves had erupted. Bones were scattered about.

Horrified, I ran around scooping up bones. I dashed from plot to plot, picking up a thighbone, an arm bone, a this bone, a that bone—fragments and shards and whole pieces. Unexpectedly, I bumped into my translator, Christopher. He was a young Brit, raised by Polish expats who had fled to England at the start of World War II. In our day trips from Warsaw, he had given me his take on the Holocaust. Yes, it was all a pity and yes the Germans were beasts, but maybe if the Jews had not isolated themselves, dressed oddly, spoken a different language, repudiated the Poles, then maybe things would have turned out differently. They had spitefully refused to assimilate. He was so Polish in his outlook. He was so British in his speech. Jews had been killed. A pity. But it was, somehow, partly their fault.

Now he was pale, the blood drained from his face. He, too, had rushed off to collect the bones. When we met, he just looked at me, wide eyed, saying nothing, cradling bones in his arms. It was stupid. So late. So beside the point. He settled the bones on the ground. I did the same. We had been lied to, he much more than me. He had believed it all, everything the mayor and the historian and the local Communist Party functionary had said about the cemetery. I had believed it, too—but why shouldn't I have? For Christopher, it was a different matter. If the story about the cemetery was not true, then it was possible that many of the other stories about Jews were also not true.

Walking out of the cemetery, we spied an old wooden house. It was a ramshackle affair, seemingly lifted from some Hollywood back lot. Smoke twirled from the chimney. Christopher knocked. A very old woman answered the door. She wore layers of sweaters; it was cold in the house. The place consisted of one long room, in the center of which was an open stove. The old woman fed it wood while she cooked something ugly on the top. Her husband talked as she worked.

He, too, was very old. He, too, wore several sweaters. His teeth were gone, but not his memory. He knew precisely what had happened to the cemetery. He had been its caretaker.

Years before, the old man had come from the countryside to tend the cemetery. It had been a resplendent place, surrounded by sentries of proud pines. He was at work the day the Germans rounded up Ostroleka's Jews and ordered them to the cemetery. The Jews were forced to topple the headstones and then marched to the forest. The Germans killed them there.

After liberation, the locals looted the cemetery. They took the headstones and shards of the crypts and used them for building materials. (This was the fate, too, of the synagogue.) The Poles were poor. They had nothing. They had to rebuild. So the living stole from the dead.

But with the headstones gone, the earth pushed back. It heaved and ejected the bones. Skulls popped out of the earth, and kids played soccer with the heads of dead Jews. The local Communist Party chief, a Jew, had hired the old man to gather the skulls and rebury them. He did so. But now that Jew was dead too, and no one cared anymore about the cemetery—so the earth kept disgorging its bones.

All this time, the old woman stirred her gruel and fed wood to the fire. She said nothing. But as her husband told of the splendor of the old cemetery, the murder of the Jews, and the macabre persistence of the bones, she sobbed. He talked and she cried. She cried for the old days and for the job her husband had once had and for the serenity of the Jewish graveyard and maybe also for the Jews. We were not sure why she cried.

This was late November, when it gets dark early in Poland. This was November, a time of cloying dampness, of a wet, insinuating cold. Christopher and I shivered in the house and then shivered some more outside. We rushed to the car, a Lada as I recall, and headed back to Warsaw. On the way, he apologized.

The death of the Jewish sawmill owner was vastly important. His murder was not an anomaly, a horrible but unique tragedy—sorry, but these things can happen—but a somewhat common occurrence. Some 1,500 to 2,000 Jews were killed in the aftermath of the war; some 1,500 Jews who had managed to stagger out of Auschwitz-Birkenau or from their hiding places in the forest or the root cellar of a kind Pole or from exile in the Soviet Union. They had almost certainly lost family, friends, businesses, or just years of their lives and had somehow made it home to places like Ostrów Mazowiecka or Ostroleka. There they were murdered by their former neighbors—sometimes for their old property, maybe to settle a debt, but also because the old hate had proved durable. Anti-Semitism, too, was a survivor.

Marek Edelman, a leader of the Warsaw ghetto uprising, insisted that the postwar murders of Jews had nothing to do with anti-Semitism and everything to do with plain theft—"banditry," he called it. Surely the killing of the Ostroleka mill owner could fall into that category, as might many of the other deaths.

It takes a certain impertinence to quibble with Edelman, but he was a vigorous anti-Zionist, a staunch Polish nationalist, who resented any attempt to incorporate the story of the Warsaw ghetto into the Israel foundation myth. Although he died in 2009 (age about ninety), his ideological roots went deep into the twentieth century and the cacophonous and nasty arguments between Poland's Zionists and its Bundists. "The Bundists did not wait for the Messiah, nor did they plan to leave for Palestine," he said. "They believed that Poland was their country, and they fought for a just, socialist Poland, in which each nationality would have its own cultural autonomy, and in which minorities' rights would be guaranteed."

Edelman notwithstanding, an abundance of evidence suggests that what fueled the postwar pogroms was not mere theft. When the killing is done in plain sight, when the police do not intervene and do not apprehend, when the fathers of the church look the other way, and the killer struts through the town the next day in the boots of the murdered Jew, then this is something more than banditry. This is banditry of a nonperson, a despised human being who has not earned the protection of the law or the respect of his neighbors. And when the reason for all that is his Jewishness, then this is not banditry, but raw Jew hatred.

In 1943 Czeslaw Milosz (1911–2004), later to win a Nobel for Literature, watched the Warsaw ghetto burn. Watching, too, were countless other people who had come for a good time. They had come by bus and tram to watch Jews incinerated—"cutlets," they called them in a jokey sort of way. In his mind, Milosz was reminded of the burning at the stake, in 1600, of Giordano Bruno, deemed a heretic by the Inquisition. A crowd came to the Campo dei Fiori in Rome to watch, to be entertained.

"That same hot wind" still hung over Poland three years later when eight-year-old Henryk Blaszczyk went missing one night. He reappeared the next day and said he had been held prisoner in the basement of a building used by the Jewish Committee of Kielce. The building was located at 7 Planty Street. It housed about 160 people, most of them Holocaust survivors. It was three stories high. It had no basement.

The boy's tale was a fib, and the police knew it. Yet when a mob assembled at 7 Planty Street, the police not only did nothing to stop it, they disarmed the few Jews who had guns and then fed them to the mob below. Jews were thrown from the second-floor window. They were beaten to death. They were stabbed. Jews who had managed to scramble to the outskirts of town were run down and killed. A Jewish woman escaped but had to abandon her newborn child. The baby was shot in the head while lying on the ground.

These examples of horror are taken from Jan T. Gross's harrowing book *Fear*. It is a vehement and convincing rebuttal to the assertion that Poles and Jews were equal victims of the Germans, when, really, the Jews were victims of both. (Five percent of the ethnic Polish population did not survive the war; the figure for Jews was 90 percent.) This is not a minor point. Nor does it deny or belittle the heroism or sacrifice of many Poles, some of whom have been honored by Israel for saving the lives of Jews during the Holocaust. And it does not in any way denigrate or diminish the suffering of Poles at the hands of the Germans or ignore the fact, a matter of enormous, justifiable pride, that the Poles—not the French or the Belgians or the Dutch or the Danes—waged Europe's fiercest and most sustained war of resistance, although you would never know it from the movies.

Yet Polish anti-Semitism was also a fact. It did not depart Poland with the retreating Germans. It persisted. And while the Holocaust made it impossible for anti-Semites still to argue that Poland had too many Jews, it was still possible to argue that those who were left were disproportionately communists, many of them returned from exile in the Soviet Union. Since the founding of the Soviet state, Jews had been disproportionately represented in both its leadership and its terror apparatus, and the same thing was apparently about to happen in postwar Poland.

The perception that an alien people—not, mind you, Poles of a different religion or, in the case of communists, no religion at all—were taking over Poland was widespread. The Roman Catholic primate, August Cardinal Hlond, put it this way in explaining the reason for the Kielce pogrom: "Jews today occupy leading positions in Poland's government." He went on, "In the fatal battle on the political front in Poland, it is to be regretted that some Jews have lost their lives. But a disproportionate larger number of Poles have lost theirs."

The boy in the basement was a reprise of Kishinev. The Poles, however, were not all that fastidious in their use of the blood libel. For one thing, it was July, way past the Passover season. For another, the boy had come home intact. He had lost not a drop of blood.

Word of the pogrom spread. People came from all over to participate or watch. Trains braked when they approached Kielce so the mob could board and search for Jews. Some were found and killed. In the end, about forty Jews, and even a few Christian Poles who had the misfortune of looking Jewish, died.

These were not the killings committed by bureaucrats—no banality of evil here. No. These were the killings of raw, unmitigated hatred, of fun and excitement, of homicide chosen and carried out gladly, of sexual or emotional release, of lackadaisical stoning conducted out in the open so everyone could watch, of uniformed Boy Scouts and police officers taking part, of the poor Jew running around in an ever-closing circle until he ran out of space and out of life. There was nothing banal about this evil.

It had been fourteen months since the Nazis had killed their last Jew.

It was 1946.

In 1939 there were about three million Jews in Poland, composing about 10 percent of the population. By 1945 and the end of the war, there were about 200,000, and most of them were running for their lives, seeking safety in Occupied Germany, of all places. For Europe's remaining Eastern European Jews, the choices were stark. They did not want to go to the Soviet Union, an oppressive and cruel communist dictatorship, nor any of the other countries that the Red Army had conquered and was unlikely ever to leave. Poland, home to the largest number of Jews before the war, was out of the question. The war had changed little. Jews were still being killed there.

There were other options. But the one place that really wanted Jews, that reached out for them, that beseeched them to come, and where Yiddish was understood if not spoken, was Palestine. Britain, which administered Palestine on behalf of the United Nations, was alarmed by the situation. It tried to keep Poland's Jews in Poland—and out of Palestine—by pressuring the new Warsaw government to make Poland more hospitable to Jews. But neither London nor, for that matter, Warsaw could materially affect matters. Poland remained dangerous for Jews. The postwar exodus to Palestine was under way.

If you ask virtually anyone about the moral justification for Israel, he'd invoke the Holocaust. The Holocaust begat Israel. Everyone knows that. The world atoned for the murder of Six Million Jews and in recompense awarded other Jews a parched piece of land more or less the size of New Jersey. But if you ask about the periods just before and just after the Holocaust, you would probably get blank stares. Wasn't the Holocaust the entire answer?

Yes. Yes and no. Yes, between 1933 and 1945, 73 percent of Europe's Jews were murdered. But there was a time before that when Jews were murdered sporadically and a time afterward when the sporadic murder of Jews resumed. This time of before and after is not, I think, well known to most people, including many Jews. The immensity of the Holocaust obscured what preceded and followed it.

For Polish, Ukrainian, Lithuanian, Latvian, Estonian, Yugoslavian, or Russian Jews, the Holocaust was both an unprecedented departure from what preceded it—and much more of the same. The killing of Jews was administered by the organizationally diligent Germans, but the murders themselves were sometimes carried out or merely witnessed passively by the local population. Jan Gross tells of peasants politely asking Jews for their boots as they were being marched by Germans to a massacre site. He tells also of these same peasants arriving at the killing fields even before the Germans, waiting patiently like vultures on a fence for the slaughter to begin.

When the war was over, the Germans were gone, but the anti-Semites remained. Some of them, including some ethnic Germans who had helped with the killing, went to work for the American military in the newly established displaced persons camps, mostly in Germany. Little wonder, then, that they were likened to Nazi concentration camps—an exaggeration, to be sure, but an understandable one. The Jews within them were still guarded, still fenced in with barbed wire, still wearing their tissue-thin concentration camp outfits, and, if those would not suffice, given the uniforms of captured SS officers. When they looked at one another, they saw the horrifying visage of the enemy.

Outside the camps, they could see local Germans living in relative comfort in their own homes, free to come and go as they pleased, their anti-Semitism now seemingly confirmed by a new authority, the US Army and its policy of incarcerating Jews. In some camps, Nazis or collaborators—not necessarily Germans, but often Balts—were put in positions of authority. The Americans praised them for their neatness, their pleasing looks: so Midwestern, so virtually American and yet not German.

American military administrators had no idea they were befriending people who had not been forcibly brought to Germany as slave laborers (often the story they told) but had come either of their own accord or because, as Nazi collaborators, they were afraid for their lives at home. Their very appearance struck terror in the hearts of Jewish DPs. To the clueless Americans, they were simply Lithuanians or Latvians or Estonians, which meant that they were not Germans and thus could not be war criminals—just harmless refugees, displaced persons themselves.

At the top of the military's chain of command in Bavaria was one of America's most storied commanders, General George S. Patton. In his cinematic incarnation, he was headstrong, impetuous, and dashingly reactionary. Much of that is historically accurate, but an element of his character is missing from the movie: his repellent anti-Semitism. It had been Patton's job to fight Nazis, but his battlefield enemy was not the one he hated most. That was the Soviet Union, his erstwhile ally, and communists everywhere. For them, he harbored a volcanic bitterness. The Nazis, anticommunists all, had at least that going for them. Patton gave them some slack.

It was only with great reluctance and a good deal of foot-dragging that Patton implemented the de-Nazification policy that the victorious Allies had agreed upon in their various meetings, particularly the postwar conference at Potsdam. For Patton, the policy was an irritating impediment to efficient administration of the conquered territories. The Nazis, after all, had been the administrators. They knew how to do the job, and many if not most were not hardened ideologues but bureaucrats who had felt compelled to join the party. Patton found them not all that different from the people back home who felt compelled to join one political party or another to get a job. So when he was asked at a press conference held at his headquarters in Bad Tolz why de-Nazification was proceeding so slowly, he explained casually: "This Nazi question is very much like a Democrat and Republican election fight."

The remark made for explosive headlines back in the United States and all but ruined what was left of Patton's military career. Privately he was saying even worse. In a letter to his wife, Beatrice, he blamed his image troubles not on his own statements but on the machinations of "the Devil and Moses." In his diary, he noted "a very apparent Semitic influence in the press" and observed that Jews and communists were attempting "a further dismemberment of Germany." Patton was appalled at what the Nazis had done, but the Jews, he felt, sort of had it coming. He wrote to his wife that the Jewish DPs were "lower than animals," and he could not fathom how they could have lost their "sense of decency . . . during their period of internment by the Germans."

"My personal opinion is that no people could have sunk to the level of degradation these have reached in the short space of four years," he wrote in another letter.

In their book *A Safe Haven: Harry S. Truman and the Founding of Israel*, Allis Radosh and Ronald Radosh make copious use of Patton's diary entries regarding DPs. He wrote that while others might "believe that the Displaced Person is a human being," he knew "he is not." He had placed them under armed guard lest they flee, "spread over the country like locusts," and then have to be rounded up and shot because they had "murdered and pillaged innocent Germans."

Patton was an ugly anti-Semite, but his views about Jews were not all that different from those of the ordinary GI. Surveys tell us that many thought there really was a category called "innocent Germans." Whatever the truth of the matter, the victorious Allies at the Potsdam Conference had stated explicitly that there was no such thing. In the summer of 1945, the United States, Great Britain, and the Soviet Union had in effect convened as a jury and found all Germans guilty of both the war and the mass murder of innocents. The Nuremberg war crimes trials would come later, but those were for individuals.

Most of the DP camps were located in Bavaria and Austria (there were some in Italy as well), and they served as catch basins for a mass of battered and disoriented people from all across Europe. The American zone of occupation, along with those of Britain and France, amounted to havens. The Soviet zone in Germany and the Soviet-occupied lands to the east were considered little more than death traps. A mass of desperate humanity fled west, collecting in what had just been Nazi Germany. Now, under American or Allied auspices, they were nominally safe, but the Americans, intent on replicating the American experience, reconstituted the vaunted melting pot. Military authorities recognized national differences but not religious ones. So Jewish Poles were housed with Christian Poles, never mind that the former considered the latter to be either hostile or dangerous. The same held for other nationalities, some of which harbored Jew killers. It seemed to these Jews that the killers had followed them out of the gates of the concentration camps, stalking them all the way. In their barracks, they could see the face of the enemy.

Branda Kalk, a seventy-three-year-old Polish Jew, lost her husband to the Germans in 1942. Along with the rest of her family, she fled east to Russia, where they remained for the rest of the war. With the capitulation of Germany in May 1945, Kalk and her family returned to Poland. Eight months later, a pogrom erupted, and her remaining family was wiped out. Kalk herself was shot in the eye.

Kalk was interviewed by a United Nations Special Committee on Palestine. The committee toured Palestine and Jordan and visited European DP camps as well.

"I want to go to Palestine," Kalk told members of the UNSCOP subcommittee, according to Jorge Garcia Granados of Guatemala. "I know the conditions there. But where in the world is it good for the Jew? Sooner or later, he is made to suffer. In Palestine, at least, the Jews fight together for their life and their country."

Kalk's story might not have been typical, but her desire to go to Palestine certainly was. When a survey was conducted of more than eighteen thousand Jewish DPs, only thirteen said they wished to remain in Europe. To the consternation of Harry Truman, another survey suggested that the Jewish DPs did not even want to immigrate to the United States. They preferred a place where Jews would be in control. They preferred Palestine. They were not, strictly speaking, Zionists seeking to make a new nation. They were, strictly speaking, victims, seeking only to be left alone. They wanted to go to Palestine if only because they could effectively go nowhere else. All that stood in their way was the swiftly collapsing British Empire. Britain ruled Palestine, and Britain, to put it mildly, had simply had it with the pesky Jews.

13

A Bald-Headed Son of a Bitch to the Rescue

By 1945 and the end of World War II, Arthur James Balfour had been dead for fifteen years and so, in a way, was his eponymous declaration. The British, once so gushingly and fervently pro-Zionist, were severely cramped with second thoughts. Not only were they more reliant on Middle Eastern oil than Balfour could have ever imagined—after all, he was born in 1848, still the age of sail—but the areas they felt obliged to govern were teeming with Arabs and Muslims of all types, none of whom wanted any more Jews in their neck of the woods.

Britain continued to have the burdens of a colonial power, but it no longer had the assets of one. Two world wars had devastated it; the winters of 1945 and 1946 were brutal. The country was cold, gray, and depressed. Churchill and his exhortations of greater glory seemed anachronistic. Britons yearned for someone and something new—for socialism, as it turned out. In the election of 1945, Churchill and the Tories were defeated, surprisingly and stunningly so. Clement Attlee and the Labour Party took over, a change so abrupt and unexpected that the postwar Potsdam Conference of victors—all but France, that is—began with Churchill in Britain's seat and ended with Attlee in the same chair.

Initially, the Zionists had no qualms about Labour. The party had eleven times over the years committed itself to the establishment of a Jewish state in Palestine, and it had a comradely affinity with the dominant political establishment of Jewish Palestine, which was also socialist. But that was a somewhat different Labour Party. It was the party in opposition. Now that it was suddenly governing, having to administer Palestine (not to mention India, Burma, and an always restive Northern Ireland) and needing to appease Palestinians, Arabs in general, and Muslims the world over—including the many millions on the Indian subcontinent—it had a different perspective. Wherever Labour's heart might be, its head was now at Number 10 Downing Street and its responsibilities were to govern. Essential to that task was keeping 100,000 Jewish DPs out of Palestine.

The figure 100,000 became the idée fixe of both Zionists and their foes. It originated, apparently, with Earl G. Harrison, one of those public-spirited men of achievement who once seemed common in America: a liberal Republican whose causes included racial justice. President Truman chose him to inspect America's DP camps in Europe and report back as quickly as possible. At the time, Harrison was the dean of the University of Pennsylvania's law school. In no time (only about a month after V-E Day), he was on his way to Europe, and once there, he got straight to work. He had been appointed on June 22, 1945. By the end of July, he had inspected thirty camps, about one a day, ignoring and departing from the itinerary given him by the army.

What Harrison saw appalled him. The living conditions were pitiful. He commiserated with Jewish DPs. He understood their fear; he appreciated their well-earned paranoia. He knew they could not be lumped in with their fellow Poles or Hungarians. The physical and psychological conditions for Jews were so bad that his description of them and his recommendations for their alleviation made a profound impression on Truman. This was one report that made a difference.

On August 31, 1945, only about two months after Harrison had arrived in Europe, a peeved Truman already had Harrison's report and had written a tough letter to his commander in Europe, Dwight D. Eisenhower. He wanted the DPs out of the camps while they awaited repatriation or evacuation. "These houses should be requisitioned from the German civilian population," Truman wrote. He reminded Ike of the agreement reached by the Allies at the postwar Potsdam Conference. "This is one way to implement the Potsdam policy that the German people cannot escape responsibility for what they have brought upon themselves."

Truman quoted directly from Harrison's report: "As matters now stand, we appear to be treating the Jews as the Nazis treated them except that we do not exterminate them. They are in concentration camps in large numbers under our military guard instead of SS troops. One is led to wonder whether the German people, seeing this, are not supposing that we are following or at least condoning Nazi policy."

The letter was in no way a personal reprimand. It was, though, an order to get on with the job of making life better for all DPs and to pay particular attention to the Jews. This was because Harrison himself had paid particular attention to the Jews by having Dr. Joseph J. Schwartz, the European director of a Jewish organization called the American Joint Distribution Committee, join his mission. Even with the war over, Jews were dying from the maltreatment they had received from the Nazis.

Harrison not only came up with the figure of 100,000 but also insisted that the naive policy of grouping refugees by nationalities not be applied to Jews. And it was also Harrison who said quite simply that these Jews ought to be allowed to immigrate to Palestine. "In conclusion, I wish to repeat that the main solution, in many ways *the only real solution*, of the problem lies in the quick evacuation of all nonrepatriable Jews in Germany and Austria who wish it, to Palestine," Harrison wrote. Over and over, he had asked Jewish DPs where they wanted to go. Palestine, he was told. Palestine, Palestine, Palestine. Harrison concurred. The Jews of Europe wanted to go to Palestine and ought to go to Palestine. That was all there was to it.

The US State Department, however, insisted that the Jewish problem must not be solved at the expense of the Arabs. To most Americans, no doubt Harrison as well, the Arabs fitted the description Neville Chamberlain once employed for the Czechoslovaks: "a far away people of which we know little." The Arabs were an even farther-away people about which most Americans knew nothing. What was known about Arabs was gleaned from the behavior of those who scavenged the World War II North African battlefield, relieving the dead of their equipment, down to their boots. (The movie *Patton* later depicted this.) Palestinians were not North Africans, of course, but such distinctions were lost on most Americans.

Whatever the case, Palestinians could never have won over the American political elite. In the first place, they made a horrible choice with Husseini as their nominal leader. More important, there were simply too few of them in the United States to have any political impact. Truman made that point himself. Speaking to American ambassadors to Arab countries who complained about a pro-Zionist tilt in the administration, he said, "I'm sorry, gentlemen, but I have to answer to hundreds of thousands who are anxious for the success of Zionism; I do not have hundreds of thousands of Arabs among my constituents."

Truman's Jewish constituents, however, were hardly in the bag. Nowadays, it's a given that Jews vote Democratic almost no matter what. Indeed, the only Democratic presidential candidate to get less than 50 percent of the Jewish vote was incumbent Jimmy Carter in 1980. (He got 45 percent, down from 71 percent four years earlier.) Truman received 75 percent of the Jewish vote in 1948, seemingly a healthy-enough figure. But just four years earlier, Franklin D. Roosevelt had won an astounding 90 percent.

So not only had a hunk of the Democratic vote abandoned the Democratic Party, but also it had done so in the key state of New York. It was, in fact, the Jewish vote that cost Truman New York's forty-seven electoral votes, according to the historian Rafael Medoff. New York was the big prize (California back then had only twenty-five electoral votes), and New York was, politically speaking, a strange animal indeed. Uniquely among the states, it had a significant Jewish vote, and according to an analysis by Professor Herbert F. Weisberg of Ohio State University (cited by Medoff), just 45 percent of that vote went to Truman. Thomas Dewey, the Republican candidate and the state's governor, got 22 percent of the vote. Where did the remaining votes go? They went to Henry A. Wallace.

Wallace had been Roosevelt's secretary of agriculture and his vice president and then Roosevelt's and Truman's secretary of the interior. In 1946 Truman fired him, and in 1948 Wallace became the standard-bearer of the Progressive Party, which managed to win not a single electoral vote but did garner half of the popular vote in New York state. Wallace was a leftist, totally dreamy and enthralled with the Soviet Union (he later recanted), and he blamed American policy, not communist mendacity, for the eruption of the Cold War. At the same time, like many leftists, Wallace was an integrationist in an era when Jim Crow was the law of much of the land.

Many New York Jews shared those positions as well. They had come from European socialist stock, and they, too, were inclined to look sympathetically at the Soviet Union. Jews were also in the vanguard of the civil rights movement. Not only was that in conformity with the egalitarian nature of socialist-tinged Judaism (or the other way around), but it seemed only logical to make common cause with yet another loathed minority group. These were good and sufficient reasons, and Jews were already gaining the reputation of voting against their economic interest—"Jews earn like Episcopalians and vote like Puerto Ricans," in the pithy phrase of the sociologist Milton Himmelfarb. But there was something more.

In the 1940s and even later, the Zionist cause was embraced by the left. And while the cause was also embraced by the Republican Party, it was Henry Wallace and the Progressive Party that gave Harry Truman and his Democrats the most to worry about. Left-wing Jews were not under any circumstances going to vote Republican. But they might vote Progressive, especially as Wallace was foursquare for the establishment of Israel, while Truman, the president with more than politics on his plate, dawdled and did not show his card until late in the game. Wallace had no such compunction. Language calling for the establishment of a Jewish state was included in the party's platform. And the party, and Wallace, favored lifting the arms embargo, which had been placed, in a parody of balance, on Jew and Arab alike. For these reasons, Jewish voters—particularly left-leaning unionists—flocked to Wallace. In the end, he cost Truman New York state.

New York was important, but not the whole picture. Jewish voting power, while growing, was insufficient to have America's immigration laws repealed but enough to gain entry into the White House and make their voice heard at the State Department. Not only did the growing number of Jewish members of Congress press for American support of a Jewish state, but so did non-Jewish members from states with substantial Jewish populations. As in England, Christian Zionism exerted a strong influence. The story of the Hebrews was deeply embedded in Christian lore. It was "Let my people go"—and the people were Jews going to Israel.

Still, London balked. It not only insisted that the Jews of Europe remain in Europe but even argued that Europe needed the talents and abilities of the Jews—a sort of human natural resource, like hydroelectric power. The statements of one Labour official after another were clumsy, insensitive. In Washington, the ambassador, Edward Frederick Lindley Wood, 1st Earl of Halifax, characterized (actually, mischaracterized) as a rank appeaser in the novel and film *The Remains of the Day*, found himself mouthing absolute inanities. Among them, expressed to US Secretary of State James Byrnes, was the conviction that Jewish DPs were really no worse off than any of the others. It was therefore the policy of his government to insist that these Jews remain in Europe "to play an active part in building up the life of the countries of which they came." At another point, he argued that to agree that the Jews should leave Germany and other European countries would constitute an acceptance of Nazi race ideology—that the Jews were indeed racially or genetically distinct.

Britain's main and obvious concern was not, of course, its commitment to a European version of the melting pot but its need to appease the Arabs. To do so might not have been heroic or even admirable, but it was understandable and consonant with British interests. Britain's representatives should have stopped right there. Instead, they made one ploddingly dumb remark after another, sometimes belittling reports of pogroms—"The same monotonous story about pogroms," said Lieutenant General Sir Frederick E. Morgan—or in the case of Labour's foreign secretary, Ernest Bevin, making a classic gaffe by telling an unpalatable truth. Referring to the incessant pressure from the United States, he told the annual Labour Party conference, "There has been agitation in the United States, and particularly in New York, for one hundred thousand Jews to be put into Palestine. I hope I will not be misunderstood in America if I say that this was proposed with the purest of motives. They did not want too many Jews in New York."

As he evidently feared, Bevin was misunderstood—or understood—in New York and elsewhere. Henceforth, there was no convincing many American Jews that Britain's Palestine policy was just the consequence of rational but unfortunate self-interest and not Anglo-Saxon anti-Semitism. Bevin's remark put Truman on the spot. He was caught between his supporters in the Democratic Party—and the importance of the Jewish vote—and America's wartime allies.

Bevin's gibe might seem cruel and stupid, but in the context of its time, it had a certain exculpatory meaning: the United States was itself unwilling to admit the very Jews it wanted Britain to permit into Palestine. The irony of the situation was not lost on *Commentary* magazine, published by the American Jewish Committee: "The readiness of the United States to tell others what they ought to do, while doing little or nothing itself, had long been one of its less endearing characteristics in the eyes of other nations. Britain, an especially favored recipient of this country's unsolicited advice, has never learned to live with it."

Commentary was then a new magazine (editor: Elliot Cohen), founded in the maelstrom of what was emerging as a robust period of political lunacy. The magazine was liberal and anticommunist, while a small but disproportionately influential segment of the American Jewish community had either communist sympathies or little sympathy for anticommunists. It was still a fact that Jewish membership in communist and affiliated organizations was out of proportion to the American Jewish population as a whole. This was the case in Europe, too.

The postwar anticommunist hysteria, the witch hunts, blacklisting, and everything that came to be called McCarthyism, was fueled to an alarming degree by anti-Semitism. (Wisconsin senator Joe McCarthy himself seemed free of the taint.) To many Americans, particularly in the South and the West, the words *communist* and *Jew* were interchangeable and were synonymous with *traitor*. It therefore made no sense to admit those 100,000 Jewish DPs because they were, probably, communists of one sort or another.

This was an almost universal sentiment. You could, apparently, hear it expressed everywhere; even on Capitol Hill, according to Senator Carl Hatch (D-NM): "I have heard it said—and I am ashamed to say that frequently it is said in the Hall of Congress: They are nothing but communists, nothing but Jews—hated, despised, unwanted spawn from the Old World." Or, as Senator Burnet R. Maybank, a South Carolina Democrat, put it, "We have too many foreigners here already, and I think we should get rid of them rather than bring in additional ones." For his time, Maybank was considered a racial moderate.

Immigrants had long been distrusted for their exotic beliefs, both religious and ideological, so in a sense, this was nothing new. But Jewish immigrants represented both an alien religion and a downright frightening ideology. There could be no doubt to some that Jewish communism was no canard. The Soviet government seemed to be nothing less than a Jewish creation—as was the short-lived post–World War I communist uprising in Bavaria or the radical Hungarian regime under Béla Kun (born Béla Kohn), who had a Jewish father, a Christian mother, and no religion to speak of, but an indelible identity as a prototypical Jewish communist. Common sense said, "Beware."

The Red Scare that followed World War II was similar to the one that followed World War I but with one significant exception. When the armistice was signed in 1918, there was only one communist country, the Soviet Union, and it was embroiled in a civil war—the outcome of which was in doubt. About a quarter century later, the Soviet Union had emerged at the end of World

War II as a major military power, the only one capable of challenging American leadership. It was poised to demand and impose a sphere of influence that encompassed all of eastern Europe as well as the southern Balkans (Yugoslavia, Albania) and the eastern part of Germany. What's more, communist movements were active elsewhere, including Italy, Greece, France, and China, where a civil war was raging. Communism was on the move.

And moving your way, wherever you happened to be, whether in Shanghai or San Francisco. Moreover, it moved in mysterious, creepy ways. Unlike the immediate threats posed by former enemies Germany and Japan, it conquered not just by military force but also by subversion. The enemy was both within and without; they were exotic peoples from "over there," as well as prosaic-looking-and-sounding Americans who were "here," often, if not frequently, burrowed deep in the government, taking a salary from fellow citizens but reporting to a foreign power.

By the end of World War II, the harsh light of recent events had exposed communism as a monstrous and murderous fraud. The Soviet Union was a brutal dictatorship; possibly millions had perished in the Gulag; certainly millions had perished in the Ukrainian famine. Countless thousands were convicted (and later executed) at show trials that fooled no one. Germany had been mercilessly pillaged by the Soviets, its women violated, its factories hauled off to the east. Most Americans, for very good reasons, loathed communism.

The writer L. P. Hartley opened his novel *The Go-Between* (1953) with a line so useful that it has been honored by becoming a cliché: "The past is a foreign country; they do things differently there." The America of the late 1940s and 1950s was indeed a foreign country. It was one in which racism, sexism, and anti-Semitism were commonplace, unexceptional—just the way things were done. These were not secret vices, prejudices that were whispered by one American to another. They were all expressed openly—statements of obvious, incontrovertible fact, nothing more.

Racism and sexism retain some currency, but anti-Semitism is so spent as a force that it can be found only in the fund-raising material of various Jewish organizations. Anti-Semitism has become like the polio scare of distant summers, tales told by the old for the entertainment of the credulous young that have no real-life application at all. It is difficult now for anyone to appreciate the vehemence, the energy, and the sheer ubiquity of anti-Semitism in the 1940s and how to a Jew just one generation out of the shtetl, it was experienced with concussive force. (Jewish DPs who immigrated to the segregated American South were terrified by signs barring African Americans from this or that public accommodation. To them, it was frighteningly familiar.)

The midcentury America of my parents was a different place. Not only did my mother have to seek work under the assumed name "Patricia Tyson"—she had reddish hair and a freckled complexion—but she even had to work for a Jew who would not hire Jews. My father had no such experience, but he worked all his life for a firm founded by Jewish immigrants. Things changed, of course—my mother worked for many years at a Catholic hospital—but both parents stuck pretty close to a Jewish universe. They vacationed in the Catskills, had not a single gentile friend, belonged to Jewish organizations, and conducted themselves always as if the twin calamities of their lives, the Great Depression and the Holocaust, could swerve in history and, like a boomerang, return. The scent of both always lingered for them.

All during the war and postwar years, American Jews retained a keen fear of anti-Semitism. There was plainly much of it around. Postwar America was not a tolerant, welcoming place. Poll after poll showed scant support for admitting additional refugees. Toward the end of 1945, Gallup asked, "Should we permit more persons from Europe to come to this country each year than we did before the war, should we keep the number the same, or should we reduce the number?"

A minuscule 5 percent said that more immigrants should be admitted, while 32 percent said the number should remain the same. But a plurality, 37 percent, wanted fewer immigrants, and 14 percent wanted none at all—in all, a majority affixing another lock to the door barring refugees from America.

In actual fact, the numbers were undoubtedly worse than presented. It's likely that the 32 percent who opted for no change were in effect calling for keeping the numbers low. When the question was put another way—"Would you support President Truman's proposal to allow more Jewish and other European refugees to come to the United States?"—72 percent said no and 12 percent had no opinion. The yeses amounted to 16 percent, which, to any politician, is a minority so small you might as well be talking about the dead. There simply was no movement to bring Jewish refugees to America and considerable, overwhelming opposition instead.

Patton's anti-Semitic observations were not confided to his diary out of shame. In fact, had he made the same observation to his staff officers, they probably would have just nodded in agreement. Leonard Dinnerstein, in his *America and the Survivors of the Holocaust*, cites a postwar poll of American soldiers in which a "very high proportion of GIs indicated that Hitler was partly right in his treatment of Jews."

Right in what way? It had to be Hitler's emphasis on Jews being a people apart, immensely talented and therefore immensely dangerous: clever, devious, mischievous, and adept at both manipulating money and making revolution. If the average GI thought that, then, it seems, so did his commander in chief. At the Casablanca Conference of January 1943, Franklin Roosevelt was asked by French general Charles A. Noguès about the newly liberated Algerian Jews, who wanted their full civil rights restored, particularly the right to vote. The minutes of the meeting do not reflect well on Roosevelt:

> The President stated that he felt the whole Jewish problem should be studied very carefully and that progress should definitely be planned. In other words, the number of Jews engaged in the practice of the professions (law, medicine, etc.) should be definitely limited to the percentage that the Jewish population in North Africa bears to the whole of the North African population. Such a plan would therefore permit the Jews to engage in the professions, at the same time would not permit them to overcrowd the professions, and would present an unanswerable argument that they are being given full rights.
>
> To the foregoing, General Noguès generally agreed, stating at the same time that it would be a sad thing for the French to win the war merely to open the way for the Jews to control the professions and the business world of North Africa.

Whether Roosevelt nodded or not, the minutes do not say. From what they do say, however, it is not too much to infer that the president voiced no objection.

> The President stated that his plan would further eliminate the specific and understandable complaint which the Germans bore towards the Jews in Germany, namely, that while they represented a small part of the population, over fifty percent of the lawyers, doctors, school teachers, college professors, etc., in Germany were Jews.

The lunch break could not come soon enough.

Oddly enough, the British government never seemed to grasp that the American government, particularly under Truman, was in thrall to the same brand of Christian Zionism that had prompted a previous generation of Englishmen to issue the Balfour Declaration. Truman himself was an inveterate Bible reader, and it seemed to him only natural and right that the Hebrews return whence they had come. Among the biblical psalms, his favorite was number 137, with its eulogistic reference to the lost Israel: "By the rivers of Babylon, there we sat down, yea, we wept, when we remembered Zion."

Throughout his political career, Truman had been a Zionist in sentiment, if not in name. Both Kansas City and St. Louis had important Jewish communities, and so it could always be argued that Truman was simply voting his "district": the state of Missouri. Maybe. When it comes to a politician, it is usually foolish to discount sheer opportunism, and Harry S. Truman was not only a politician but also a product of conventional machine politics—the storied and tainted Kansas City organization of Thomas "Boss Tom" Pendergast. (For a while, Truman was dubbed "the senator from Pendergast.")

Still, there is abundant evidence that when it came to the Zionist cause, Truman was swayed more by his religious upbringing and his sense of justice than by sheer political opportunism. One might nevertheless wonder where Truman would have come down on the question of Palestine if there had been a considerable Arab constituency in Missouri and, later, when he was president, elsewhere in America. The question, of course, is moot—no such Arab populations existed—but a glimpse into Truman's true belief can be obtained by seeing whom he chose for his staff. As Allis Radosh and Ronald Radosh point out, Truman retained only two of FDR's aides, and one of them was the extremely instrumental David K. Niles. Before the war, Niles was indifferent to Zionism. After the war, his commitment was absolute.

Niles was not only a Jew but also a reliable pipeline into the White House for leaders of the American Zionist movement. He wore his sympathies on his sleeve and often badgered Truman with his arguments in favor of, first, pressuring Britain into increasing immigration into Palestine and, later, recognizing the new State of Israel.

Possibly even more influential was Clark Clifford. The young, tall, and infinitely dapper aide was not a Jew and therefore could argue that he came by his Zionist sympathies through the application of a logic as cool as his mien. Whatever the case, Clifford argued incessantly on behalf of the Zionist program: first, the admission of more Jews to Palestine, and then the partition of the former British mandate, and, finally, the creation of a Jewish state.

This, in a nutshell, is what most American Jews had come around to supporting. By the end of the war, the shocking realization that most European Jewry no longer existed left the anti-Zionist elements marooned. Purely in domestic political terms, it made no sense to Clifford to stand with Britain and the Arabs against the politically influential and highly energetic Jewish community. Beyond that, Clifford was convinced of the moral correctness of post-Holocaust Zionism. It was clearly the right thing to do. He had a great influence on Truman.

But the person who had the most influence on Truman was not a White House aide at all. It was his old army buddy and partner in a failed Kansas City haberdashery, Eddie Jacobson. Unlike Franklin Roosevelt, who was the product of the insular and rarefied Hudson River aristocracy and inclined at times to indulge in country club anti-Semitism (Eleanor, early on, did the same, but later, appalled by slights to her friend Elinor Morgenthau, she became sensitized to the issue), Truman actually had a friend who was Jewish: a buddy, not a grandee like FDR's fellow Hudson River estate owner Henry Morgenthau; a buddy, not an aide; a buddy, not an ally; a buddy who had spent countless hours with him behind the counter of the haberdashery they owned jointly. Eddie Jacobson was probably Truman's closest friend, and Eddie Jacobson was a proud and unapologetic Jew.

When Eddie Jacobson came to the White House, it was always as a friend. For understandable reasons, the other Jews who met with Truman—in fact, almost any Jew he met with—had an agenda. Some of them pressed their cases with an energy and forcefulness that Truman found off-putting. They were, to resort to an anti-Semitic caricature, pushy. And who could blame them? Six million Jews had recently been murdered. The United States, the Western democracies in general, had done precious little to save them. Now the pitiful remnants of that community were being barred from immigrating to Palestine (as well as to the United States) and being confined to DP camps. American Jewish leaders had learned a lesson. Submissiveness, meekness, and knowing their place had not saved lives. They were prepared to be obnoxious, and Truman, ultimately sympathetic, understood.

Still, when Rabbi Abba Hillel Silver pounded on Truman's desk and yelled at him, Truman was both appalled and angered. He was fed up with the Jews, telling a cabinet meeting, "Jesus Christ couldn't please them when he was on earth, so how could anyone expect that I could have any luck?"

Truman voiced similar sentiments to others—his sister, for instance—and eventually refused to see any representative of the Zionists. The intense lobbying campaign was turning out to be counterproductive. Truman was mad: mad at the Jews, mad at the Zionists, and mad at members of his own staff who pressed the Zionist cause. He was so thoroughly tired of grappling with Palestine that he absolutely refused to see Chaim Weizmann, who had come to America specifically to meet with Truman and press for partition. Jacobson pleaded with Truman to see Weizmann. Truman rebuffed his old friend.

So Jacobson, at his own expense—he took no funds from Jewish organizations—flew from Kansas City to Washington and, without any appointment at all, walked right into the White House. After checking with Truman's appointment secretary, Matt Connelly, Jacobson breezed into the Oval Office.

To Jacobson's consternation, Truman not only stuck to his refusal to see Weizmann, but also forcefully denounced what he called the extreme Zionist leadership. "I suddenly found myself thinking that my dear friend, the president of the United States, was at that moment as close to being an anti-Semite as a man could possibly be," Jacobson recalled. Then he spotted a small bronze bust of Andrew Jackson on a table to the right of Truman's desk. It was a replica of the statue that Truman had commissioned for the Jackson County Courthouse in Kansas City. Ol' Hickory was Truman's hero.

"Harry, all your life you have had a hero," Jacobson began. "I too have a hero, a man I never met, but who I think is the greatest Jew who ever lived." With that, Jacobson launched into an aria on Weizmann and how, although his health was broken, he had come all the way to the United States to meet with the president. "Now you refuse to see him just because you are insulted by some of our American Jewish leaders, even though you know that Weizmann had absolutely nothing to do with these insults and would be the last man to be party to them. It doesn't sound like you, Harry, because I thought you could take this stuff they have been handing out."

All this time, Truman had been facing the Rose Garden, his back to his old friend. At first he responded to Jacobson's plea with silence; what to Jacobson seemed "like centuries" passed. Then Truman swung around to face Jacobson. He fixed him in the eye.

"You win, you bald-headed son-of-a-bitch," the president said. "I will see him."

This story, so touching, so endearing, and so very, very "Truman," would be none of those things to a typical Arab, especially a Palestinian. It says nothing about the justice or fairness of splitting Palestine in two, the inevitable first step toward statehood, and everything about the power and influence of what would later be called the Jewish or Israel lobby. Jacobson might have been a humble and endearing figure, but it was his proximity to Truman that mattered—and it is almost inconceivable that any Arab could have gotten as close or that the Palestinian cause would have resonated forcefully with a Midwestern American and Southern Baptist.

As it happened, the Arab argument was made forcefully not by any Arab domestic constituency but by the State Department. Against a gale of vituperation and charges of anti-Semitism, the department essentially kept making the case that while there may not be many Arabs in New York or Chicago, there were literally millions of them in the oil-rich Middle East.

The Arabs had more than oil on their side, although that should have been sufficient. They also had a potent political and moral argument. Palestine, after all, was the land of the Palestinians. Whether Muslim or Christian, they were not Jews, and they had not just recently come from Europe. Partition, which increasingly seemed the inevitable solution—one state for Jews, another for Arabs—had to mean that some Arabs would lose their lands, their homes, their fields, and their mosques. Partition could mean—might mean—the loss of Jerusalem, a holy city that the Ottoman sultan not that long ago had told Theodor Herzl was sacred to all Muslims.

At the State Department, Secretary George C. Marshall and his deputy at the Bureau of Near Eastern Affairs, Loy Henderson, argued that the United States was risking its position and prestige in the Middle East just to placate a domestic lobby. They were right. They further insisted that the beneficiary of the Truman administration's Palestine policy would be the Soviet Union. They were right about that, too. Already Moscow was up to mischief in the Middle East. It had seized—and then relinquished—Iranian territory and was demanding that Turkey surrender control of the Dardanelles Strait.

Henderson had served in Moscow and Iraq. He knew the Russians. He knew the Arabs. He predicted that Moscow would make inroads in the region. It did. He predicted that the partition would not work and war would follow. He was right: five full-scale wars, several limited ones, and incessant terrorism. He stuck to his guns despite knowing that Truman was leaning the other way and that key White House aides, including the increasingly important Clark Clifford, firmly endorsed the Zionist program, partition, and the creation of a Jewish state.

All the issues, all the problems, all the conflicting claims, were present from the beginning. The Arabs were implacably opposed to the creation of a Jewish state. For them, this was not a matter of mere policy but a humiliating slap in the face by the insolent Western powers. They seethed. They threatened war. They promised annihilation.

Britain paid heed. But Britain was a spent force. Bit by bit, the empire receded. It could not keep the subcontinent, India, and what became Pakistan and Bangladesh. It relinquished its interest in Greece; it wanted out of Palestine as well.

Only the United States had the power to impose its will on distant places of the world—and then very, very conditionally. It was not Truman's intention to take Britain's place in the region. He feared direct American involvement and the need to dispatch troops. He wanted none of that.

Truman's decision to support partition, his decision to recognize the newly created State of Israel moments after its birth—all this appalled what he called the "striped pants" set at the State Department. But these were the right decisions; right as in correct or moral but not right as pragmatic or hardheaded. Those 100,000 Jewish DPs might not seem like much, but the Jewish population of Palestine was less than 500,000 before the war. That 100,000 represented a tipping point. With more than a half million or so Jews in Palestine, there would be no turning back—and there wasn't. By 1946, the Jewish population stood at 543,000 (about 30 percent of the country); by 1948 and independence, the figure was 716,700. Jews were more than 80 percent of the new country. Herzl's mad plan had worked.

At the State Department, it was Marshall's job to pursue policies that were in America's pragmatic interests. To him, siding with a handful of Jews against millions of Arabs, choosing a country barren of oil over those countries that had it in abundance, made no sense whatsoever. Speaking only in terms of national interest, Roosevelt had been right in ensuring that America did not appear to be fighting World War II on behalf of the Jews. But his decision—cold, chillingly so, and a kind of politically induced amorality—has slowly tarnished his reputation. There is nothing brave or admirable in doing nothing. There is nothing heroic in not doing everything imaginable to stop the slaughter of innocents.

Increasingly, the Holocaust looms larger than the war itself. Increasingly, too, the Russian role in the war—the Russians did most of the fighting and most of the dying—has reduced the relative importance of the Western Front. The Soviet Union lost almost 14 percent of its population in the war; the United States, about 0.32 percent.

What remains for America is a retrospectively diminished role and the stench of moral failure. The war itself—as big and grand as it was—was just another war, a resumption, after a pause, of World War I. What distinguishes it is the Holocaust. It is the Holocaust that is absent from World War I (not even the immense atrocity perpetrated on the Armenians qualifies) and that occupied the moral heart of World War II. The Holocaust was a departure. Nothing like it had happened before, and the United States did little to head it off and almost nothing to hamper it—no bombings of the camps, for instance.

Oddly enough, the State Department's refusal to take the side of the Jews against the Arabs got some support from precincts that today would not be remotely possible: elements of the Jewish community. There were not many anti-Zionists in the American Jewish community, but they reflected the larger concern about dual loyalties—or, when you came right down to it, that the bulk of American Jews were more loyal to their fellow Jews than to the United States of America. American Jews never quite saw things that way, of course. They did not understand why loyalty to one meant disloyalty to another. Their dilemma was made inestimably easier because the United States was so powerful and so swimming in its own oil that it could afford a minor mistake. It could help Israel and, if you will, hurt the Arabs, and there was nothing the Arabs or anyone could do about it. Might in this case may not have made a right, but it sure made policy.

To many American Jews, Zion was America itself. After some initial difficulty, it turned out that the streets really were paved with gold—if not gold itself then with golden opportunities. Jews had advised Roosevelt. They were advising Truman. They sat on the Supreme Court. They were elected to Congress, both the House and the Senate. They had reached critical political mass in New York and other states. They could not be ignored. They had to be courted, cultivated. In a tight race, they could make a president. They had the votes. They had the activism. They had the money.

The obliteration of the European Jewish community was more than sufficient proof that Europe was no place for a Jew. But for the Eastern European Jew, the Holocaust was unique only in extent, in depth, in the paradoxical purging of visceral religious hatred from traditional anti-Semitism and making the killing oddly antiseptic, scientific—a very tough job that, as Heinrich Himmler himself said, just had to be done. Still, watching the job being done, approving of the job being done, often helping to do the job, was the same old peasant for whom killing Jews was not an exercise in social Darwinism, not something out of Joseph Chamberlain or any other anti-Semitic theorist, but a violent act of sulfuric hatred.

It was this that remained. It was this that survived the war and preceded it, too. It was this and not the Holocaust that compelled Herzl to write *Der Judenstaat*. It was the pogroms of 1881 and similar outbreaks of anti-Jewish violence. It was not Auschwitz that inhabited Herzl's imagination and propelled his movement, but the much more prosaic violence of daily life for Russia's Jews and the outburst of Jew hatred he had seen in Paris, the capital of liberal France, if not of Western civilization. Poor Dreyfus, the single most unimportant-important man of the nineteenth century—the inadvertent catalyst in the creation of Israel—had gone off to Devil's Island, innocent of treason but guilty of being a Jew.

The Jewish problem that Herzl set out to solve was based on his conviction that Europe was quite capable of isolating or ghettoizing its Jews but not assimilating them. They had to go somewhere else. It hardly mattered to him where. Palestine? Yes. Argentina? Why not? The issue was not so much where Jews should go but the dangers they faced if they stayed.

These emigrants from Europe, these immigrants to nowhere, hurled themselves at Palestine. Later they would be characterized as colonialists, haughty

First Worlders who came to the Third World and pushed its people around. These were the foul whites, the zealous ideologues who made the innocent Arabs pay for the crimes of the Germans. One of them was the sawmill owner from Ostrolenka.

He had survived. I insist on it. His family was gone: his wife, his children. He no longer had any friends or relatives. He was a stranger in his own town, utterly alone. His mill had been looted. The equipment was gone and the office furniture, too. Where his desk chair had once been—the ruts from the wheels still visible in the floor—was a small mound of shit. It was human.

That night, the sawmill owner slept on the floor of the office. He had gone to his old house, but he saw the weak light of a candle and smoke coming from the chimney, and out of caution and courtesy, he had not demanded entry—these things would be settled somehow.

In the morning, three men came to the office door and ordered the Jew to leave. He protested that the place was his. He was the owner, the proprietor. He knew how to sharpen the teeth of the huge saw, which was now gone—Do any of you gentlemen know what had happened to it?

The men did not answer, but they asked about the house. Did he want it back, too? The Jew nodded. The men scoffed, and one of them punched the Jew hard in the face. He fell down, and all three men kicked him over and over again in the head. He did not lose consciousness. He felt no pain, just a kind of sorrowful resignation. Life could never disappoint him. He had not died before. He would not die now.

This is not the story the old Jewess told. Hers had been very sketchy, just that the Jew had been murdered upon his return from the camps. The rest of the story, the details, I made up. I did so because the man, maybe a relative of mine, deserved more than a fleeting mention and because, too often, we come to talk in statistics: the famous, incomprehensible, virtually astronomical Six Million, a light-year of deaths. The immensity of the figure overpowers the suffering, the pain, and the horror and hurls the victims into the heavens, twinkling angels without dysentery.

Over the years, the man and his story started to fill out. I came to know him, to envision him not, for some reason, emaciated as he would have been, but stocky and strong and dressed in an undershirt and slacks. He seemed somehow to take the shape of the Lithuanian man who was photographed killing Jews with a crowbar—the so-called Garage Massacre of Kovno. He was beefy and holding the crowbar in two hands, swinging it with enormous force as the Jews were taken, one by one, to be fatally battered. I had inadvertently given a victim the strength of his killer, superimposed one on the other, made the man strong and alive. I could not bear his murder. I made him live. I made him Israel.

The man wended his way to Warsaw and from there to Germany and the American zone of occupation—over forty DP camps. In the night, he was smuggled out by renegade units of the Jewish Brigade, a contingent of the British Army consisting of Jews from Palestine, hopped a requisitioned (stolen) British army truck, and wound up days later in Marseilles. There he boarded a derelict steamer, and in days it stopped, engines still, off the coast of Palestine.

He got into a dinghy and, along with other men, rowed to the beach and tumbled into the surf. He stood in the shallow water, waded to the beach, and collapsed into the wet sand, exhausted—no fat on his body, no money in his pocket, no wife, no children, no parents, no relatives of any kind. He went to sleep, a sleep so sound that he did not hear history telling him that he had made a mistake.

14

Ethnic Cleansing for a Better World

In March 1946 a group of prisoners of war rebelled as they were being loaded onto ships in New York Harbor for repatriation to their homeland. Oddly enough, they were not Germans, Italians, or Japanese—the very recent enemies—but what the newspapers called Russians, our erstwhile ally. Some were undoubtedly Ukrainians or Byelorussians, but whatever the case, they, as well as genuine Russians, had been taken prisoner after going over to the German side and were eventually incarcerated in the United States.

Undoubtedly, some of the POWs were genuine Nazis or Nazi sympathizers, but probably most of them were ordinary Soviet soldiers who had been captured by the Germans and given the choice of remaining POWs—tantamount to a death sentence—or fighting for Germany. All together, the Germans killed 3.1 million Soviet POWs. Many simply starved to death. Another 1 million accepted Berlin's offer, and it was some of these men who ultimately were sent to camps in America.

These Soviet POWs were under no illusion that they would be treated humanely if they were returned to their homeland. The Kremlin was determined to deal with them ruthlessly—as pitilessly as Stalin had dealt with his own son, Yakov, who had been captured by the Germans. Stalin not only rejected an offer to swap Yakov for the captured Field Marshal Friedrich Paulus—"I will not trade a marshal for a lieutenant," he supposedly said—but for good measure dispatched Yakov's wife to Siberia. (Yakov died in Nazi captivity.) At the Yalta Conference, the Allies found out firsthand just how strongly Stalin felt about his turncoats. He was determined to kill them all. The Allies, for their part, were determined to placate Stalin. The POWs were doomed.

The March 1946 rebellion by Soviet POWs was hardly the first. A mass suicide had been attempted nearly a year earlier at Fort Dix, New Jersey: three Soviets had managed to hang themselves. The ones who had rebelled in New York had been held at Fort Meade, Maryland, where they had been sent to work in a local paper mill and on nearby farms. The *Washington Post* quoted Lieutenant Colonel John P. Byrnes as calling the Russians "exceptionally willing and able workers."

At dockside, the Russian POWs made their stand. They fought with dull mess kit knives and with "clubs improvised from furniture." In the end, three hanged themselves. The furious fight by the desperate men, the trio of suicides, the horror of their plight, and the barbarity of the Soviet Union made a riveting story—just the sort of news that would make any cinematically inclined editor yell, "Stop the presses!" Yet, no such order was shouted in the *Washington Post's* newsroom. The story was played on the third page of the second section of that day's newspaper. In other words, it was buried.

One can understand. Sympathy for anyone who had fought for the Nazis must have been hard to come by. More to the point, yet another outrage, yet another horrific episode, yet another example of cruelty was not news. News was what was unique, different—out of the ordinary. The deaths of three men, three non-Americans, were nothing out of the ordinary. The world had just been through a bloodbath.

A world war had just been concluded in which up to seventy million people had been killed—an estimate of appalling and telling inexactness. The loss of life was numbing: twenty-six million in the Soviet Union alone, six million Poles, possibly fifty million deaths in China's civil war and the one with Japan, and, of course, six million Jews, considered Poles or Russians when dead, but rarely counted as such while alive.

Whole cities had been incinerated—Hamburg, Dresden, Tokyo, Hiroshima, Nagasaki—and earlier in the war, Coventry, Rotterdam, and others by the Germans. Earlier still, Guernica had been bombed during the Spanish Civil War by German and Italian warplanes—a clear attack on a civilian target. On that market day, something significant had happened. War had become total.

The United States suffered 460,000 military deaths, a modest amount by European or Asian standards, but still a big number. (Not as big as the Civil War's 640,000, but in that war, Americans killed Americans.) Still, the presence of death was ubiquitous—every town, every village, and quite a few households. And many of those households were just recently American—first- or second-generation emigrants from Europe. For them, the battles and bombings and massacres had not happened "over there" to "them," but "back home" to grandpa or a cousin. This was especially true of American Jews. Hardly a family was not touched by the Holocaust. Death was commonplace. It was a time of plague.

So the deaths of a handful of Slavic fascists could not have mattered much. All the rules of journalism said so. Dog bites man? No story. Man bites dog? That's a story! A handful of deaths in a world awash in them? No story. Ethnic Germans dying on the road to Berlin? No story. Czechs pushing Germans over the border? No story. Ukrainians and Poles hacking each other to death? No story. Romanians and Ukrainians murdering one another with glee? No story. Indian Hindus and Indian Muslims killing each other in fierce eruptions of hate? No story. The Chinese communists and the Nationalists murdering one another? Not a story.

No story for any of this. No interest. Nothing new. Nothing odd. No reason to stop the presses. No reason even to look up from an easy chair.

Jews pushing Arabs out of Palestine?

No story.

Not until recently.

All over Europe, it was payback time. The Second World War did not end with everyone shaking hands. Instead, it was time to settle scores, to deal with collaborators and old enemies. Another bloodbath commenced. It was not as great as the one that preceded it, World War II and the Holocaust, but it was substantial nevertheless.

In France, collaborators—alleged, rumored, or actual—were executed, occasionally on the slimmest of evidence. In Greece, communists and anticommunists killed one another with abandon—and killed Albanian Muslims, too.

The Poles turned on Ukrainians, and Ukrainians had a beef with the Romanians, and the Romanians in turn had a score to settle with the Hungarians. And all over Eastern Europe, ethnic Germans were pushed over the border to Germany, raped, or murdered—very often both.

There was one additional horror. The huge entity called the Raj, an imperial concoction of Muslims, Hindus, some Christians, and a scattering of others, was getting its independence. In recognition of the fact that Muslims had no wish to live in a Hindu state, and Hindus felt just as strongly about a Muslim state, the British, as was customary, had recourse to the map and started drawing lines. When they had finished, they had a concoction called Pakistan, which sat, like shoulder pads, straddling either side of India, and would have a Muslim majority. Needless to say, this bizarre cartographic creation did not last—East Pakistan became Bangladesh—but it did get the British out of India with dispatch. It also necessitated a population transfer. More than five million Hindus and Sikhs moved from what is now Pakistan into what is now India, and about six million Muslims went the other way. This was not some orderly swap, but a movable pogrom of Muslim killing Hindu and Hindu killing Muslim. In the end, more than one million people perished.

The Muslim-Hindu swap on the Indian subcontinent occurred in 1947, about two years after the end of World War II and the same year that the new United Nations authorized the partition of Palestine into Jewish and Arab states. It happened a mere three decades after the Young Turks had sent much of their country's Armenians into the Syrian desert, there to starve, to perish from lack of water, to be shot—a huge crime, an attempted genocide, that claimed as many as 1.5 million lives. When ordering the slaughter of the Poles, Hitler supposedly asked, "Who, after all, speaks today of the annihilation of the Armenians?" and whether he actually said such a thing or not, the answer for the longest time was plain: only the Armenians.

On and on it went, continentwide payback, a settling of scores and a general cleaning up. As much as possible, the new nation-states would each speak one language and revere one set of myths. In these arrangements, there was, of course, no place for the Jews and, really, no place that the Jews wanted to go. Home was out of the question. Israel! Israel looked good.

For the leaders of Zionism—indeed, for Jews in general—the horrors just kept on coming. It is impossible to imagine how some of them kept going. Their world was Hobbesian squared—"solitary, poor, nasty, brutish, and short" to a degree once thought unimaginable. The calamity was man himself, an evil leviathan that had risen out of the filigree and pastries of a cultured and refined continent and had slaughtered every Jew in sight.

And then, when it was over, it was not over. The killings continued—not as they had before (after all, the numbers of killers and victims were greatly diminished and some understandable exhaustion had set in), but enough so that it could be said that the Holocaust had not come to an end, it was merely running out of gas, pausing for what could be a second wind.

For the Jews of Palestine as well as those of the Grand Concourse in the Bronx not to have drawn lessons from what had happened and what was happening would not be possible. Jews had learned all the appropriate lessons and learned them the hard way. Why should they be different? Why should they of all people be crippled by sentimentality, by a touching consideration for the feelings and pain of others? Why were they not entitled to a victor's hypocrisy, to wax Wilsonian and prattle on about Four Freedoms while at the same time employing violence, settling scores, and clearing the fields for a whole new crop? Why were they not entitled to play by the rules others had established? They had to use power and force and violence too. Sorry, it was unavoidable.

The bloodbath that followed the bloodbath of World War II is now being rediscovered. A number of books have recently been published about an era for which there is no name. It followed the war against Nazi Germany and Japan (Italy hardly mattered) and preceded the Cold War between the Soviet Union and the United States. It not only lacks a name, it lacks pictures. It's not that none exist, it's rather than they don't celebrate victory and the uplifting fictions about the nobility of the common man and the inevitable victory of virtue. More to the point, possibly, is that fact that the United States was only tangentially involved. It participated in the conferences at Yalta and Potsdam that both enabled and authorized a fair amount of ethnic cleansing, but it left the dirty work to others. To Americans, the scores being settled had nothing to do with them and everything to do with the strange, incomprehensibly barbaric peoples of Eastern Europe and Asia. For the peoples of Central and Eastern Europe, the war ended in an orgy of revenge and casual murder. For Americans and other fortunates, it ended with pretty pictures. For the longest time, the images prevailed.

The image was Alfred Eisenstaedt's picture of a nurse and a sailor kissing in Times Square. It was of ecstatic crowds in front of Buckingham Palace, King George VI and Queen Elizabeth decorously waving to the throng. It was of Allied troops, led by the Free French forces, marching proudly on the Avenue des Champs-Élysées, given pride of place in an early example of affirmative action. It was a Soviet soldier exuberantly waving the hammer-and-sickle flag from the gutted Reichstag in just-liberated Berlin—a staged propaganda photo by the Soviet military photographer Yevgeny Khaldei.

Those nice pictures told a nice story, and while that story was true, it was far from the whole story. In Prague, for instance, had there been an image, it would have been of a charred human torso, its limbs chopped off, dangling from a street lamp. It would have been of men, women, and even children marched to cellars and makeshift abattoirs so they could be executed with a single shot to the back of the neck—a method perfected by the just-departed Nazis. It would have been of people forced to clean latrines with their bare hands and then beaten to death with crowbars, and others being forced to wear armbands announcing who they were. And if they were women, it was permissible to rape them—over and over. Some women crawled away to kill themselves in disgust, and others had to be surgically reconstructed, and some died of primitive abortions.

These—the raped, the beaten, the tortured, and the dead—were not Nazis or former Nazis or collaborators. Not necessarily, anyway. They were ethnic Germans, the so-called *Volksdeutsche*, a once politically useful term popularized early in the twentieth century. It referred to the German-speaking peoples living outside Germany proper. There were some sixteen million of them, most in nearby Poland and Czechoslovakia, but still others in Hungary, Romania, and even deep into the Caucasus. These were German-speaking communities, some dating to medieval times, which like the Jewish ones they were supposed to hate, had obstinately refused to assimilate.

Prior to the war and Hitler's annexation of the Czechoslovakian regions of Bohemia and Moravia, 23 percent of Czechoslovaks were ethnic Germans. They were concentrated in the west, the so-called Sudetenland, which comprised the areas of Bohemia and Moravia. But even the capital city, Prague, located to the east in the Czech-speaking region, had a large and culturally important German minority, anywhere from 10 percent to 20 percent of the city. Not included were the Jews, most of whom also spoke German. The Prague resident Franz Kafka wrote in German.

The ethnic Germans were of great value to the Nazi occupiers of Eastern and Central Europe. Not only were they often enthusiastic Nazis or German nationalists themselves, but they knew the lay of the land—what was around the next corner and who the likely resistance fighter might be. They spoke the language, they knew the people. They were useful collaborators. So it was understandable that when liberation came, a certain amount of score settling would occur.

What actually happened—an eruption of hate and violence hidden in the shadow of the Holocaust—amounted to a vast and prolonged pogrom. In his account of those days, *After the Reich*, Giles MacDonogh calls it "ethnic cleansing," and he is exactly right. As with almost all examples of ethnic cleansing, encouragement came from the top. The government—the new, postwar democratic government—was as intent as some liquored-up goon on ridding the country of its ethnic Germans. The government and the mob were as one.

The difference between the ethnic cleansing of Czechoslovakia and what happened later in the twentieth century in, say, the Balkans and Rwanda (among other places) is that explicit permission for it was granted by the Great Powers and by their intellectuals. Writing during the Second World War, the eminent British historian Hugh Seton-Watson devoted himself to the imminent problem of what to do with all those ethnic Germans who were about to find themselves in the wrong parts of Europe. He raised the possibility of "the exchange of population," not because he approved—he most certainly did not—but because what he termed "the attractive simplicity" was bound to be found irresistible by the Allies, who were then on the verge of defeating Hitler.

Despite the "unspeakable suffering" that Seton-Watson predicted, this is precisely the remedy the Allies chose—initially reluctantly in some cases and later with some alacrity. From the very beginning of the war, in 1939, governments in exile were already looking forward to ultimate victory and the chance to clean up their ethnic messes. The Czechoslovaks were intent on ridding themselves of their Germans, who were, after all, the cause of their country's woes. It was the *Sudetendeutsch* who had agitated for union with Germany and who played the victim for Hitler to rescue. Their loyalty to the state was always in question, and during the war, they both greeted the Nazis as liberators and joined their fellow Germans in conquering their own country. There were, however, many exceptions to those generalizations—not that it mattered any. A whole people had been found guilty of treason and were to be banished accordingly.

162

The Poles, too, had a German problem, and they too were determined to fix it once and for all. But the leader of the Polish government in exile, Wladyslaw Sikorski, had more than Germans in mind when it came to tidying up. R. M. Douglas reports, in his book *Orderly and Humane*, that Sikorski told Anthony Eden, Britain's foreign secretary, that in addition to the Germans, the Jews would also have to go. "Room must be found for them elsewhere," he said in 1942. He apparently did not know that the Germans were at that moment rendering that problem moot.

The Germans, in fact, seemed to have accustomed even their enemies to massive population transfers or the murder of ethnic undesirables. Stalin in the Soviet Union was doing his own ethnic cleansing, sometimes moving peoples, sometimes just killing them off. For his usual paranoid reasons, he turned on the Poles who had sought shelter in his country, and killed some 85,000 of them with abandon, if not relish.

Population transfers were in the air. A good many figures in public life supported them, Churchill being the most prominent of all. "Expulsion is the method which, insofar as we have been able to see, will be the most satisfactory and lasting," he told the House of Commons in 1944. "There will be no mixture of populations to cause endless trouble. . . . A clean sweep will be made. I am not alarmed by the prospect of disentanglement of populations, not even of these large transferences, which are more possible in modern conditions than they have ever been before."

Those "modern conditions" produced a humanitarian calamity, a debacle of extraordinary horror that for many years was virtually ignored. Still, as Churchill foresaw, the policy—while significantly more brutal than he predicted—worked. Except for the Balkans and the occasional victimization of the Romani (Gypsies), Eastern Europe has been largely free of ethnic strife since the 1950s, and, afterward, largely free of discussing how that was accomplished.

But in postwar Czechoslovakia, ethnic cleansing was not the product of some sotto voce understanding or, as with the Final Solution, a policy emanating from the top but not acknowledged. In Czechoslovakia, it was the audaciously proclaimed policy of the new political leadership. "Woe, woe, woe, thrice woe to the Germans, we will liquidate you," pronounced the Czechoslovakian prime minister, Edvard Beneš, in April 1945. The effect was immediate. The wanton murder of Germans had begun.

The next month, Beneš repeated his threat. "We have decided . . . that we have to liquidate the German problem in our republic once and for all," he said. And a month later, in June, he issued probably the most draconian of all his so-called retribution decrees: it stripped all Germans and Hungarians (as well as traitors) of their land. The land of the Czechs and the Slovaks was fast becoming the land of the Czechs and Slovaks only.

Astonishingly, Beneš's various threats—although not necessarily the manner in which they were implemented—were compatible with the policies of the wartime Allies and anticipated by them. ("Many [Sudeten] Germans will be killed in your country as well," Churchill told Beneš. "It cannot be helped, and I agree with it.") It seemed so did the other world leaders.

Meeting at Potsdam, Truman, Stalin, and Churchill and his successor, Clement Attlee, agreed that for the sake of a safe and stable Europe, Germans had to be collected from wherever they resided outside Germany and deposited in their ancestral fatherland. Article XII of the Potsdam Declaration stated: "The Three Governments, having considered the question in all its aspects, recognize that the transfer to Germany of German populations, or elements thereof, remaining in Poland, Czechoslovakia and Hungary, will have to be undertaken."

As befitting democracies, the United States and Great Britain (joined by the Soviet Union) asked only "that any transfers that take place should be effected in an orderly and humane manner," and they further asked both Poland and Czechoslovakia to "suspend further expulsions pending an examination by the Governments concerned of the report from their representatives on the Control Council."

In the end, as many as 95,000 ethnic Germans were killed by the Czechoslovaks, the Russians, or a combination of the two. Across Europe, as many as fourteen million ethnic Germans were banished from their native lands and sent packing to Germany. Of these, possibly more than two million died along the way. How many more were raped or beaten is impossible to know—as is the number who were innocent of any crime, political or otherwise, or who might actually have opposed the Nazi regime that was imposed on their country. The expulsion of the Germans was as monumental an example of collective punishment as the sorry twentieth century can offer—not nearly as horrendous as the Holocaust but not nearly as remembered or memorialized, either.

I don't remember hearing the terms "ethnic cleansing" or "population transfers" in Hebrew school, although Jews seemed always on the receiving end of one or the other. The applicable term was "exiled," which is what happened twice to the Jews of ancient Israel, forcing them into a Diaspora that ended only in 1948 with the (re)creation of Israel itself. Even before the twin exile, though, came a succession of bloody battles, invasions, and genocides in which the Jews, initially, were not the victims. The exodus from Egypt was followed by an epoch of war making in which the biblical Jews conquered the land promised them by God. They slew and they annihilated and they smote and in other ways showed little mercy for the unlucky people who either blocked their way to the Promised Land or, as with the Canaanites, occupied it. The God of the Israelites could be short on compassion. The Amalekites were eradicated—"man and women, child and infant, oxen and sheep, camel and donkey." As a child in Hebrew school, I shuddered.

As if in recompense, God turned the tables on the Jews. That He did so— that He was complicit in the exiles and all the rest that was awful—there was no doubt, at least in Hebrew school. God was in charge of everything, and while the calamities that befell the Jews were their own fault (they were forever disappointing the Almighty), He allowed it all to happen. Being the Chosen People came with certain obligations. Meet them or suffer terribly.

The suffering went on and on. The ancient Israelites were promised a land of milk and honey, but, as if in some fine print, lots of difficulties as well. It was a spot on the ancient world's highway between Asia and Africa, and the Jews, geopolitically insignificant, were an obstacle for whatever army wanted to get at whatever army. In 722 BC, the Assyrians decided to move most of the Jews out of the way. This was the first exile. The Babylonians compelled the next one, the banishment of the remaining tribes. After that, the miseries continued: a dirge, a lamentation, an incessant rending of garments that ended, if indeed it has, in the Holocaust. Ethnic cleansing, population transfers, and genocide—these are areas about which Jews have a tactile knowledge. We know the feel of it.

Jews have suffered frequently and inordinately, but hardly uniquely. The same year they were expelled from Spain, 1492, European-style ethnic cleansing commenced in the New World. Spain and its European diseases decimated the Arawak Indians. It was an ominous and trend-setting development. Europeans then embarked on a colonization and settlement effort that featured all sorts of ethnic cleansing and population transfers—one or the other, whatever worked at the time. The result was that an Indian population in North America once esti-mated at anywhere from 10 million to 12 million, and even as high as 16 million, was down to exactly 237,196, according to the Census of 1900. The word *geno-cide*, used so often in a hyperbolic sense, is in this case a virtual understatement.

Some of that genocide was accomplished inadvertently through the spread of European diseases against which the Indians had no defenses. Where and when the tribes were not decimated by either disease or warfare with whites, they were occasionally moved out of the way. The Choctaw were sent west of the Mississippi, and the astonishingly adaptive Cherokee were rewarded for their success by being forced from the mountain south to Oklahoma: the aptly named Trail of Tears. Much of this was done on an ad hoc basis, some by government edict; but cer-tainly by the twentieth century, the barbarism of population transfers had become accepted government policy. It was a solution, no matter how ugly, to the problem of certain peoples being in certain places—a coldly pragmatic way of dealing with a combustible mix of peoples. The population transfers that followed World War I were sometimes executed under League of Nations auspices, and those that fol-lowed World War II were the product of wartime treaties or agreements.

Earlier in the century, Greeks and Turks exchanged populations, with about 1.5 million Greeks going west and about 500,000 Turks going east. Before that, a similar swap had been arranged between Bulgaria and Turkey, but the one with Greece was far larger. It amounted to a humanitarian catastrophe, but an instructive one. Once Christian Greeks had become disentangled from Muslim Turks, they ceased killing one another. (This process was made even more complicated by Turks who had adopted Christianity and Greeks who had adopted Islam.) The lesson from this, the first significant population transfer of the twentieth century, was that ethnic cleansing worked.

The Germans under Hitler applied the lesson in ways heretofore unimag-inable. Western Poland was made free of Poles (and Jews). In the eastern half of the country, the Soviets did something similar. They plunged into Poland sev-enteen days after the Germans had and, in accordance with Stalin's agreement with Hitler, simply absorbed the eastern part, restoring as best they could the old empire as it had been under the czars. (When the Baltic states followed, the job was nearly completed.)

Both Nazi Germany and the Soviet Union were ruthless dictatorships that, especially in the case of the Soviet Union, treated their own people with a pitilessness other nations reserved for their enemies. While nationalism played a role in their respective conquests, it was not the paramount mover. The average German had no overarching desire to conquer Norway or France, and the average Russian probably felt the same way about Finland or Poland. The words *reuniting* or *restoring* have little application here. Both nations were rogue regimes that were simply building empires.

The Russians who died in New York Harbor, like their comrades who made it back to the Soviet Union, were grains of sand on the bloodiest beach of all time: the wars of the twentieth century. Lives were wasted for monstrous political reasons; Stalin paused the Russian advance outside Warsaw to provide the Nazis with the time to eliminate the Polish underground, a nationalist anticommunist force that might have opposed the eventual establishment of a communist regime. Earlier he killed about 22,000 Polish officers and others in what is now called the Katyn Forest massacre. (Actually, the prisoners were shot one by one, an astounding seven thousand or so by a single man, the security service's chief executioner, Vasili Mikhailovich Blokhin. He used a German pistol.)

Toward the end of the war, about seven thousand Jews were marched into the frigid Baltic Sea off East Prussia and either machine-gunned or drowned. They had originally come from a concentration camp where about 87,000 people had died. The camp's name was Stutthof, almost unheard of.

In 1943 several high-ranking Nazis, including Adolf Eichmann, offered to swap one million Jews for ten thousand trucks and other material. The Germans called this *Blut gegen Waren* (blood for goods). The offer was rejected and over 400,000 Hungarian Jews died at Auschwitz. Maybe nothing would have come of the offer, and maybe the Jews would have died anyway, but it was just one of several times the Nazis offered to bargain for the lives of Jews.

In most of the major ghettos, the Nazis appointed Jews to do their bidding. These Jews often had to decide who would die and who would live, if only for a while. Some of them truly believed they were doing good, making impossible choices but doing what had to be done.

Between 1939 and 1945, about seventy million people died on account of the war and the Holocaust.

Almost thirty thousand people died every day.

This is the era when Israel was born. This is the era that shaped its leadership and its people. This was an era unlike any other. Israel was born in hell.

15

Nakba . . . or Not

In November 1947, the newly created Central Intelligence Agency issued a report entitled *The Consequences of the Partition of Palestine*. A civil war between Palestine's Arabs and Jews was imminent, and so the American government, as well as the British one, set to work to determine who would win. Both the CIA and Whitehall predicted an Arab victory—if not in the civil war then certainly in the war with the Arab states that would follow shortly. In its report, the CIA said it had "coordinated with the intelligence organizations of the Departments of State, Army, Navy and Air Forces," so its judgment represented the collected wisdom of virtually the entire United States government. If there was any dissent, it is not mentioned, and if there was any doubt, it is not reflected in the conclusion:

"Without substantial outside aid in terms of manpower and material, they [the Jews] will be able to hold out no longer than two years."

Whitehall phrased it this way: "In the long run, the Jews would not be able to cope."

The CIA classified its report "Secret," but, really, its conclusions were banal—nothing less than conventional wisdom. After all, not only did Palestinians outnumber Jews two to one, but beyond Palestine itself were an additional forty million Arabs determined to push the Jews into the sea. The combined armies of Egypt, Saudi Arabia, Iraq, Jordan, and Lebanon would join with the Arab Liberation Army (ALA) of Palestine and end the Zionist dream once and for all.

Just to make matters worse (for the Jews), one of those Arab armies contained a particularly formidable unit: Jordan's vaunted Arab Legion. It was British trained and led by the honorifically festooned Lieutenant-General Sir John Bagot Glubb KCB, CMG, DSO, OBE, MC—better known as Glubb Pasha. It possessed armored cars and tanks, formidable weapons in that region at that time. The legion was a thoroughly professional force, and while it was tough in battle, and Jews came to fear it, they also came to appreciate it. On more than one occasion, the legion stepped in to thwart the massacre of Jewish POWs by the ill-trained or untrained ALA.

On paper, the Arabs had it all over the Jews. In the romanticized estimation of the CIA, they were "good guerrilla fighters" who would be "well supplied with small arms" as well as "some planes and tanks." Given the lineup, given the well-known Arab (especially Bedouin) facility for warfare and mayhem, the United States would be plain foolish to back the Jews—not that there was any reason to do so. The Arabs had the numbers, the choice location (the Suez Canal), and, of course, all that oil. The CIA kissed off Israel.

Not surprisingly, many Jews were in agreement. They too could do their sums—so many Arabs, so few Jews—and their sense of foreboding was understandably exacerbated by their own recent history. They mostly were, either in actual fact or by one or two degrees of separation, Holocaust survivors. The unimaginable had already occurred, and the world, as far as they could tell, had not given a damn. It would no doubt react no differently if the Arabs attempted to finish the job.

It is easy enough at this remove to talk of Jewish paranoia and to see the Yishuv, as the Jewish community of Palestine was called, and the nascent Israel of 1948 as the powerful state it later became. Certainly some Jews and others felt confident that the Arabs were not as strong as the CIA thought, and that a total population of forty million or so did not mean that they could put anywhere near that number in the field. For many reasons, the Jews would win both wars: the initial civil war with the Palestinians and the later one with the combined Arab army. It soon became apparent that the Arabs were disorganized, poorly led, underfinanced, undisciplined, and not much interested in a fight.

The Palestinian Arabs were ill prepared for war. Although they had an advantage in manpower and often held the high ground, they lacked what many Jews had purposely and with intentional foresight gained in World War II: combat experience. And what the Jews did not have, they could get. They not only went on an arms-buying spree, but their cause also attracted volunteers from abroad—particularly South Africa and the United States. (The Israeli air force wound up with more pilots than it had airplanes.) Probably the most famous of the volunteers was David (Mickey) Marcus, a former colonel on General Dwight Eisenhower's staff, who became Israel's first general and was killed by friendly fire. (He was played by Kirk Douglas in the 1966 movie *Cast a Giant Shadow*.) He is buried at West Point.

The Arabs, too, had volunteers. Some were former British army personnel who genuinely favored the Arabs (the British military never shared its political leadership's enthusiasm for Zionism), and some were just sincere former Nazis. Volunteers also came from the Islamic world—some even from Bosnia—but these never amounted to much. All in all, the Jews got immeasurable help from their coreligionists in America and elsewhere, as well as huge shipments of weapons—some bought illegally but many more sold by Czechoslovakia in that period when the Soviet satellites, taking their cue from Stalin, were briefly pro-Israel.

Anti-Semitism was hardly the Middle East's sole import from Europe. The region was a European creation; even the very term *Middle East* is Eurocentric. (So is *Near East*.) Israel, too, is Europe's creation: the work of Europeans with their particular culture and know-how. It's not merely that founders of Israel were born in Europe but also that they had within them whatever it is that consists of culture. They were Jews, of course, but that is not what mattered so much in the actual creation of the state. What mattered more is that they were Western.

In the end, the organizational abilities of the Jews, resulting in an eventual ability to field an army that outnumbered the Arab army, created Israel. Nowhere was this clearer than in the run-up to the 1948 war—which the Israelis call the War of Independence and the Arabs simply call the War of 1948. This is more than a semantic distinction. It is about outcome, and that outcome was a consequence of the Jews' ability to plan and organize, to prepare for a war that everyone knew was coming. The Jews had no population advantage and no tactical advantage—such as a better knowledge of the land or control of the high ground—although they did have more at stake, since they were either fighting for their lives or thought they were. In the end, desperation and know-how made all the difference.

The Jews of that era actually fought two wars. The first was a civil war: Palestinian Jews against Palestinian Arabs. The end of this war coincided with the end of the Mandate when Great Britain, with much relief, brought its troops home. The second war commenced immediately: the Jews of the newly proclaimed State of Israel versus the Arabs of six armies—from neighboring Lebanon, Syria, Iraq, Egypt, what was then called Transjordan, and, of course, Palestine.

In both wars, the Jews prevailed; and in both wars, they were aided enormously by the incompetence and misplaced confidence of the Arab countries. They, too, were relatively new countries, newly independent or newly created. They had small, untested armies. All together, these countries fielded a maximum of only 25,000 men and failed to establish a unified command. Israel, in contrast, initially managed to raise an army of 35,000, which grew to 96,000 by the end of the war, and had a centralized command. It was not five armies, but one.

At first, though, there was little reason for confidence and plenty of reason for fear. After all, the Arabs intended to fight a war of extermination, or so they said. And while in retrospect that seems ludicrous, it was no laughing matter at the time. The presence on the Arab side of the grand mufti himself, Mohammed Amin al-Husseini, seemed to attest to the intent of the Arabs. He personified the Holocaust continued. To the Jews, it hardly seemed that the Arabs merely wanted to reclaim some territory or even conquer and occupy them. The Arabs' rhetoric proclaimed something else: an attempt to finish the job that Hitler had started. This was 1948, not 1984. The future had not yet happened, and the past was not yet over.

The civil war that preceded the war with the five Arab states was of maximum importance. Contemporary critics of Israel choose to downplay it or ignore it entirely, sometimes making it seem that there was only one war that the Jews were always going to win. But the civil war, which proceeded while the British were still nominally in charge of Palestine and the Arab states hovered but did not join in, was in some sense the more important of the two. Like so many civil wars, it was immeasurably ugly and chaotic. As Benny Morris points out in his account of both wars, *1948*, neither army made provisions for prisoners. Since they had no POW camps and could not really have constructed any, both sides sometimes executed prisoners. Morris says that the Jews probably murdered more POWs than the Arabs did, but this, he adds, is because they took more prisoners. As for the Arabs, they not only retaliated in kind but also occasionally sexually mutilated the dead—a bit of gratuitous barbarity suggesting that the enemy was no mere opponent but a contemptible alien.

By 1947–48, Arab-Jew enmity was almost a half century old. Jews had sometimes killed Arabs and even mounted what could be called pogroms. But anti-Jewish violence was far more frequent and far more devastating in a relative sense (few Jews, many Arabs) and in an absolute sense as well. Not only were there many more Arabs than Jews, but Arabs had a sense of ownership—it was their country, after all—and a concurrent familiarity with the land. Jews mounted operations to punish this or that Arab village, tribe, or family, but their default posture was defensive. In time, that too would change.

If the Arabs did not hate the Jews before the civil war, they surely did afterward. This presented the emerging nation with an insurmountable problem: what to do with a hostile population that would almost certainly comprise a fifth column if and when peace came? Surprisingly, some in the Yishuv leadership counseled accommodation—an admirable but wholly unrealistic option. They were not persuasive. Others understood instantly what had to be done: the Arabs had to go.

Often, that was accomplished easily enough. The massacre at Deir Yassin and other examples of Jewish brutality caused many Arabs to flee in panic. Others were pushed out by Jewish military and paramilitary forces, particularly units of the Irgun and Stern Gang, which were quickly earning the label *terrorist*. Horrible things were done. Arabs were murdered, their homes torched, and women raped. Morris gives example after example of this sort of thing, as does Ari Shavit in *My Promised Land*. His account of the purging of Palestinians from Lydda in 1948 is both harrowing and beyond rebuttal. For anyone, particularly a Jew, who believes that Jews do not do that sort of thing, Morris and Shavit make for disturbing reading.

At the same time that Arabs were being forced out of their villages or homes in the cities (Jaffa, or Haifa, for instance), others—many others—fled of their own volition. Some were told to do so by their local or national leadership. Some merely took their cue from the Palestinian elite, significant portions of whom left the country. Many, however, left convinced they would soon return home. The Arab armies were massing. Help was on the way.

In the summer of 2010, the *Financial Times* newspaper had historian Avi Shlaim review Martin Gilbert's book on the history of Jews in Islamic lands. Gilbert is both celebrated as a biographer of Winston Churchill and a staunch defender of Israel—complementary obsessions, to be sure—while Shlaim is an equally well-known critic of the Jewish state. (He is an Iraqi-born Jew who was raised in Israel.) The review was softly hostile. Gilbert, Shlaim said, had tried to balance what had happened to Palestinians with what had happened to the 850,000 Jews who had once lived in the Islamic world. "Nowhere is Gilbert more strikingly one-sided than in his account of the consequences of the 1948 Arab-Israeli War," Shlaim writes. "In the course of this war, the name Palestine was wiped off the map and 726,000 Palestinians became refugees." This, succinctly put, is the New Narrative.

The New Narrative is an increasingly successful attempt to rewrite history. Its practitioners—and Shlaim is one of the most prominent—do not question the legitimacy of Israel, just the manner of its birth and its subsequent behavior. Had they simply argued that Israel was a colonial enterprise, rooted in cultural arrogance, they might well have an unrebuttable argument. After all, the facts are the facts: European Jews, no matter how noble their cause, established themselves in a part of the world occupied by another people and, by dint of their advanced culture (for that is what it was), forced those occupants to make way. This, essentially, is the argument made by the enemies of Zionism, and they are right. Only religious Jews can differ, but I am not one of them.

But once you concede the right of Israel to exist—once you lack the stomach to either deny the Holocaust or argue its irrelevance—then you are stuck with what for some is an unpalatable reality: the nascent state simply could not afford a large and hostile minority/majority within its borders. Both the Palestinian-Jewish war of 1947–48 and the Arab-Israeli war of 1948 had aspects of a civil war. The ultimate losers, the Palestinians, had not invaded and therefore could not be driven back to their homeland. They were *in* their homeland.

What to do with them? The twin wars had not been something like the American Civil War, which was fought mostly over an issue, slavery, and pitted one region against another. Here the "issue" was ownership—whose land was this anyway?—and the "regions" were intermixed. (If anything, the Arab-Jewish fight was like the Civil War in the Border States, particularly Kentucky and Missouri, which were almost evenly split between Union and Confederate sympathizers, and the warfare, often conducted by guerrilla forces, was especially violent and bestial.)

In Palestine, Jews and Arabs lived among one another. Some separation started to occur after the violence of 1936, but for a long time, some cities (Jaffa, Haifa) were mixed, and so were some villages. Even where separation had occurred, an Arab village and a kibbutz might still be close to each other.

In other places, in other times, the remedy to this situation had been both apparent and implemented: separation and population transfer. In a way, the latter was accomplished when 800,000 Jews from Arab lands were swapped for 770,000 Palestinians from Palestine. But no one had quite intended for that to happen. It was done chaotically, across national boundaries, and at a considerable loss of life. The Jews who arrived, like most of the Arabs who had left, came with nothing but pressing needs. The Jews, though, were assimilated by their host country. The Palestinians, for all the hosannas to Arab unity, still largely live in refugee camps, and in almost all the host nations, they have either a restricted citizenship or none at all.

Almost instantly, the Yishuv's leadership sensed an opening. Once it became clear that annihilation was not in the offing—indeed, the war was going to be a triumph—it became equally clear that the Palestinians had to go. They could not, as was done in America, be relegated to reservations; or, as in South Africa, to synthetic homelands called Bantustans and townships; or, as was done in Europe, to some ancestral homeland; or, as was done on the Indian subcontinent, swapped for another population also under the control of the colonial authorities. They simply had to be pushed out. The very people who had made war—who had initiated the war and sometimes conducted it in barbaric fashion—could not be permitted to stay in place or to return to their old homes. This was not a case of racism or colonialism but of security based on common sense. The Palestinian was the enemy, and the enemy had to go.

The plan—or, if you will, The Plan—took shape over time. It was calculated and extemporaneous: planned in the sense that a blueprint for the ethnic cleansing of Palestine did exist, and extemporaneous in the sense that it was never deemed practical or likely, and it was never implemented. It existed, as plans do, because there are planners, and they must plan. Surely during the Cold War there were plans for the nuclear annihilation of the Soviet Union and for its occupation. Those plans probably still exist.

The plan the Jews drew up was called Plan D. It is the centerpiece of *The*

Ethnic Cleansing of Palestine, Ilan Pappe's provocative book. Pappe is another of the so-called New Historians, who, like Shlaim, no longer teaches in Israel. His book argues that the separation of Arab from Jew was done by design and with much malice aforethought. "The main goal" of the two wars "was the ethnic cleansing of Palestine," he writes, and he likens the effort to the Serbian attempt to oust Muslims and Croats from Bosnia and Herzegovina during the 1992–95 wars of the former Yugoslavia. In his telling, the Zionists were bent on genocide.

But Pappe's allegations do not pass what newspaper people call the "smell test." In the first place, it's quite clear from the CIA report alone that any planned ethnic cleansing of Palestine amounted to a dark kind of wishful thinking. Jews were hardly confident of victory and were, in any case, cognizant of how much they relied on sympathetic world opinion. Maybe more to the point—a point that Pappe, Shlaim, and others manage to overlook—it was the Palestinians, not the Jews, who initiated hostilities.

That's understandable. After all, to the Palestinians, the war amounted to a counterattack. They had already lost the first round by failing to defeat the UN resolution establishing two states. In fact, they had been losing consistently since the nineteenth-century trial of a French army officer in Paris had planted the idea of Zionism in the fired-up imagination of an out-of-town journalist. None of what happened in Paris had anything to do with Palestinians, yet the consequences for them were baleful—and no matter what happened, the Jews kept on coming.

From the Palestinian point of view, the war made sense—not, though, how it was planned or conducted. Had the Arabs abided by the UN resolution and accepted the partition plan, they would have been left with a truncated state on about 42 percent of the original territory, with the Jerusalem area, including Bethlehem, declared an international zone under the UN Trusteeship Council. The apportioning of the land was somewhat misleading, since the Jewish 55 percent included the arid Negev, but all in all, the Jews got the better agricultural land and, adding insult to injury, international recognition of their claim. Henceforth, Palestine was theirs too.

Still, the fact remained that the Palestinians had fought and lost: fought in the Arab Revolt of 1936–39 and in countless clashes with the Jews. Had they accepted this outcome—had they accepted the rule of law—there would not have been a *nakba*, and 770,000 Palestinians would not have been displaced.

In fact, had the Palestinians acceded to the wishes of the international community, they might have come to predominate in the new Israel. Instead of being 20 percent of the population as they are today, they might be a majority. The Jewish state might not be Jewish after all.

None of that happened, of course. And once the Palestinians took up arms, the die was cast—at least for the next sixty or so years. On November 30, 1947, one day after the UN had voted for partition, eight Arabs ambushed a Jewish bus and killed five people. Thirty minutes later, the gunmen struck again—yet another bus. This time, two Jews were killed.

Morris says it is not at all clear that the Arabs were anything more than thieves looking for some loot. It is also possible that they were seeking to revenge the killing of some Bedouins by Jews who themselves were seeking to revenge an earlier incident. Whatever the case, the civil war was on—and it was on at the insistence of the Arabs.

The war had two phases. The Arabs gained the advantage, and then the Arabs lost their advantage. There matters stood until the British pulled their troops out of their old Mandatory Palestine and sailed home. On May 14, 1948, David Ben-Gurion declared Israel independent. The surrounding states promptly began phase two. They invaded. Once again, the Jews did not take the initiative, and once again the outcome was hardly the sure thing that some contemporary writers now insist it was. Both the British foreign office and the CIA thought the Jews would lose.

The new nation of Israel, like the old nations of Central and Eastern Europe, had an intractable ethnic problem. By 1946, Jews and Arabs had been killing one another for more than fifty years, living a whole lot less peaceably than had ethnic Germans and Czechs. The remedies were obvious, and the blunt instrumentalities available to the victors of the European war were, of course, available to the Jews of Palestine as well. By 1945–46, they had not yet triumphed, and maybe they never would—they lacked allies and manpower—but if they did win, what would victory look like? The Zionist dream was not to establish a timorous Jewish minority in an Arab nation—an untenable arrangement, even if possible. The nebulous Zionist fantasy had, in fact, been quite specific: all those Viennese cafés for all those Viennese émigrés, with Herzl undoubtedly getting the best table. This was going to be a Jewish state, a state run by Jews—

European Jews, to get a bit more specific—and *enlightened* European Jews, to get even more specific.

What should be done? Should a stronger and better-organized Jewish community either shove the Arabs out of their country—no less their country than Bohemia had been for Germans—or should they make some sort of accommodation: an accommodation that had failed in the past and was being attempted nowhere else in the world? Should the Jews of Palestine, some of them recent arrivals from Bergen-Belsen or Dachau, some of them survivors of the Polish pogroms of 1946, all of them aware of what had just happened and what was still happening, be expected to abide by rules that elsewhere had been suspended or simply violated? Should they not invoke the permission and the example of the Great Powers to make their land ethnically pure? Could it be that the law of the jungle applied to everyone but Jews? Could it be that they alone were expected to lie down with the lion? They decided otherwise. Once was enough.

It is of more than incidental interest that most of Israel's early political leaders once had Polish or Russian names. David Ben-Gurion had been born David Grüen, and Golda Meir was Golda Mabovich (later Meyerson), and Ariel Sharon, who took his name from the valley in Israel, had been Scheinermann. Benzion Netanyahu, the father of Binyamin Netanyahu, had been born Benzion Mileikowsky in Warsaw and changed the family name upon their arrival in Palestine to mean "God-given."

The significance of these name changes is obvious and their importance great. Shimon Peres, in his biography of Ben-Gurion, mentions that Ben-Gurion lost family members in the Holocaust. So did Peres, born Szymon Perski in Poland. This means that for virtually an entire generation of Israel's leadership, the Holocaust did not happen "over there" to fellow but distant Jews, but in their own place of birth to relatives—often siblings or parents who had stayed behind. The victims were not landsmen, fellow Jews of some abstraction, but loved ones with a name and a face, such as Ben-Gurion's beloved niece, whose studies he had supported. These leaders had an intimate familiarity with the twin barbarities of extermination and ethnic cleansing. It had been done to them. Why should they not do it to others?

In the telling of some critics of Israel, Arab as well as Jew, they did. The *nakba* was a calamity on a vast scale, an ethnic cleansing and an immense crime against humanity. The hyperbolic adjectives are appropriate, we are told, because the event itself was overlooked for so long, ignored in the euphoria over the creation of Israel, and because the scale of it was huge and its methods monstrous. It was not quite a Holocaust—no one could possibly argue that—and yet it was *almost* a holocaust if only because its perpetrators were the *victims* of the Holocaust. By implication, by indirection, by insidious association, the *nakba* not only condemns its Israeli perpetrators but suggests something about the Holocaust itself: the victims-cum-victimizers had it coming.

Alas, for the more idealistic or naive defenders of Israel, it is indisputable that some ethnic cleansing was not only attempted but effectuated. The various Palestinian refugee camps, not to mention the burgeoning population of the Gaza Strip and, to a lesser extent, the West Bank, seem to testify to it. The standard exoneration that all these Arabs fled at the insistence or suggestion of an Arab leadership that was certain of victory does not hold up under examination. Too many eyewitnesses, Jewish as well as Arab, testify otherwise.

Reality, however, is not necessarily what happened; it is also what is *said* to have happened. What is said now is that the creation of Israel was a bloody horror, awful in its aspect, virtually unprecedented, cruel and oppressive and racist in the way that these colonial matters invariably are. In these accounts, the birth of Israel was not an ordinary historic event—a triumph for some, a tragedy for others—but a horrendous act of colonial impudence that was accomplished by the promiscuous use of force, culminating in a victory of the First World Jews over the Third World Arabs that can be likened to Hernando Cortés's conquest of the Aztecs in 1521.

The Jews of Palestine were Europeans once removed. Had expulsion or something like it not occurred to them, they could not be living in the middle of the twentieth century. Expulsion was all around them. People were on the move everywhere. And everywhere, it was condoned. The most advanced nations in the world not only permitted it but also advocated it. Expulsion made as much sense to Palestinian Jews and, later, Israelis as it did to Churchill and other world leaders sitting around the table at Potsdam. And yet the Jews of Israel hesitated and, in the end, did not order the expulsion of the Arabs. There is no record of an important Jewish leader echoing what Czech president Beneš said regarding his ethnic Germans—although Ilan Pappe quotes from a 1937 letter

Ben-Gurion wrote to his son: "The Arabs will have to go." He writes that Ben-Gurion "masterminded the ethnic cleansing of Palestine."

Whatever Ben-Gurion set down in a letter in 1937, Shimon Peres never heard him utter anything similar in public: "I was at Ben-Gurion's side for much of that time, and I never heard him speak in favor of expelling the Arabs from Israel. On the contrary, during the war, I heard him speak in condemnation of this practice."

Peres is no naïf. In his own black-and-white telling of this history, he concedes that others might see some gray. He mentions an incident in which Ben-Gurion was informed that Arabs were being evicted from Lydda, and "Ben-Gurion made a gesture with his hand that implied approval." On the other hand, Ben-Gurion ordered the mayor of Haifa, a mixed Arab-Jewish city, to discourage the flight of Arabs.

Common sense suggests that Israel's leaders were torn between the pragmatic and inhumane, and the humane and somewhat impractical. One solution was, however, discussed, and that was an exchange of populations. This once had the support of the British Labour Party—it was implemented in India, after all—but nothing came of it. Sheer expulsion, though, was never on the table. "That would have been against our fundamental ideology," Peres writes, "and I don't think Ben-Gurion would have countenanced any ideological compromise in this matter." Expulsion was for others, not for a Jewish state.

Israel mainly kept its virtue but may well have lost its future. Expulsion of the Arabs would have been horrible, and if I were writing at the time, I would have condemned it vociferously. But it would have worked. Israel would now be as Jewish as the Czech Republic is Czech or Hungary is Hungarian. In Europe, the passage of time has dissipated anger and soothed hates so that, for instance, the association of Germans expelled from the east (Poland, for example) has played a diminishing role in German politics. In these cases, though, the refugees found a home in the new/old country, even though their ancestors had left it hundreds of years ago and they themselves spoke an odd German, the product of isolation and a long separation from the mother country.

No doubt the same process could have applied to Palestinian exiles and refugees. But *could* is not the same as *would*, the distinction here being one of culture, not grammar. The Arab societies back in 1948 had just recently been organized into nations. They were still largely tribal—and some of them still are. Palestinians may be Arabs, speak Arabic, and mostly practice Islam, but they have not been welcomed into the neighboring states. The Arab nation exists mostly as a rhetorical device.

The Germans, with considerable reluctance, became resigned to the mass immigration of the *Volksdeutsche*; Israel's neighboring Arab states never accepted their Palestinian brothers. For that reason, it is not clear that a massive population transfer would have worked. Certainly it would have rid Israel of a possible fifth column, but Palestinian tenacity and the tribal realities of the Arab world would have kept the issue alive. While it is true that no one comes to Hungary and demands to know what happened to the Romanians or asks the Czechs to account for the missing Germans, the Arab world is a different matter. No law of return applies to the *Volksdeutsche*, but in the rhetoric of Palestinian leaders, it would apply to the Palestinians. Hundreds of thousands of exiles ought to be allowed to return to Palestine, swamping the Jewish state, obliterating its national character so that it is no longer Jewish.

To the extent that the Palestinians were indeed expelled, it was not only a hardship for the actual victims but also a moral failure for the many Jews who not only wanted to avoid such an outcome but sincerely thought it would never happen. What's striking about the sentiments of so many Israeli leaders was not their hatred or even fear of Arabs but an incomprehensible naïveté about a people who didn't like them from the start. Palestinians—from the upper-class effendis to the lower-class fellahin—realistically assessed the threat posed by Jewish immigration and understood what the outcome would be. Never mind that this was often accompanied by raw hatred, prejudice, ignorance, and all sorts of repellent actions: petty murders, inept insurrections, and an embrace of Hitler. The fact remained that Palestinians were dead right about Jews and their intentions. Arabs understood what the Jews wanted even if some of the Jews did not.

Jews indulged in all sorts of fantasies, as much captives of various ideologies as were the Arabs of tradition and religion. Early on, Jews were so intent on casting off what they considered the ghetto stigma of avoiding manual labor that they made a fetish of Zionist self-sufficiency. This insistence on working the land meant that Arabs were displaced. Those Arabs were not the owners of the land, but peasants, tenant farmers, fathers, then sons, then fathers again working the same land. For obvious reasons, these Palestinian peasants were not willing to give the Jews credit merely because the land was bought—often at inflated prices—rather than seized by force. All they knew was that they were out of a job, and they hated the Jews accordingly.

The inadvertent creation of enemies is a feature of cultural clashes, and the harsh truth is that Arab and Jew were and remain two different cultures. They were destined to clash. Some Jews recognized that right off and said so. But a significant number, most of them socialists and members of the dominant Labor movement, adhered stubbornly to the dream that Arab and Jew could work together and—in a spot-on example of noblesse oblige—that the Arabs would come to appreciate how much they could benefit from the Jews. (Indeed, many Arabs came from surrounding countries to seek employment in Jewish Palestine, just as West Bankers do today.) The Jews' argument fell, as it was destined to fall, on deaf ears. In effect, the Arabs were saying they would rather be poor in their own land than rich in a Jewish one.

This, of course, is the truest example of the colonial mentality: the conviction that the "colonialist," so labeled by virtue of skin color and national origin, is the sole agent of change. This naïveté was a tick of the Jewish left. The Jewish right was much more willing to give the Arabs their due: their religion, their nationalism, their tribalism, and their history. Hate (or fear) can be a function of respect. Love (or tolerance) can be condescending.

As a result, the Jewish political and intellectual leadership of the pre-independence era could be fairly accused of retaining a touch of the ghetto mentality they so abhorred. They cared so much for what others thought of them (and what they might think of themselves) that when it came to the Palestinian challenge, they produced a mishmash: a desire to see the Palestinians gone and, simultaneously, a reluctance to do what was necessary to make it happen. Ben-Gurion, who loathed that arch-rightist Jabotinsky, nevertheless recognized in him and his approach to the Arabs a total lack of ghetto demeanor.

The solution that now seems obvious, and which was entailed in every mention of population transfers—separation of the two peoples—was slow to become accepted and even slower in coming. For a long time, it seemed possible that Jew and Arab could live together, but the Hebron pogrom of 1929 changed all that. It was not only that sixty-seven Jews were killed but also the sheer bestiality of the attack. Women and children were murdered, and when Rabbi Slonim Dwek refused to turn over Yeshiva students to the mob, he was killed on the spot. The pogrom, followed by the Arab Revolt of 1936, put an end to any thoughts of peaceful coexistence.

Despite all this, in their diaries, their newspapers, their letters, and their speeches, Jews for the most part failed to leave any evidence of a consuming animus toward Arabs or a determination to drive them from the land. Instead, the record is replete with statements from the leadership—the very same people who would assume political and military power in the new state—suggesting appreciation for the Arabs and their plight. This one, from the future prime minister Moshe Sharett (then Shertok), is fairly typical: "There is not a single Arab who has not been hurt by the entry of Jews into Palestine; there is not a single Arab who does not see himself as part of the Arab race. . . . In his eyes, Palestine is an independent unit. Previously, it had had an Arab face, and now it is changing."

David Ben-Gurion, destined to be Israel's first prime minister, made similar remarks, and he pleaded with his fellow Jews not to denigrate the Arab Revolt by ascribing it to hooliganism. He acknowledged Arab nationalism. "An Arab national movement has been discovered, a mature and militant movement." Missing—at least in these statements—is any suggestion of Arabs benefiting from the Jewish influx. A tragedy was in the making.

As a child, I was always told that I could not excuse something bad I had done by claiming that everyone else had done it. For this, I got the unassailable Brooklyn Bridge riposte: If everyone jumps off the Brooklyn Bridge, does that mean you should too? I got the point. The point in defending (or, as I prefer, *explaining*) what Jews did to Palestinians is not to suggest that it was virtuous because it was common—*because others did it*—but rather to emphasize that others *did* do it. And while they sometimes did it out of vengeance or for the sheer ugly fun of it, they more often did it because they had to or because they thought they had to. The tribes of the world sometimes get along, but more often they do not. Hungarians, Romanians, Poles, Germans, Czechs, Slovaks, Croatians, Slovenians, Montenegrins, Albanians, Kosovars, Bosnian Christians and Bosnian Muslims, Greeks, Macedonians, Ruthenians, Tutsis and Hutus of Africa, and all the peoples of the Caucasus have had to be separated from one another. The differences sometimes can seem minor. Bosnian Muslims speak Serbo-Croatian and so do Bosnian Christians; Croats and Serbs are both Christians. Yet they all spent part of the twentieth century trying to kill one another.

To the outsider, the differences separating these groups are imperceptible. This is not the case—and it certainly *was* not the case—with Palestinians and Jews. They dressed differently, and they spoke different languages, and they treated women differently, and they observed different days for the Sabbath, and Palestinians were mostly rural whereas Jews were mostly urban, and many of them lived, at least in the beginning, in different centuries.

Some of these differences have lessened. A contemporary Palestinian is likely to be a city dweller and to dress in a contemporary fashion and even speak Hebrew. He or she would be indistinguishable from a Jew of Moroccan or Yemenite heritage; neither one would have the stereotypical physiognomy of the eastern European Jew—the stuff of a *Der Stürmer* caricature. But that was not the case in the 1920s, 1930s, and 1940s, when Israeli society was taking shape and had few Jews from North Africa or the Middle East. The Yishuv, a bit like Australia or, more ominously, South Africa, was culturally European.

Had these Jews not foisted the *nakba* on the Palestinians, the state would not have survived. It is one thing, of course, to hold that the state *should not* have survived—that it was nothing other than a racist, colonialist enterprise— but should you hold otherwise, then you have bought into a chain of events that entails a certain amount of ethnic cleansing. Once again, the driver of events was not, as is almost universally argued, the Jews, but the Arabs. Had the Palestinians and the nearby Arab states agreed to the United Nations partition plan, had they acceded to the creation of the State of Israel, the rationale for the *nakba* would have been avoided. ("It was our mistake," the Palestinian leader Mahmoud Abbas said in late 2011. "It was an Arab mistake as a whole. But do they [the Israelis] punish us for this mistake for sixty-four years?")

Demography compounds the mistake. Had the Palestinians acceded to the wishes of the international community, they would have come to predominate in the new Israel. Instead of being 20 percent of the population as they are today, they might now be a majority. The descendants of the original refugees now number almost five million. Added to the 1.5 million Arab citizens of Israel, they would outnumber Israel's six million Jews. Given the different fertility rates, Israel would have become yet another Middle East Arab nation over time—either that, or an apartheid nation in which a minority of Jews ruled a majority of Arabs, and not by democratic means, either. But that did not happen, and a civil war ensued. Palestinian Jews and Palestinian Arabs killed one another with impressive ferocity. Prisoners of war were executed; women were raped. Children were killed, sometimes purposely.

Had the Palestinians won, a Jewish *nakba* would surely have taken place; it was, after all, the whole idea behind Arab intransigence. If they could have done it, the Arabs would have forced the Jews into the sea—back to Europe on boats that might or might not have been given a berth in European ports. Things did not turn out that way, of course. The Jews have to be pardoned, however, for thinking that defeat would not just have pushed them into the Mediterranean but back into history: coffin boats, extermination, and a world that did not give a damn. History would double back on itself, finally extinguishing the Holocaust not by some international fire brigade but from lack of fuel.

It's been a long time since the convulsions that followed World War II. Most of the exiled or transferred people have settled in. The Germans are assimilated into Germany (the Sudetens mostly in Bavaria), the Hungarians into Hungary, and the Romanians into Romania. Even the Muslims and Hindus of India and Pakistan, while doggedly persisting in hating each other, do not demand to go back from whence they came. They seem resigned to hate from their respective sides of the border.

Palestinians have been welcomed nowhere—not, anyway, as full-fledged citizens. They remain Palestinians, generation after generation, a people who nurse an understandable grudge, who are contained either physically or culturally in camps in which hate festers. They have been wronged, no doubt about it—not just by Jews but by their leaders and their fellow Arabs as well. They are stuck in the amber of grievances. They want a nation they never had. They want to return to a place where most have never lived. It may seem like folly, but history argues otherwise.

They have seen it done.

16

Two Grandmothers and a Lake

The road from Beirut to Rashidieh winds along the Mediterranean, past Sidon and then Tyre. The cities and towns are ugly with the utilitarian use of cement, but the countryside is lovely and the sea resplendent. Rashidieh itself was a surprise, a long-established (1963) Palestinian refugee camp of precisely 25,580 UN-counted souls and placed next to one built years earlier for Armenian refugees from yet another regional debacle. It is, all things considered, not such a bad place, hardly squalid like some other camps, and tucked into a scenic spot. The day I visited was sunny and warm, the only discordant note being the Kalashnikov rifle that a pudgy Palestinian boy kept poking in my stomach. It was his idea of a joke. He laughed, and I, with little choice, did the same.

Rashidieh's residents are poor and their living conditions somewhat primitive. But like most of the refugee camps, it is something more than a "camp" and something less than a town or village. Somewhere along the way, tents were replaced by cement structures. When I visited years ago, the homes lacked running water—a hose sufficed—and consisted of one large room that served during the day as a living room and at night as a sleeping quarter.

I toured the camp in the company of an armed guide supplied by what was then Yasser Arafat's Palestine Liberation Organization. Nonetheless, I was allowed to go where I wanted, and so, on a whim, I stopped at a one-room house and asked to talk to one of the residents. He was a young man, not in the least hostile to me, a (Jewish) reporter for the hated Western media, but, in truth, I don't remember what we talked about. I do remember the old woman I saw over his shoulder. She was inside the house, cleaning up.

First, she rolled up the sleeping mats. There were six or more of them—one for each member of the family. Everyone slept in the single room. Then she grabbed her broom and swept the floor. When she was done, the young man and I stepped into the room, and I spied something familiar: a gaudily colored picture, a scenic view of the Sea of Galilee. For a moment or two, I could not place it. Then I remembered: my grandmother! She had had the same picture. It was the top half of a wall calendar.

"Why does she have that picture?" I asked my guide, and he, stunned that I was asking about such a banal item, asked the young man. He didn't know. So he asked the old woman, and she replied.

"It's where she used to live," he said.

Bingo! There it was: the story of the Israeli-Arab conflict in one kitschy picture. My grandmother, an immigrant to America who had never seen the Sea of Galilee, cherished it as much—no, not as much, but dearly and fervently—as the woman who used to live there. And to both of them it was an idealized, Technicolored place. A placid, serene sea. Jesus had walked on it (not that either grandmother cared or probably even knew) and it was deep blue, surrounded by a shoreline of vibrant green. And the sky, of course, was an endless azure. The place had taken on mythical qualities.

The old woman had probably been in the first exile from Palestine. Possibly, she had a farm, some land that had been in her family for generations. Possibly, she had had a husband and possibly he had been killed in the '48 war. Or—again, possibly—he had gone off to Tyre or Sidon, where there was some work, or maybe even Beirut, where, again, there was work and all the distractions of a big city. Whatever the case, she had last seen the Galilee in 1948, which was a very long time ago.

By now, that old woman is more than likely dead, and possibly so is her son. For the surviving family—now at least three generations into exile—the Galilee exists in memory, in tales told of the old days, of a longing that brings on sobs and impedes breathing. It has become an abstraction, a myth, a symbol of all that was lost.

For my grandmother, it was the same—*somewhat* the same. Her house had not been by the Galilee, nor her farm, and the land had not been in the family for generations, not even one. But that picture, with its colors bleeding one into another, had represented a fervid dream—not just Israel, although that would have been enough, but relief from oppression, from fear of pogroms, from a lid placed on aspirations, from a world where Jews were killed not for any crime but just for being Jews. She covered her eyes when she prayed, and above her, on the wall, was the calendar, the picture, and beyond that Israel itself. Next year. Next year. And then in 1948 next year came. One grandmother had the Sea of Galilee. The other had the picture.

But this story, this tragedy, is not yet complete. It is presented as the other shoe that dropped: first the Holocaust and then the *nakba* and the implication of a kind of symmetry. At the time, however, something else was happening—the uprooting and eradication of the Arab world's Jewish communities. As many as 866,000 Jews left, fled, or were expelled from Arab countries. This, too, was not an orderly transfer of volunteers eager to live in the new land of Israel but a wrenching uprooting conducted, in some cases, in a faux-Nazi style, complete with the standard document attesting to the fact that the bearer was *voluntarily* choosing to leave behind his home, his furniture, his business, his bank account, his cash, his synagogue, his school, his father's school, his grandfather's school—all the way back for hundreds of years—in exchange for which he would happily live in a tent.

The inducement consisted of sporadic pogroms, mob violence, and the absolute loss of citizenship. Israel was both the cause of their expulsion and their haven, doing for the imperiled Mizrahi (Sephardic and indigenous Jewish) community what it could not do for the endangered Ashkenazi one. For these Jews, without Israel, Israel would not have been necessary.

Compared with what had just happened in Europe, the suffering of the Mizrahi community might seem minor. The numbers of dead were *relatively* few, as were stores looted or buildings burned. But within those countries and, particularly, within the communities themselves, a broad and horrible terror had swept the region, and its prime cause was the creation of Israel. It started with the UN's partition vote of November 1947, which triggered a pogrom in Aden, Yemen's port at the entrance to the Red Sea. There eighty-two Jews were murdered and most Jewish-owned stores looted. In a very short period of time, a thousand-year-old Jewish community as well as the larger one of Yemen itself was gone.

Pogroms erupted across the Arab world and far into the Maghreb. In Egypt, sporadic pogroms and isolated murders culminated in an outright expulsion order following the Suez crisis of 1956, when Israel joined Britain and France in attacking Egypt. (The Israelis' so-called false flag operation of 1954—the infamous Lavon affair, when Israel used Egyptian Jews to conduct bombing that could be blamed on the Muslim Brotherhood—did not help matters any.) By then, the Jewish community was widely seen as an Israeli fifth column; Jews were declared Zionists and ordered to "voluntarily" leave the country. Since they had ostensibly chosen to abandon Egypt, they were forced by the Nasser government to leave behind their wealth. By century's end, an Egyptian Jewish community once numbering 75,000 to 80,000 was reduced to several hundred.

The richly textured Jewish community of Egypt is now only the stuff of memoirs. Jews had had a long and decidedly mixed history in Egypt—possibly the first pogrom took place in Alexandria in the first century AD—but by the 1956 Suez War, that history was mixed no more. By diktat of Gamal Abdel Nasser, it was over. He expelled the lot of the Jews, proclaiming for simplicity's sake that there was no difference between Zionism and Judaism. For the Jews of Egypt, the Second Exodus had come.

This experience was duplicated throughout North Africa and the Middle East. The large Moroccan Jewish community of about 250,000 was dispersed in the late 1940s and early 1950s—some to the United States and Canada (particularly French-speaking Montreal), many to France (then a colonial power), but most to Israel.

Iraq was as congenial a place for Jews as Morocco, but by the 1930s, Nazi-style fascism had made inroads there. From then on, Iraq practiced European-style anti-Semitism. With the creation of Israel, life in Iraq for Jews became utterly untenable, and they fled—often from gracious upper-class villas to tents in dusty immigrant centers.

Like the Arabs displaced by the creation of Israel, the Jews who fled Arab lands left everything behind. In this way, Arab and Jew were alike. Where they were different was in how they were received in their new lands. The Jews were greeted as the building blocks of a nation under construction. They were needed if only for manpower, and despite some difficulty—the Arab Jews (a designation once reserved for the Jews of Iraq) were not, after all, longing to re-create Herzl's Vienna—assimilation proceeded, sometimes painfully and never really totally; but by the end of the century, Sephardic Jews were in the political hierarchy and held senior positions in the military.

The Palestinian immigrants got no such reception and had a distinctly different experience. They were not, after all, beginning a new life but supposedly just interrupting an old one. Their plight was supposedly temporary, and their welcome was grudging. They spoke the same language and practiced the same religion, but they were considered different. Their welcome, consequently, was restrained. The Palestinian cause was embraced, but not the Palestinians themselves.

Lebanon, a country with a surfeit of ethnic groups, was none too happy when Palestinians started streaming over the border. They came first in 1948 and then again in 1967, until there are now possibly 400,000 of them, although the inexactness of that figure testifies to their somewhat stateless status. Whatever the case, they represent a significant portion of Lebanon's four million residents but hardly a corresponding portion of its economic life. They are banned from participating in seventy-two professions, including law, and they are either discouraged from owning or forbidden to own property.

The Jewish *nakba*, a word that an Egyptian Jew might feel just as entitled to use as a Palestinian Arab, is one of those events, like the displacement of the ethnic Germans, that have dropped down the proverbial memory hole. One reason for this, surely, is that just as the ethnic Germans assimilated relatively quickly into German society, so did the Jews of the Arab world in Israel. This does not mean that there are no longer Ashkenazi and Sephardic communities; it means only that they live in peace, and neither one has a monopoly on the instrumentalities of power.

No Jew whose family since time immemorial has recited the Passover hope, "Next year in Jerusalem," can disparage or belittle the Palestinians' longing for Palestine. One or two generations have elapsed since the Palestinian *nakba*, but countless generations have elapsed since the Babylonian exile and the origins of the Jewish Diaspora, and yet for much of that time the longing for Israel seemed encoded in the DNA of religiously inclined Jews.

On the other hand, it's not likely that assimilated German Jews longed for Israel. (In fact, we know from the trouble early Zionists had with this community that Zion had little allure for the shopkeepers and bankers of Germany.) The same could be said for the Jews of Britain, Canada—even Argentina or, until relatively recently, South Africa. Certainly, that is the case for the country where nearly half the world's Jews live. In the United States, the longing for Israel, the urge to make aliya and move to the Holy Land, is virtually nonexistent. Only some twenty thousand of the approximately five million Jews in the United States have actually pulled up their roots and moved to Israel, and many of them are members of ultraorthodox religious communities. To put it another way, of the world's eleven million Jews, only five million or so live in Israel. The rest—the majority—choose not to.

So where Jews are assimilated, where they feel secure and are able to be Jews or practice Judaism, they stay put. They do not seek to "return" to Palestine. The same is undoubtedly true for the Palestinian Diaspora. Where Palestinians can assimilate—the United States, western Europe, South America—they do and have done so. (There are some 72,000 Palestinians in the United States and, astoundingly, more Palestinians in Chile—as many as 500,000—than in Lebanon.) The Palestinians in the United States do not campaign overtly to return to Palestine.

A diaspora is no single thing. The urban Christian Arabs who left Palestine for economic reasons—the overriding reason before 1948—can hardly be considered in the same category as rural or village-based Muslims who fled in 1948 or after. The latter ran to safety and camped, waiting for an imminent return. It has been a long wait—in some cases, more than sixty years. All together, the eight camps of the Gaza Strip, originally controlled by Egypt, house nearly a half million people.

These camps have gone from being an indictment of the Arab governments and their indifference to Palestinian suffering to an indictment of Israel, which, unfairly and irrationally, is held solely responsible for the sorry way things have turned out. The Palestinian *nakba* has become the semiofficial narrative, the one that is increasingly preferred to the founding myth best depicted in the book and movie *Exodus*. The stirring story of Holocaust survivors creating a nation without racist rancor now seems laughable, and indeed it is. But that story is truer than it is false, just as it is not true that the early Zionists proceeded as if no people occupied the land now called Israel or as if the occupants had no claim to it. Not even Herzl was so blind, although in truth he did not give the Palestinians much thought.

Herzl's pamphlet *The Jewish State* is an odd document. With clichéd Teutonic thoroughness, he enumerated all the challenges and problems he could think of down to the design of the flag ("a white one with seven golden stars") and the language to be spoken. (Anything but Yiddish or Ladino—"those are miserable, stunted jargon"—and probably not, for practical reasons, Hebrew. "Who among us has a sufficient acquaintance with Hebrew to ask for a railway ticket in that language?" he wrote.) But not a word about the Palestinians. Presumably, Herzl intended to emulate the American model, with Palestinians playing the part of Indians. Jews would simply buy land and move into the supposedly empty spaces.

Two years after Herzl's death in 1904, Weizmann was on his way to visit Palestine for the first time. He stopped in Beirut and met there with a man named Victor Jacobson, the director of the local branch of the Anglo-Palestine Bank. "It was from him that I first learned something of the nascent Arab national movement," Weizmann wrote.

Weizmann's naïveté or maybe plain ignorance is shocking on the surface, but Palestine was a long way from Great Britain, and the era—pretty much the high-water mark of colonialism—was one in which anything other than a superficial knowledge of indigenous populations was not in any way essential. At that time, the Middle East was an inchoate collection of tribes and clans, substantially without borders and still not understood. With the exception of Egypt and Turkey, none of the area's modern nations existed yet. Turkey ruled most of the region, Britain some of it, the rest was the domain of tribes—and Jerusalem was a backwater with a population of about 33,000. All that changed pretty quickly with the conversion of Britain's fleet from coal to oil by Winston Churchill in 1911 and the realization, not long afterward, that the Middle East was where the oil was. Control of that oil and access to the strategically important Suez Canal moved the Middle East and its peoples up several notches during World War I. Palestine, near the oil and the Suez Canal, was obscure no more.

The very year, 1948, that South Africa was herding its people into ethnic pens—setting up its apartheid system—Chaim Weizmann became Israel's first president. For more than a year, he had been working on his memoirs, in which he outlined what he hoped would be the new state's approach to its own minority problem. "There must not be one law for the Jew and another for the Arabs," he wrote. "We must stand first by the ancient principle enunciated in our Torah: 'One law and one manner shall be for you and the stranger that sojourneth with you.' In saying this, I do not assume that there are tendencies toward inequality or discrimination. It is merely a timely warning, which is particularly necessary because we shall have a very large Arab minority." He concluded with a prescient warning: *I am certain that the world will judge the Jewish State by what it will do with the Arabs."*

17

Jabotinsky Was Right

In 1948 Hannah Arendt, Albert Einstein, and other prominent American Jews wrote to the *New York Times* to denounce Menachem Begin. Begin was then the leader of Israel's right-wing Freedom Party and on the very fringes of Israeli political life—so far to the right that the letter's signatories said that the party was "closely akin in its organization, methods, political philosophy, and social appeal to the Nazi and Fascist parties."

Einstein, Arendt, and their colleagues had not taken leave of their senses. Begin *had* been a terrorist, a militant, and an extreme Jewish chauvinist. He *had* been associated with all sorts of violent acts: the 1947 retaliatory kidnapping and hanging of two British army sergeants and, the previous year, the infamous bombing of the King David Hotel, which took ninety-one lives. (The two sergeants were murdered after two Jews, Meir Feinstein and Moshe Barazani, blew themselves up with smuggled grenades moments before they were about to be executed by the British. Begin instructed that he be buried next to their graves. He was.)

Begin was an extremely tough man whose policies and activities as head of the ultranationalistic Irgun, a guerrilla outfit, nearly pitched Jewish forces into a civil war. He styled himself the anti–Ben-Gurion. He wore a suit and tie, while Ben-Gurion sported the open-collar shirt that for a time became Israel's standard civilian uniform. It is fair to say that no one at the time, least of all Begin, would have predicted that he would become Israel's paramount leader, its prime minister, and the first not from the dominant socialist (Labor) coalition. His triumph was so unexpected and yet complete that it may come as a surprise to know that he was not the founder of his movement but a dedicated and zealous follower—far less important in his own mind than the man who had fathered what became right-wing Israeli politics: Ze'ev Jabotinsky, the firebrand militant and ideological wanderer.

Jabotinsky was born in 1880 as Vladimir Jabotinsky, an Odessa Jew. He died unexpectedly in 1940 while visiting his organization's quasimilitary youth camp in New York state. It would be many years before his body was permitted to be returned to the Palestine he left, the Israel he never lived to see. To the Ben-Gurion government, he was an anathema.

Jabotinsky is now an obscure figure—except in Israel and for a scattering of Jews elsewhere who, many years after his death, still revere him. But for the signatories to that *New York Times* letter, he was a significant and menacing figure—the founding father of the reviled right-wing guerrilla fighters cum terrorists who were loath to accept the authority of Ben-Gurion. This was no mere political disagreement about jobs or even policy but a breach involving character and basic outlook. Jabotinsky's followers considered Ben-Gurion to be too deferential to the British, not militant enough, and, when you came right down to it, too much the sort of ghetto Jew they all deplored.

This business of who could be more gentile than the gentiles—who could be prouder and stronger and indifferent to what we would now call world opinion— ran like a leitmotif through the Yishuv into statehood and persists to this day. It allows for the outright rejection of valid criticism on the grounds that it is either anti-Semitic or, if from a Jew, an effort to please the gentiles. Early on, it surfaced in the statements and observations of various leaders. The quality of being a Jew who was unlike the stereotype of the Jew, of being a Jew who was not even what other Jews thought was a Jew, of being a Jew who was not, in the parlance of America's racial experience, an Uncle Tom, is the one characteristic that commended Jabotinsky to Ben-Gurion: "He had nothing in him of the *Galut* [Diaspora] Jew, and he was never embarrassed in the presence of a Gentile."

Jabotinsky was a divisive figure, but time has proven him to be prescient. Like Herzl, who intuited the calamity that would befall Europe's Jews, Jabotinsky also felt it coming. Jeremy Ben-Ami, the son of a Jabotinsky aide (and the founder of the left-wing Zionist organization J Street), cites a warning Jabotinsky offered the Jews of Poland in 1938. In a speech in Warsaw's Great Synagogue, Jabotinsky warned of an "impending catastrophe—a horrible vision: Listen to my words at this, the twelfth hour. For God's sake: let everyone save himself, so long as there is time to do so, for time is running short."

By then, of course, Nazi Germany was stirring with aggressive intentions, and Poland, just over the German border, had become a right-wing anti-Semitic republic. That same year, Neville Chamberlain signed the Munich accords.

Given the events of the time and what he saw coming, it's understandable that Jabotinsky was a man of little patience and less moderation. He was out to save European Jewry, to bring it to Palestine, where it would be safe. "Perfidious Albion," as Great Britain was sometimes called, was living up to its name. Not only had it sold out the Czechoslovaks but it was reneging on the promise it had made in the Balfour Declaration and the subsequent white paper. Britain was closing the door to Jewish immigration. Britain was consigning European Jews to their deaths. Britain had to be fought.

This obduracy, not to mention Jabotinsky's martial airs, gave Ben-Gurion the opportunity to heap scorn and epithets on Jabotinsky. "Vladimir Hitler," he called him, and just to make his feeling even plainer, he later would not permit Jabotinsky to be buried in Israel. (Jabotinsky specified that he was not to be buried in Palestine until independence was achieved.) In 1964 the government of Levi Eshkol finally brought Jabotinsky home to Mount Herzl.

To Arendt, Einstein, and like-minded liberal Jews, Jabotinsky was a dangerous zealot, a militant nationalist whose policies were, in fact, praised by the scattering of Jewish fascists who for a time were enamored of Mussolini. Jabotinsky was never a fascist—indeed, his virtual mantra was "Every individual is a king"—but he did set great store in uniforms, discipline, and ceremony, as did genuine fascists. And compared with the socialist-minded Jewish community, he was right wing to his core, an enthusiastic strikebreaker, for example.

The differences between Jabotinsky Revisionists and the Yishuv's mainstream political leadership were both profound and profoundly emotional. Much of it was ideological, and some of that, no doubt, was biographical. Jabotinsky and Begin were forged by Europe's white-hot anti-Semitism. Begin himself had been something of an outlaw much of his life: on the run from the Poles, the Soviets, the British, and, in a way, the mainstream Jewish leadership.

He had come to Palestine in midlife, fully formed by the Europe he had left behind.

Ben-Gurion, in contrast, had come to Palestine in 1906, when he was merely twenty years old. Unlike Begin, he did not flee European anti-Semitism; astoundingly, he had never experienced it. In his memoir, he writes, "For many of us, anti-Semitic feeling had little to do with our dedication [to Zionism]. I personally never suffered anti-Semitic persecution. Plonsk [in Poland, his birthplace] was remarkably free of it."

This was primarily a political squabble, but it engendered a visceral hatred that on occasion erupted into violence. The first dustup came in 1933 and involved the dispatch of an envoy to Berlin to negotiate with the new Nazi regime for the lives and property of German Jews. The so-called Haavara agreement would have benefited both parties. Hitler had a chance to show that he was not a homicidal maniac, merely an insane anti-Semite. As for the Palestinian Jews, they were bringing in their co-religionists.

The man chosen for the job was Haim Arlosoroff, a leader of Mapai, Jewish Palestine's most important political party. Arlosoroff is one of those historical asterisks that illuminate their times, a man who seems to have known everyone by dint of his own brilliance but also through the sort of coincidence that usually cannot be found outside of bad movies. Arlosoroff had been born in Ukraine but raised in Berlin. As a youth, he had founded a political party as well as a Zionist magazine, and his sister, Lisa, had become friendly with a certain Magda Behrend—the aforementioned coincidence. In 1931 Magda married Joseph Goebbels, an intimate of Hitler's, in a ceremony witnessed by the führer himself. And so when Arlosoroff returned to Germany to negotiate with the Nazi regime, he had a connection—if not with Goebbels, then with Magda.

Whatever the case, two days after returning to Palestine, Arlosoroff was murdered while walking on the Tel Aviv beach with his wife, Sima. Two members of Jabotinsky's Revisionist Party were arrested for the crime but later acquitted. On the left, the exoneration meant nothing. So venomous were the relations between left and right that the idea that the former would murder a leader of the latter was not considered far-fetched. Arlosoroff had been accused of making a craven, ghetto-like deal with the ultimate goys and so deserved what he got. So heated was the atmosphere that Shimon Peres, in his biography of Ben-Gurion, writes: "it came very close to exploding into serious internecine violence, if not outright civil strife."

The second—and more serious—brush with internecine violence amounted to no brush at all; it actually came off, although a calamity was avoided at the last minute. After the War of Independence, the various Jewish paramilitaries were being merged into the new Israel Defense Forces. The process was both complicated and slow. As this was happening, a prearranged shipment of arms from France was making its way to Israel on the *Altalena*, a ship named after one of Jabotinsky's pen-names.

Ben-Gurion, the former Yishuv leader and now the new prime minister, demanded that the weapons be turned over to the new state. Begin rejected the ultimatum, and Ben-Gurion, for his part, rejected any suggestion that he negotiate. Irgunists flocked to the beach near Tel Aviv where the *Altalena* was heading. Ben-Gurion ordered the army to the same beach, and Begin, not for the first time displaying great physical courage, boarded the ship. The army presented him with an ultimatum: turn over the weapons. He was given ten minutes to respond. He didn't bother to respond at all.

Ben-Gurion gave the order to open fire. The *Altalena* was shelled. A fire broke out, and the sinking ship was abandoned. The fighting continued on the beach, with Jew killing Jew. Begin ordered a cease-fire, but he remained on the ship until the last of the wounded were taken off. All together, some thirty-two Irgun fighters and three IDF soldiers died that day.

The Revisionists represented a particularly robust, almost exaggerated reaction to the ghetto experience. Nonetheless, their feelings were not all that far removed from the sentiment contained in Chaim Nahman Bialik's poem "In the City of Slaughter," written in response to the Kishinev pogrom. This abhorrence of the supposed ghetto mentality, the supine posture—a metaphorical bowing and scraping—toward gentiles led to a belligerent attitude toward Yiddish, which was a pity, but, more importantly, led to a distancing of Yishuv Jews from their brethren in Nazi-occupied Europe, which was pitiful. This was a classic, epic example of blaming the victim—if for no other reason than that the Holocaust engendered excruciating feelings of helplessness. Jews were being killed by the millions, and Jews in Palestine could do little about it. If only the ghetto Jews had been stronger, if only they had fought, if only they had died fighting rather than passively and obediently, if . . . Feelings of frustration were intense.

Jabotinsky's name is indelibly associated with strength, stubbornness, and the word *iron*, since his most famous essay was entitled "The Iron Wall." (He also wanted to establish an Iron Wall battalion under the British to fight the Turks in World War I.) Both his name and the essay are invoked by those who either think or would like to think that Jabotinsky represents the black heart of Israel. Over time, his Revisionist movement—a *revision* of Zionism—moderated, and colliding now and again with reality, dropped its insistence on reclaiming all the ancient Kingdom of Israel (both sides of the Jordan River). It evolved into the governments of Begin, his successor, Yitzhak Shamir, and, in due course, Benjamin Netanyahu. (Netanyahu's father, the scholar Benzion Netanyahu, served as Jabotinsky's secretary.) Revisionist became Likud, more centrist, more acceptable, and somewhat tamer.

It would be understandable, given Jabotinsky's background and the enemies he made, that he would turn out to be precisely the sort of muscular Zionist who advocated either a wholesale population transfer of Arabs or their outright elimination—treating the Palestinians no differently from how Greeks and Turks had treated each other or how the people of Europe had moved and massacred one another to create ethnically neater nations. To the question of why Palestine's Arabs escaped the fate of so many European (as well as Asian) minorities, there is only one answer: it just wasn't the Jewish thing to do. This was hardly the case on the Arab side. There, ethnic cleansing was policy, official policy, the stated goal. No one on the Arab side was fighting for partition, for a little bit more land, for another couple of blocks of Jerusalem, another swath of the forbidding Negev. The rallying cry was to push Jews into the sea.

Seekers of a Jewish ethnic cleanser of note would naturally come banging on Jabotinsky's door to serve the historical summons. Here was a hard man, coldly pragmatic, and what could be more pragmatic than a Churchillian separation of antagonistic peoples? It is, in fact, Jabotinsky whose works are cited by contemporary critics of Israel's policy toward the Palestinians (Avi Shlaim's *The Iron Wall: Israel and the Arab World*, for instance). But the firebrand sorely disappoints on this score. On the contrary, in his emblematic essay, "The Iron Wall," Jabotinsky reveals himself to be not an Arab hater but an Arab abider.

It begins:

Contrary to the excellent rule of getting to the point immediately, I must begin this article with a personal introduction. The author of these lines is considered to be an enemy of the Arabs, a proponent of their expulsion, etc. *This is not true.* My emotional relationship to the Arabs is the same as it is to all other peoples—polite indifference. My political relationship is characterized by two principles. First: the expulsion of the Arabs from Palestine is absolutely impossible in any form. There will always be two nations in Palestine—which is good enough for me, *provided the Jews become the majority.* . . .

I am prepared to swear, for us and our descendants, that we will never destroy this equality and we will never attempt to expel or oppress the Arabs. Our credo, as the reader can see, is completely peaceful. But it is absolutely another matter if it will be possible to achieve our peaceful aims through peaceful means. This depends, not on our relationship with the Arabs, but exclusively *on the Arabs' relationship to Zionism.*

This was an extremely important statement. It totally rejects the sweeping formulation that the Israeli-Arab problem could be solved by Jewish compromise, Jewish accommodation—Jewish *something.* No, first the Arabs must come to terms with Zionism. They must recognize it as legitimate, a nationalism as valid as their own. And if they cannot bring themselves to do that, then at least they must come to terms with reality. The Jews were going nowhere. Israel was real. The Arabs had an obligation to cope with the facts. This is not an obligation they have met.

Subsequent events would tragically mock Jabotinsky. He wrote "The Iron Wall" in 1923, when Palestine was sparsely populated by Arabs, and Europe, particularly Poland, had millions of Jews. Had Europe's Jews made aliyah (a Hebrew word meaning to "go up" to Israel), a nation with a majority Jewish population would not only have been conceivable but likely. The Holocaust changed all that: the Jewish population of Poland alone went from three million to 300,000. A prime source of immigrants was gone.

At the same time, the Jews who did manage to make it to Palestine created an economy that needed labor. Arabs, particularly Palestinians, filled the need. (A single Jew could start a factory, but many Palestinians were needed to run it.) A majority Jewish population in the Greater Israel that Jabotinsky conceived—a Jewish state from the Mediterranean to the Jordan River—was becoming less and less possible without the very expulsion that Jabotinsky himself pronounced "absolutely impossible."

In his early days, Jabotinsky had been a journalist—a brilliant one, we are told—and he had even written a novel about the biblical Samson. (Cecil B. DeMille bought the rights for $2,500 and based his *Samson and Delilah* on it; Jabotinsky got a posthumous screen credit.) In an era drenched in ideologies, he had sampled his share. He was keenly talented, capable of writing in French, Italian, German, Russian, Yiddish, and Hebrew. Whatever his writing talents may have been, "The Iron Wall," written in Russian, is short on poetry and lacks the sort of touches one might expect in a writer. Jabotinsky makes no effort to appeal to the emotions. The essay is a word train of one declarative sentence after another, one statement after another—a chain of logic that cannot be uncoupled, and for all its faults as literature, has not been repudiated by subsequent events.

Jabotinsky believed that the Arabs would never voluntarily surrender a single inch of Palestine. (Some had sold off their land, but these sales were the acts of individuals—often absentee landlords—and had no bearing on his argument.) He felt that Jews who thought otherwise were patronizing the Arabs, exhibiting a colonial mentality while at the same time condemning colonialism. Jabotinsky recognized that Arabs were no different from other peoples. They loved their land and would fight tenaciously to keep it. He had scorn for those who felt otherwise.

"To think that the Arabs will voluntarily consent to the realization of Zionism in return for the cultural and economic benefits we can bestow on them is infantile. This childish fantasy of our 'Arabo-philes' comes from some kind of contempt for the Arab people, of some kind of unfounded view of this race as a rabble ready to be bribed in order to sell out their homeland for a railroad network."

Jabotinsky had a plan. And even though he was supposedly a right-wing fanatic and the godfather of what later became Jewish terrorism, his plan was essentially a defensive strategy. He called it the "Iron Wall." The wall—much later to become one in reality, dividing Israel proper from its territories in the West Bank—was more a concept than any sort of physical barrier. Jews would simply hunker down until the Arabs, exhausted from their hopeless struggle, repudiated their radical leadership, turned to pragmatic moderates, and made peace.

Jabotinsky was emphatically an odd man out—what in America would be called a conservative in an Israel that was almost universally socialist—not just in economic terms but in outlook. The dominant Israeli weltanschauung was vehemently anticolonialist, prolabor, propeasant, and what we would today call liberal or progressive. These people did not have it in them to consciously exploit the Arabs—or perhaps they just couldn't admit that they had. Many of the Zionist leaders not only saw the Arabs as fellow workers but also as fellow victims of British colonialism. They had all sorts of dreams and aspirations for the Arabs. It was only a pity that the Arabs did not share them.

Jabotinsky understood. He did not expect the Arabs to behave differently from other exploited or colonized people. He could wait. The Jews could wait. Time was on their side. Jews needed to get behind their iron wall and just bide their time.

"In other words, for us the only path to an agreement in the future is an absolute refusal of any attempts at an agreement now," he wrote.

History, which is to say the way things turned out, has so far adopted Jabotinsky's plan.

Whatever else Jabotinsky was, he was no fool. A man such as he, a citizen of the world, was not about to put down on paper some repugnant call for a population transfer or ethnic cleansing. So maybe he was not sincere. Jabotinsky was an educated man, a journalist, a writer, and so he would have engaged in what the philosopher Paul Berman, in his book *The Flight of the Intellectuals*, calls "double discourse"—"a language intended to deceive Western liberals about the grain of his own thought." Berman was referring to the Muslim intellectual Tariq Ramadan, but the term "double discourse" is useful and might be applied to Jabotinsky as well.

Jabotinsky set down his ideas in the interwar period, after the huge population transfers that followed World War I and the earlier Balkan Wars and before the even bigger population transfers that would follow World War II. There was no reason to be coy. Population transfers were routine and openly discussed. What's more, he was not writing about Christians, the standard preoccupation of the West, but about Muslims, the loathed Saracens of yore. Had he urged they simply get out of the way, be pushed over the River Jordan or down into Egypt, few in the West would have responded with the cry of racism. This would have been the Churchillian approach, the way things were done because it was the way things *had* to be done. But Jabotinsky proposed nothing of the sort: and he, above all, is the protofascist of leftist invective, the godfather of the implacable Likud and the feverishly mad settlers doing God's work on the West Bank.

Whether it was Jabotinsky's Iron Wall plan or the dictates of "we are all brothers" socialism, the consequences for the Palestinians were about the same. A transfer or eradication of the Palestinian population did not occur. Of all the nations created or re-created or formed or constituted in the immediate postwar era, Israel is different. It retained a significant—and hostile—ethnic minority.

This was a remarkable development, or, more precisely, a remarkable *nondevelopment*. For explanation, one has to turn to what these Jews had in common: Jewishness. They were pious and they were not. They were Orthodox and they were not, and many of them were anxious agnostics or implacable atheists. But they were all Jews, meaning that no matter what else they were, they carried within them a history, a tradition, an obligation *not* to do unto others as was done unto them. (The story goes that when Hillel, the Babylonian-born scholar and sage, was asked if he could describe Judaism while standing on one leg, he said, "That which is hateful to you, do not do to your fellow. That is the whole Torah; the rest is the explanation; go and learn.")

Hillel's golden rule seemed to govern, or restrain, the leadership of Jewish Palestine. Jews had been singled out for the worst that mankind had to offer, but now they would single themselves out to show the best. They were not created in the image of their enemies or of the Old Testament God himself, but from a thousand years of tradition and learning and an emphasis on justice. They were the Israelites of the Bible, but they would smite no one.

Instead, they were so restrained by the obligations of being a Jew—not necessarily of Judaism—that they never threw the knockout punch. They were so besotted by the ethical demands of their culture, so intent on proving that they were, as their enemies had always suggested, *different*—but different as in *better*, as in *wiser*, as in more *humane*, as in the heirs of the Israelites who had given the world one God and (after a while) a good God, and then the Sabbath, that blessed day of rest for both man and beast, a salute to humanity, a respite from labor, a time to pray: all that it means, all that it has ever meant, to be a *Jew*.

Shimon Peres has written that he never once heard Ben-Gurion talk of expelling the Arabs. "There was a time when an exchange of populations was discussed, and the British Labour Party supported the idea at one point," he writes in *Ben-Gurion: A Political Life*. "But never expulsion. That would have been against our fundamental ideology, and I don't think Ben-Gurion would have countenanced any ideological compromise on this matter."

A different nation, a different victor in the wars of 1947–48, might have cleared the general area of Arabs: everything west of the Jordan River, for sure. But this one was different. Its birth was midwifed by the immense moral imperative to compensate, to express contrition and guilt and horror and shame at what had just been done to the Jews. So it was important to husband this moral authority and not be like other nations. A thoroughly admirable humanitarian policy was firmly set—sometimes violated—and secular Jews brimming with the smug righteousness that they thought was the essence of Judaism—no skullcaps and forelocks and wives walking a deferential step or two behind their husbands—created a state in which, in the not-unforeseeable future, Jews might become a minority. This policy, this refusal to engage in population transfer or ethnic cleansing so that Israel would be as free of Arabs as Hungary is of Romanians or Turkey is of Greeks, has left Israel in mortal peril.

It was a mistake.

18

Jabotinsky Was Wrong

Between June 5 and June 10, 1967, Israel fought a fierce war against Jordan, Syria, and Egypt. When it was over, Israel had conquered the Golan Heights, the Gaza Strip, the Sinai Peninsula, and the area between the old Green Line—the border established by the 1948 armistice—and the Jordan River: the West Bank. That area included East Jerusalem and the holy sites that Jordan had controlled and had barred Jews from visiting. By far the most cherished of these sites was the Western Wall, a remnant of the one that once surrounded the temple that Herod the Great is thought to have built. Suddenly all the oaths to Jerusalem came to fruition. The capture of the wall represented a rapturous moment, virtually a sign of God's approval. Israeli soldiers rushed to the site to pray, and the picture of that moment became almost instantly totemic. The people of David were back in the City of David.

And just as totemic, they had brought along their bulldozers. The area around the Western Wall was a slum, called the Moroccan or Mughrabi Quarter. Teddy Kollek, the mayor of what had been West Jerusalem and suddenly the mayor of it all, ordered the quarter leveled. The residents were given compensation—and three hours to get out. Kollek acted, he said in his memoir, because there simply was not enough space to accommodate the crowds he knew were coming. And he acted fast because he was determined to establish facts on the ground before resistance could be organized.

The sector was indeed the slum Kollek called it, but some of the houses were nearly eight hundred years old and had been in families for generations. No matter. Bulldozers were brought in—floodlights, too—and after the crew had worked around the clock, the Mughrabi Quarter and its hundred or so Palestinian families were gone: some of them to better housing, all of them with cash in their pockets. In its place, a splendid one-acre plaza had been created, and so had a precedent.

This first incursion into the West Bank was deceptively simple and remarkably noncontroversial. What followed was not. The West Bank was the Israeli version of the American West. Not only was it there for the taking, but it represented wild, open spaces. A glance at the map shows that the West Bank bulges into Israel proper. At one point, Israel is only nine miles wide, and the suburbs of Tel Aviv, which is on the sea, bleed into the West Bank. This is a very small place. It was only natural that Israel would seize parts of the West Bank. Geography demanded it.

But God had his demands too. To the religious as well as some nationalists, the West Bank—not that gaudy strip along the coast—was the Israeli heartland. Jerusalem, not Tel Aviv, is what mattered. Hebron, not Haifa, is where Abraham bought land for the burial site of his family. It is where Joshua fought the Battle of Jericho and where, ultimately, he settled and died. As is sometimes the case, the reverence that Jews had for one place or another was matched by that of the Muslims. Abraham and his burial site were holy to them too. In 1994 the American-born West Bank settler Dr. Baruch Goldstein murdered twenty-nine Arabs who were worshipping in a room of the Cave of the Patriarchs that had been made into a mosque.

The peoples that Europeans colonized are now colonizing Europe. France has a large Muslim minority from its former colonies. Britain also has considerable numbers of residents who are one or two generations removed from former colonial lands such as India, Pakistan, Jamaica, and other Caribbean islands.

Israel, too, is mightily—maybe tragically—affected by what amounts to its own colonization effort, this time of the West Bank. Some 350,000 Jews now live there.

The figures are daunting. There are 2.6 million Arabs in the West Bank, including East Jerusalem, and another 1.6 million in Israel proper. That totals 4.2 million. The Jewish population of Israel (and the West Bank) is 6 million, but of these, at least 500,000 reside out of the country. Over the course of time, the Arab population is going to overtake the Jewish one. Various dates are projected, some sooner rather than later, but the consensus was stated by President Barack Obama in 2013: "Given the demographics west of the Jordan River, the only way for Israel to endure and thrive as a Jewish and democratic state is through the realization of an independent and viable Palestine." Obama was referring to what is called the Demographic Time Bomb: the date when the fertile Palestinians overtake the somewhat less fertile Jews.

Some skeptics maintain that the Demographic Time Bomb is a dud. It will never go off because the Jewish birthrate is rising and the Palestinian rate is falling. Not likely. The long-term trends seem well established, including the one—applicable to both Jews and Arabs—that the education of women tends to depress the birthrate. (This has started to happen among ultraorthodox Jews. The birthrate declined by one baby per woman, from 7.5 to 6.5. Israeli Muslim women were also having fewer babies, down from 4.6 to 3.5. If the trends continue, they will modify—but not alter—the outcome.)

Whatever the numbers, they will not change the fundamental reality that as long as Israel controls the West Bank, it will have to deal with either a majority of Palestinians or a large minority of them. In either case, force and repression will have to be used. The result is ugly, and the outcome is going to be even uglier.

To the casual observer, it may seem obvious that for Israel, the West Bank is a demographic trap. But for certain Israelis, including the followers of Ze'ev Jabotinsky, the West Bank is nothing of the sort. It is merely a challenge, and in the meantime, Jabotinsky would counsel, do nothing. This, more or less, is what Israel has done.

In the end, it is necessary to go back almost to the beginning, to Jabotinsky's "The Iron Wall." He wrote that in due course, a moderate Arab leadership would emerge and come to terms with Israel. Jabotinsky published "The Iron Wall" in 1923. By then, the Arab-Jewish struggle over Palestine had been under way for about a biblical forty years, and it was still in its infancy. Now more than a century has passed: over a hundred years since the first Arab killed his first Jew, or the other way around. The Arab-Israeli conflict is our own Hundred Years' War.

Jabotinsky poured the concrete of an ideology on a foundation that has radically changed over the years. The millions of Jews waiting in the anteroom of Eastern Europe to make aliya were slaughtered where they waited. The indigenous peoples of the Middle East were congealing into nations, sometimes peoples, and this was happening to the Palestinians too. To some degree, they had picked up this virus from the very people they hated: Jews in general, Palestinian Jews in particular. At the same time, in Egypt, two simultaneous but conflicting movements were taking shape. The first was a nationalism rooted in anticolonialism, and the second, quite independent, was Islamic radicalism. The two remain enemies to this day. What they have in common, though, is a loathing of Israel—anything from a passing distaste to a roaring, implacable hatred.

The towering figure of the post–World War II period was Egypt's Gamal Abdel Nasser, the country's strongman for eighteen years, fourteen of them as its official president. Nasser both rebelled against the colonial era and was a product of its thinking. In an odd way, he saw his region a bit as the British once did. They envisioned an entity called Arabia, and because an Arab was an Arab was an Arab, national boundaries could be created willy-nilly and monarchies established for the undeserving sons of deserving clients. In this way, the Hashemites were deposited on the instantly created thrones of Iraq and Trans-Jordan. In Amman, the monarchy still survives.

Nasser did not exactly see the Arab world as one nation—he was hardly oblivious to ethnic and religious differences—but he did see it as one audience with one language. His radio outlet, *Sawr al Arab* ("Voice of the Arabs"), could be heard throughout the region. It was vigorously anticolonialist, anti-Western, anti-Zionist, and antiestablishment. It made Nasser the dominant figure in the region, and it induced the Syrians to approach him with an offer to merge the two nations. As it turned out, this was a preposterous proposition, since Syria and Egypt had no common border, but Nasser could not say no. He wanted to be the leader of the Arab world, and now, in effect, he was. This aspiration was based both on Egypt's traditional pride in its place as the largest of the Arab states, and also on Nasser's vigorous anticolonialism.

Nasser had earned his anticolonial and anti-West credentials by fighting for Palestine in 1948, by sending his own king packing, and, above all, by taking on the once-preeminent colonial powers, Britain and France. In 1956 he nationalized the Suez Canal, and the same year he expelled what remained of the once-vibrant Jewish community, ruling that there was no difference between Judaism and Zionism. He was a fiery opponent of the region's ancien régimes and put his money where his mouth was by intervening on the side of officers intent on overthrowing the decrepit and corrupt Hamiduddin dynasty in Yemen. The expedition was a disaster for Egypt, weakening it in advance of the coming wars with Israel—1967, 1973—but it added to Nasser's standing in the region. He had not only taken on the Yemini monarchy, but its royal backers as well, Saudi Arabia and Jordan. Nasser did not merely talk.

The United Arab Republic was a short-lived affair—1958 to 1961—because it was built upon the fiction of Pan-Arabism, which Nasser attempted to personify. (However, it was no more ridiculous than the pre–World War I belief that the workingmen of Europe would not fight one another or that Jewish and Arab workers in Palestine could make common cause.) Syria and Egypt were, in fact, not one nation. Syria was a proud, independent state with imperial fantasies of its own and a capital, Damascus, that predated even Cairo and had been, along with Baghdad, a once-upon-a-time Arab capital. Moreover, the Syrians soon realized that one of the problematic benefits of union was the python-like embrace of the suffocating Egyptian bureaucracy, renowned for its grinding inefficiency. The Syrian military wanted out, and Nasser, for once being realistic, relented.

The Pan-Arabists had the right idea but the wrong vehicle. What truly united the region was not Arabic or Arab nationalism, but Islam. There were divisions, of course: Sunni and Shiite, Druze, and various sects such as the Alawites of Syria, as well as a scattering of non-Islamic religions, such as the Maronites of Lebanon and the Copts of Egypt. These divisions should not be minimized—they were sufficient cause for mayhem and murder—but even those breaches could, maybe for only a while, be bridged by the threat of a common enemy.

All of Islam could agree upon the importance of Jerusalem and the grave injustice of Israel's very existence. An Arab nationalist can live with the reality of Israel—an issue of decreasing importance that, really, has no impact on his daily life. But the injury to Islam is a different matter. It is grievous, present in one's spiritual life, which is the life that matters most. It can affect one's being, since one is first and foremost a Muslim. A Muslim and not a Shiite. A Muslim and not a Sunni. A Muslim and not an Arab and not an Egyptian and not a member of one clan or another. All Muslims can agree on the importance of Jerusalem and that a person is first, foremost, and above all a Muslim.

✡   ✡   ✡

Israel (Palestine) has Jerusalem. Saudi Arabia has Medina and Mecca. Damascus and Baghdad are older capitals than Cairo, but the city by the Nile is the real capital of the Arab nation. It contains the Al-Azhar Mosque, premier in the Islamic world, and is the capital of the region's most populous country (about eighty million), not to mention its most ancient civilization. For thousands of years, much of the world recognized Egypt as both a world power and a center of learning. So it seemed only natural that the modern Islamic fundamentalist movement would originate there.

In 1928 a schoolteacher named Hassan al-Banna created the Muslim Brotherhood. His intention was to replace the secular state with an Islamic republic and rule according to the dictates of the Qur'an and the Sunnah, a pious lifestyle based on the one Muhammad had led. It was an idea whose time has not quite come.

Soon enough, the Brotherhood clashed with the monarchy and its government. The Brotherhood was suppressed, and, in apparent retaliation, the prime minister, Mahmoud an-Nukrashi Pasha, was assassinated. Al-Banna denounced the murder, an act of imprudent moderation that might have cost him his own life. In 1949 he was assassinated, supposedly by extremist elements in the Brotherhood but possibly by the government. In the hospital, according to one account, he was allowed to bleed to death.

By 1952, a whole new cast of characters was in place. Nasser, a mere lieutenant colonel, was effectively head of state, ruling through a front man, the more senior General Muhammad Naguib. Initially, the Brotherhood thought it had a brother in Nasser, but it soon found out otherwise.

For Nasser as well as most of the other Arab rulers, religious zeal was not their cup of tea. They were unwilling to share power with anyone, even Allah, and they distrusted and considered subversive the truly religious who, after all, considered Sharia (religious law) paramount and wanted a religious figure as the head of state—the Supreme Leader, in the language of the Islamic Republic of Iran. That being the case, it was just a matter of time until Nasser, as had King Farouk before him, butted heads with what we now call Islamists.

Nasser saw radical Islam as a threat, if not an impediment to modernity. He had fought in the 1948 war against Israel and came away both furious and mortified. The Egyptian army, supposedly the mightiest in the Arab world, had performed ineptly. It needed modernizing, a dose of Western efficiency. To Nasser and many of the Arab leaders to come, Islam was a religion, not a political ideology—no way to run a government, not to mention an army. He and the others might well have wanted to push Israel and its Jews into the sea, but they appreciated that this was not going to happen soon.

The Islamic radicals had a different priority. They wanted the Islamization of their own country. For Nasser, urgency was linked to anticolonialism. He was remarkably nonideological, and when he and his colleagues in the Free Officers Movement first came to power, they did so with no plan. Bit by bit, they tilted statist, gnawing at the Egyptian economy, nationalizing banks and insurance companies, and proceeding from there until the state had become a sluggish leviathan: owner of so much, capable of so little.

If the state was expanding at the expense of private enterprise, it was also doing so at the expense of religion. Nasser had his eyes on Al-Azhar, the university-mosque complex founded in AD 970 and without a peer in the Muslim world. He not only brought it under state control but also added secular subjects such as engineering to the curriculum, yanking the institution into the twentieth century, where it distinctly did not want to go.

Nasser was proceeding determinedly in one direction, and the Muslim Brotherhood wanted to go just as fast in the other. Compromise was not possible. On August 29, 1966, he hanged an Islamic radical named Sayyid Qutb.

Qutb is a historic figure. From him and his writings, according to many authors and experts, there is a material link to the general rise of Islamic radicalism and in turn to the attacks on the World Trade Center and the Pentagon. The United States invaded both Iraq and Afghanistan in part because of the man who was hanged in 1966 by Nasser. In that sense, only one of them is dead.

Al-Banna might have been the founder of the Muslim Brotherhood, but Qutb was its intellectual godfather. The Oxford University scholar Eugene Rogan, in his book *The Arabs*, calls him "one of the most influential Islamic reformers of the twentieth century." His literary output was vast: twenty-four books, some of them written while he was in wretched health and under horrendous conditions in Egyptian prisons. One of those books was called *Our Struggle with the Jews*. It argued that Judaism was at war with Islam in a fight to the finish. "Jews will not be satisfied until this Religion [Islam] has been destroyed," he wrote.

Qutb was born in the Egyptian village of Musha in 1906, and if that was all one knew of him, one could conjure up a provincial figure, ill educated, ill traveled, cossetted by ignorance, and leave it at that. Not so. Qutb was a precocious child, recognized for his brilliance at a young age and sent early on by mentors and admirers to Cairo. There he caught the attention of the government, both for his Islamist writings and for his contempt for King Farouk.

The portraits of Farouk and Qutb in Lawrence Wright's *The Looming Tower* show polar opposites. The king was a spendthrift, a glutton, obese, and given to sailing the royal yacht *al-Mahrusa* to the French Riviera. As befits a stereotypical oriental monarch, if not quite a despot, Farouk had monarchical tastes. He had a fleet of two hundred cars, all of them red—the only ones in Egypt permitted to be that color. He had a gargantuan appetite, mostly for food but also for women. He was a renowned, even legendary, gourmand and womanizer.

Qutb, on the other hand, seemed to live in dread of a sexual encounter. He related with horror how a drunken woman, apparently intent on seduction, had tried to enter his stateroom on his voyage to America. You would think he narrowly escaped with his life. He bitterly condemned the provocative way that American women dressed and the way they danced. He seems to have been refreshingly innocent of Freudian notions regarding repression and the thin border between love and hate, lust and revulsion.

But Qutb was hardly a hick. When his early writings got under the skin of the Farouk government, he booked passage to the United States, arriving in New York City in November 1948. He became intrigued by America and its culture. He dressed in Western clothes and collected European classical music. Qutb spent almost two years in the United States, much of it at Colorado State College of Education in Greeley. (He also spent time in Washington, DC, and Palo Alto, California.) It was enough to confirm him in his fundamentalism, his anti-Americanism, and his general loathing for the West and its way of life. With Qutb, familiarity did indeed breed contempt.

When he returned to Egypt, Qutb published an article entitled "The America I Have Seen," which is virtually a parody of classic sexual repression. The American "girl," he wrote, "is well acquainted with her body's seductive capacity. She knows it lies in the face, and in expressive eyes, and thirsty lips. She knows seductiveness lies in the round breasts, the full buttocks, and in the shapely thighs, sleek legs—and she shows all this and does not hide it."

There wasn't much about America that Qutb didn't deplore, including its "poor" haircuts; and while he didn't hesitate to express racist views himself—

"Jazz," he wrote, "is that music that the Negroes invented to satisfy their primitive inclinations, as well as their desire to be noisy"—his dark, exotic skin proved a problem for him in the United States. Qutb learned firsthand about American racism, but nothing, it seems, about his own. He was a colossal anti-Semite.

Qutb expounded his Jew hatred not in some early, supposedly innocent, time, but in the years immediately following the Holocaust, when the world was coming to grips with the appalling consequences of anti-Semitism. To Qutb, the trouble with the Final Solution was that it was in no way final. He lived, after all, in a part of the world where the Holocaust was widely dismissed as an exaggeration or a myth concocted by Jews for Zionistic purposes—or, if true, just deserts.

Whatever the case, his ravings about Jews, not to mention his eccentric beliefs about African Americans, have done nothing to discredit him in the Arab world or, for that matter, with scholars of the Arab world. Usually his bigotry is just plain ignored, as if it's an odd tick that's extraneous to the man's larger accomplishment—as is, for example, Henry Ford's anti-Semitism to the creation of the assembly line and the Model T. In Qutb's case, though, the "product" was thought, ideas, an original interpretation of Islam. For Jews, Qutb was dangerous. For Muslims, he should have been an embarrassment.

In July 1950 Qutb returned to an Egypt on the verge of revolution. The Farouk monarchy was teetering. It was associated with corruption, colonialism, and foreign dominance. (It didn't help Farouk any that his line had originated in 1805 with an *Albanian* commander in the Ottoman army.) The French had been Egypt's original colonizers, but the British soon supplanted them, buying a controlling interest in the French-conceived Suez Canal.

The Muslim Brotherhood, officially dissolved in 1948, moved into the vacuum created by the crumbling and inefficient state. It was by now not only a fundamentalist religious organization but also a social-service entity. A showdown was near.

In July 1952 the army finally acted. Nasser and the Free Officers Movement overthrew Farouk, depositing him on the royal yacht and forcing him into an arduous exile of lasciviousness and gluttony on the French Riviera.

Farouk had had a solid Islamic education and was at least a genuine Israel hater. With Nasser, things are not so clear. Certainly he had no love for the Jewish state, but he was first and foremost an Egyptian nationalist. Sinai, Gaza, and, above all, the Suez Canal Zone were of utmost importance because they were Egyptian and somehow had fallen under the thumbs of the British and Israelis. Above all, Nasser wanted the British out of Egypt. Jews and Palestine were less important. In the manner of Atatürk, the creator of modern Turkey, and for the same nationalist reasons, Nasser was a committed secularist.

Initially, Qutb considered Nasser an ally, and Nasser, aware of the Brotherhood's popularity, encouraged that belief. Qutb and others in the Brotherhood thought Nasser's Free Officers Movement would establish an Islamic state, and Nasser, hiding his cards, even offered Qutb a government position—almost anything he wanted. Qutb was beyond blandishment or bribery, however, and eventually, realizing that Nasser's aspirations were for a secular state, he broke with him. An attempted assassination of Nasser in 1954 brought things to a head. The Brotherhood was blamed and outlawed. Qutb was jailed and tortured. After about three years, however, conditions improved, and Qutb was permitted some freedom—including, notably, the freedom to write. He did so copiously.

When he was finally freed in 1964, it was only to serve as bait. He was followed everywhere, possibly leading Nasser's secret police to other members of the Muslim Brotherhood. When his utility was exhausted, he was rearrested, tried in the fashion of the day, and sentenced to death. By then, 1965, Qutb was an immensely important figure, renowned for his purity and the zeal of his religious conviction. He could be hanged, but not silenced.

Nasser hesitated. His vice president, Anwar el-Sādāt (a devout Muslim), went to see Qutb in prison with an offer. In exchange for appealing his sentence—an appeal whose outcome was presumably guaranteed—Qutb's life would be spared. Qutb declined. He was in failing health—all that time in prison had taken its toll—and his work, he knew, was done. (Among other things, he revived the concept of excommunication, by which it was permissible once again for Muslim to kill Muslim—which, in short order, they did.) Qutb knew that he would be more influencial in death than he was in life. His sister, also in prison, was brought to see him and pleaded with him to accept Nasser's deal.

"Write the words," she said. He refused.

"My words will be stronger if they kill me," he told his sister.

On August 29, 1966, Qutb was hanged. He was right about his words being remembered. He was right, too, in understanding that his life would become mythologized. His jailing, his torture, his ill health, his indomitable ability to turn out book after book, his saintly asexual character, and his choosing a death that could have been avoided—all of this was evocative of Gandhi, the saint of India, or Christ. Qutb left no heirs, just an Islamist movement that is now much more of a force than Nasser's secular Pan-Arabism, nowadays little more than the occasional poster of the still-revered Egyptian leader, peeling from a wall.

At the time, Qutb was advocating something that did not exist in the Middle East. None of the region's nations qualified as Islamic republics. Turkey, the onetime colonial power, had been a secular republic ever since Mustafa Kemal, the later Atatürk, westernized the country. Iran had been ruled by Mohammad Reza Pahlavi, another modernizer, and Syria was governed by one strongman or another before the Assad family settled matters under the rubric of the Baath Party. The Baath also ruled Iraq under Saddam Hussein, hardly an Islamist. Lebanon was an uneasy and unstable condominium of Muslims, Christians, Druze, and their constituent sects. As for Jordan, it was a monarchy, and while the Hashemites claimed direct descent from the Prophet Muhammad, none of them were particularly pious.

Saudi Arabia was somewhat the exception, but even here the ruler was not a Muslim holy man but a desert warrior with his many (thirty-seven) sons, some of them given to an opulent lifestyle not to the liking of religious leaders. The rulers of Saudi Arabia retained their power through an understanding with the religious authorities. Saudi Arabia is the closest of the Arab states to being an Islamic republic but it is not a republic, and the ruler is chosen not for his piety and theological knowledge but for the happenstance of his birth.

Qutb's time may yet come. Iran, though not Arab and not Sunni, is nonetheless an Islamic republic. The shah as well as his maddening modernizing is gone and with him his ersatz monarchy, proclaimed to be two thousand years old and altogether truly, if you include a missing nineteen hundred years or so. The other countries of the region remain despotic regimes of one sort or another and of varying severity. But throughout the region, whether in kingdoms or pseudodemocracies, rulers look over their shoulder at the Muslim Brotherhood or similar organizations.

It is Palestine—half of it, at least—where the Muslim Brotherhood has come to power. In Gaza, it is called Hamas, and Article Two of its charter specifically states it is "one of the wings of the Muslim Brotherhood in Palestine." The document itself is a hodgepodge of history, myth, truth, and lies, and while here and there it pauses to pay homage to human rights, religious freedom, and even the legitimacy of Judaism, in its totality it is quite insane. Among other things, it accepts the authenticity of *The Protocols of the Learned Elders of Zion*, not in part but as a whole and in spirit, and in strenuous disregard of its many inanities and its authorship by the czar's secret police.

"Today it is Palestine, tomorrow it will be one country or another," the charter says. "The Zionist plan is limitless. After Palestine, the Zionists aspire to expand from the Nile to the Euphrates. When they have digested the region they overtook, they will aspire to further expansion, and so on. Their plan is embodied in the 'Protocols of the Elders of Zion,' and their present conduct is the best proof of what we are saying."

The authors of the Hamas charter, proclaimed on August 18, 1988, literally saw Jews no differently than did the Nazis: so immensely powerful, not to mention evil, that it is an unexplained mystery as to how they have been contained in tiny Israel.

With their money, they took control of the world media, news agencies, the press, publishing houses, broadcasting stations, and others.

With their money, they stirred revolutions in various parts of the world with the purpose of achieving their interests and reaping the fruit therein. They were behind the French Revolution, the Communist revolution and most of the revolutions we heard and hear about, here and there.

With their money they formed secret societies, such as Freemasons, Rotary Clubs, the Lions, and others in different parts of the world for the purpose of sabotaging societies and achieving Zionist interests. With their money they were able to control imperialistic countries and instigate them to colonize many countries in order to enable them to exploit their resources and spread corruption there.

You may speak as much as you want about regional and world wars. They were behind World War I, when they were able to destroy the Islamic Caliphate, making financial gains and controlling resources. They obtained the Balfour Declaration, formed the League of Nations, through which they could rule the world. They were behind World War II, through which they made huge financial gains by trading in armaments, and paved the way for the establishment of their state. It was they who instigated the replacement of the League of Nations with the United Nations and the Security Council to enable them to rule the world through them. There is no war going on anywhere, without having their finger in it.

The Hamas charter is a stunning document. It is the work of provincial, insular minds—men who were very comfortable in their anti-Semitism and did not have to account to a world where such beliefs are abhorrent. It is therefore the work of an insurgency, a movement, and not a government—of men who talked among themselves, nodding to one another in agreement as sweet as their coffee.

Things changed when in 2007 Hamas became the government of the Gaza Strip and started to seek a semblance of respectability. It could no longer be little more than a nasty Jew-hating terrorist group. If it was to get international aid, if it was to earn the goodwill of other governments, nongovernmental organizations, and even the Israeli left, it had to moderate its message and approach. Little by little, it did so, and with the inadvertent cooperation of an implacably hostile Israeli government and the ingenuousness of some peace activists, Hamas managed to transform itself into a victim. Its rocket attacks on Israel, not to mention its anti-Semitism, got treated as an idiosyncratic folkway, a kind of innocence of the naive.

The question is whether the charter has become mere boilerplate or represents the dark heart of Islamic zealotry. Whatever the ultimate answer may be, the current situation is not only deeply perturbing but deeply insulting as well. Yet no Arab government shuns Hamas on account of its anti-Semitism, and the representatives of nations, their historical knowledge seemingly checked at the airport, tour Gaza, shake hands with the leadership, and offer not a whisper of rebuke. It's not as if the leadership has ordered a purge of anti-Semitism from Gaza's textbooks and has ordered the Friday-afternoon sermons to be free of anti-Jewish vitriol. Nothing has changed: not Hamas's ideology and not, either, the willingness of much of the world to overlook it. Sampson went eyeless in Gaza. Now it seems everyone does.

19

Dinner with Sinatra and Tracy

In the spring of 1980, I took my first trip to the Middle East—and for an American Jew, did it backward. I toured the Arab world before going on to Israel. I went first to Egypt, flying to Cairo from Paris on an overcast day made even blurrier by sand blowing in from the Sahara. I tried to make out the pyramids, but they were obscured. Still, I was thrilled. Somehow I had a job where I was being paid to see the world—all expenses paid. The newspaper business for me was once a grand adventure, a wonderful way of life.

The *Washington Post*'s Cairo bureau was housed in a gracious two-story home located on Mossadeq Street in the Dokki District. It had working areas on the first floor and living quarters on the second. I was on the first floor, talking to a colleague, when my attention was drawn to the window. A small blizzard of what looked like scrap paper whirled around the outside courtyard. "What's that?" I asked. My colleague, an old Middle East hand, just shrugged. Cairo was a mysterious city, full of the inexplicable, and this was just another mystery.

One of the scraps settled on the window ledge, and I went to take a peek. I noticed my handwriting. I bolted out the door and into the courtyard. The papers were my notes. The maid was cleaning my room upstairs by throwing everything out the window. It was a lesson: the Middle East was different.

The bureau had three employees: the maid, an office manager who was a young Coptic woman, and a driver nicknamed Salah, short for Salāh ad-Dīn (Saladin), the name of the Kurd who became Egypt's first sultan. They all provided lessons.

Salah had the look of a headwaiter in a cheap Italian restaurant: black, silky, tight shirt and pants; black pointy-toed shoes; and hair the same color. He knew no English. Yet he dressed Western, he could drive a car, and he hung out, for hours on end, in the lobbies of Western hotels—outposts of the decadent West. So when he invited me home for dinner—fish, he offered—I accepted. I wanted to see how an average Egyptian lived.

Salah lived, it turned out, in one room. To get there, we drove to a part of Cairo where the streets narrowed and converged until we had to leave the car. We then walked, alley after alley, climbing all the time, until we reached a spot where we could look down on parts of the city. The houses were piled on top of one another, steps leading to still more steps.

By now it was nighttime, and in the darkness a squatting woman lurked at the side of the street. Salah stopped and said something to her, and she scurried off. We went on our way—up some stairs and then over a roof and then into Salah's apartment. It consisted of a single room. Two beds, running parallel to facing walls, served as couches. A refrigerator, the sole appliance, stood along one wall. Off to the side, a blanket hung from a rail. Behind it was the cooking area.

Salah's eight-year-old son joined us. Salah had a daughter, but she was already asleep, although where she slept I could not figure out. Behind the blanket, I could hear the fish sizzling. Salah took the frame of an old table and placed it between the beds. He then set a sheet of glass over it and covered it with newspaper. The boy took a seat.

A hand reached out from behind the blanket. It held a plate of fish. Salah took it and set it on the table. When we finished the fish, Salah parted the blanket and offered the dirty plates to the hand. The hand belonged to his wife, of course, the lurking woman whom I had met earlier and who I'd naively expected would be joining us for dinner.

Salah played music from a boom box and later switched on the TV set. *The Devil at 4 O'Clock*, a 1961 movie with Spencer Tracy and Frank Sinatra, was playing in English with Arabic subtitles.

"You spit your Ts," Tracy said to Sinatra. "That'd be Jersey, I guess, maybe

Jersey City. Hunh! I came from just across the river: Hell's Kitchen. We used to eat punks like you." "Maybe that's when you had your teeth," Sinatra responded.

Salah laughed.

The next day's newspapers had an account of a speech that the American feminist Gloria Steinem gave at the American University in Cairo. She said that Egyptian women should do something outrageous in the name of feminism—like refusing to pick up something a man had dropped. Or coming out from behind the blanket, I thought.

In Cairo, the poor lived in the City of the Dead, the huge cemetery in the southeastern part of the city. They joined the deceased in their crypts.

In Cairo, traffic lights often did not work, and when they did, they were widely ignored. Green meant go; so did red. Telephone service was sporadic, and old buildings collapsed out of exhaustion—more went down than went up, I was told. Elevators stopped between floors, and it could take a day to get a car tire changed.

The Copt office manager said that female genital mutilation was still common among Muslims—this was the first I'd heard of it, I think—but she was clearly uncomfortable talking about it. The subject came up because the bureau chief and I confessed ourselves dense on the subject of Egyptians' sexuality—their romantic life, if any. Men held hands with each other on the street, but never with women. We were told there were places where couples in cars could go and neck, but that required a car, and most Egyptians didn't have one. Whatever the case, the office manager pronounced herself ignorant on the subject. She was a Christian, after all—not only a different religion from that of most Egyptians, but a different social class as well. Copts were the Jews of Egypt now that the Jews of Egypt were gone.

On the airport road, young boys dashed into traffic to sell Marlboro cigarettes and Kleenex tissues. The peace with Israel was still fresh, and so the boys assumed that any non-Arab coming from the airport was a Jew. They sold their goods as they spouted anti-Semitic curses in Arabic. My colleague explained the hierarchy of Arab curses, with the top two rungs occupied by sisters and mothers. He responded with the ultimate one: the M-bomb. "Your mother's cunt," he said in Arabic. The boys recoiled as if shot.

At the Cairo airport, my flight to Beirut was overbooked. This was ex-

pected. The flights were always overbooked, I was told, which is why it was ad-
visable to buy a first-class ticket. There was no first class on the plane itself, but
having the ticket got you on board, which is all one could ask for. I did not have
a first-class ticket, so when the bus arrived at the departure lounge to take us to
the airplane, I was part of a mob that lunged for it, jostling, elbowing, pushing, shoving. I went for that bus the way I used to go for a New York subway.
The melee was repeated at the airplane itself. A woman broke down and cried.
A well-dressed man simply sat down on the ramp, spread his legs, and tried to
block everyone from boarding until his mother made it up the stairs. I stepped
over him. He did not complain. I did not look local, after all.

In Beirut, my cab was pulled over by the police as it was leaving the airport.
It was a routine kidnapping check. My name and the cab were recorded. If I did
not make it to my hotel, the cabdriver would be held accountable. The hotel itself was considered safe. It was the Commodore, located in the Hamra District
of West Beirut, which was controlled then by the Palestine Liberation Organization. (Christian militias controlled East Beirut.) Mean-looking militiamen
patrolled the streets. Many of them were teenage boys with flat, expressionless
faces, armed with the ubiquitous AK-47. They looked as if they knew nothing
about life. They looked as if they knew everything about death.

Many of Beirut's buildings were partially destroyed. Squatters lived on the
upper floors of the bombed-out and windowless Holiday Inn. Laundry flapped
from blown-out windows. The St. Georges Hotel and others along the once-
resplendent Corniche—so reminiscent of Monte Carlo—had been gutted. The
various militias had fought for control of the hotel district, utilizing the height
of the buildings for a line of fire. The Muslims had eventually won.

The Commodore was not in the hotel district itself, but it was said to be
under the protection of the PLO. For this reason, it became the headquarters
of the hacks, which is what foreign correspondents call themselves. At night,
they would meet at the bar and tell war stories. I listened, but had nothing
to contribute, and besides, I did not want to give myself away. The Beirut-
based corps of foreign correspondents, Brits as well as Americans, were no-
toriously cynical about Israel. Or, to put it another way, they were distinctly
unsentimental about the Jewish state. For the most part, they were non-Jews
and hugely unaffected by what some others, and certainly Jews, thought
was a stirring story of a nation's creation from the ashes of the Holocaust.
Throughout the Middle East, Israel was seen not as the besieged nation of

hora-dancing warriors but as the region's dominant power. It did not hesitate to throw its weight around.

In the Middle East and elsewhere, I encountered a smug grudge against Israel. The hacks acted as if they knew Israel in a way that others, particularly American Jews, did not. For instance, they knew it tortured prisoners. I remember when a story to that effect arrived at the *Washington Post*. It shocked me. I drifted over to a senior editor, acting as if I had a kind of passing interest in the story. Actually, I didn't trust it, and then, when I was convinced of its veracity, I wished it didn't need to be published. I still believed in the Israel of my Passaic (New Jersey) Hebrew Day School and, after the third grade and our move back to New York City, the Israel of Shaaray Tefila, the after-school program I attended until I was thirteen and bar mitzvahed. That Israel was not only a miracle but a miracle that performed miracles—made the desert bloom; drained the fetid Hula; welcomed and assimilated countless immigrants; beat the pants off the Arabs in the wars of 1948 and 1956; started a symphony orchestra, a university, a cancer center, and . . . But it was, above all, a nation of good people, wonderful people: Jews. Like me. Like my father and mother. We did not torture.

But we did. The senior editor insisted on it. And when I turned to other editors, *Jewish* editors, they smiled, they turned away. This was truth. This was journalism, and we were a newspaper. Damn you! Damn you, I thought. What is truth compared with the suffering of the Jews? What is truth compared with the satisfaction and ammunition the story would give Israel's enemies? What is truth if it gives the lie to Israel? For me, this was what was meant when critics of Israel suggested that American Jews had dual loyalty. What nonsense! When would the average American Jew have to choose? Why not wonder about dual loyalty between Britain and America, or Ireland and America?

But for me, the question was apt: Was I loyal to Israel or to journalism? In the view of some American Jews, it was clearly an either-or proposition. The feeling was so strong that once, over the strenuous objection of some key editors, the *Washington Post* allowed a representative of the Washington Jewish community to sit at the foreign desk and watch how decisions were made. Was there an anti-Israel bias or was there, instead, a policy of merely reporting the news? To the disappointment of some, the observer—Michael Berenbaum, a rabbi, scholar, and specialist in the Holocaust—found the *Post* not guilty of bias. Some days, the news from Israel was simply bad.

This was what the hacks knew. But they also knew—or thought they did—that some of the bad news would never make it into the paper or onto the air. A vigilant and powerful lobby stood sentry. It could block stories that were, to use a cliché, bad for the Jews. Barring that, it could insist on a level of accuracy or certainty that, even if possible, was arduous. Some stories were clearly not worth the effort. Why waste the time? Why risk a career?

The hacks never won me over—and besides, I think they were careful around me. But touring the Arab Middle East before seeing Israel did, in fact, reorient me. There was no exact moment, but I do remember a day when an Israeli fighter plane boomed its way over Beirut. It did no damage and did not intend any. But it showed that it could inflict harm if it wanted to, and Lebanon could do nothing about it. Israel could do pretty much as it wanted. (Imagine the United States sending a jet zooming over Mexico City or Toronto.) For Israel, it was an impressive show of force. For Lebanon, it was an infuriating violation of its sovereignty.

My first night in Beirut, storks flew over the city, and some militiamen opened fire on them. This in turn prompted other militiamen to open up, either on the hapless storks or on one another, and soon the city was at war with the birds. All of this was reported in the next day's newspaper and on the radio. The radio also said which streets to avoid on account of snipers. This was a daily event, sort of like the weather report.

Later that day, in crossing from West to East Beirut, my colleague, the *Washington Post*'s Nora Boustany, missed an exit, and we found ourselves the lone car on the causeway, which is called the Ring Road. To the right and left were gutted buildings, sniper nests for sure. We both realized we were on one of the forbidden highways. Nora froze at the wheel. She was a brave woman, a Beirut resident who had coolly covered mayhem and murder for years, but this day it all seemed to come down on her. Instead of flooring the accelerator and scurrying to the nearest exit, she let up on it and slowed the car, as if the police were clocking us for speed. We maintained a maddening pace of twenty-five miles per hour or so. I could not tell if Nora was purposely driving slowly so as to not seem provocative or whether, as she later admitted, she had simply frozen.

"Oh, shit, we're going to die," she said, more to herself than to me.

I didn't know what to do. I considered ducking under the dashboard, but some ludicrous sense of chivalry—not to mention some doubt whether it would do any good—kept me in my seat.

"Oh, shit, we're going to die," she repeated.

I scanned the imagined sniper nests to my right: gutted building after building, window after window. I wondered if I could get a glimpse of a weapon, the sun reflecting off the barrel, but I saw nothing. The car plodded along—provoking, not provoking, noticed, not noticed. I scanned the road up ahead, hoping to see cars. Nothing. We were alone.

Soon, though, we glided onto an off-ramp and descended into East Beirut and a kind of weird normalcy: shops, people on the street, cars. A camera went off in my mind. *Snap.* I can still picture the street where we exited and a woman, dressed in black, crossing the road.

Lebanon in those days was an odd country. Powerful sectarian militias had had their way with it. Syria and Israel exerted inordinate influence as well. Syria had always considered Lebanon to be part of what it called Greater Syria, a fabulist concoction that included hunks of Turkey, Jordan, and, of course, Israel as well. An Israel-supported Christian militia was ensconced in the south along the Israel border, and to the north of that was the territory the PLO controlled. It was known as Fatahland, after the main Palestinian faction, Fatah. There, Yasser Arafat reigned.

And yet as dystopian as Lebanon was, it nevertheless was where the reality of modern Israel was most apparent. It was where the Palestinian refugees numbered about 400,000—most from 1948, some from subsequent wars or incursions—and where victims of Israeli aggression or self-protection could easily be found. Here was the father who had lost his family in some recent or distant bombing. Here was the orphan, the amputee; and in Beirut proper were the camps of Shatila and Sabra, where in the summer of 1982, the Christian militia had massacred upward of seven hundred people—as the Israeli army, to its everlasting shame, stood by.

Touring three Arab countries taught me a little about them but much about Israel. It worked; the Arab countries didn't. I knew that by the time I reached Jordan, where, after some days, I planned to take the Allenby Bridge over the Jordan River to the West Bank and from there hop a cab to Jerusalem. Only, things kept going wrong. On the day I had wanted to leave, the Allenby

Bridge was closed for a Muslim holiday—not that a crossing was possible, anyway.

I always traveled with a dozen or more passport photos, but the Jordanian bureaucracy exhausted my supply. I needed a photo for this document and another for that document—and still more and more. I had to go to a photo studio in Amman, where the photographer exulted in the bonanza that had come his way. Instead of merely popping off some Polaroids, he scheduled a studio session. I got an appointment—a sitting, actually—and had to pose this way and that, full face and profile. He arranged the lighting. I protested, but to no avail. All I needed were snapshots, passport photos. Nonetheless, the strobes flashed on and off—mini lightning bolts zapping through the room. My exasperation did not matter. I only wanted to get across the bridge. The photographer brushed aside my protestations. Face right. Face left. Finally the session was over.

I'll wait for the pictures, I said.

Oh, no, sir. It will take two days, the photographer insisted. This was a matter of pride. I was evidently an important man, someone who had been to the palace. (I had.) He was a professional, something of an artist. These things can't be rushed. My wife and my eight-year-old son were waiting for me in Jerusalem. I took the next flight to Cairo, spent the night at the house on Mossadeq Street, and flew to Tel Aviv the next day.

Israel was a respite. There everything worked. The Third World had become the First. With the lift of the receiver, telephones came alive. Traffic lights functioned. Crowds did not inexplicably congregate in front of shoe store windows, as they do in Cairo, and no one lived in the cemetery. Israel was Europe or America. It was not the Middle East, which is why it dominates the region. It is strong in absolute terms. In relative terms, it is a superpower.

Within a couple of days, my family and I were in the north of Israel, pressed up against the Lebanese frontier in the town of Metulla. Some days earlier, terrorists had slipped across the border and killed three people at a settlement. They entered the house where children slept and took them hostage. The army responded and killed the terrorists. One child and one soldier also died. The purposeful killing of children is an outrage, and it drives this children-obsessed land crazy. What kind of people kill children?

What kind of people bomb them?

The two are not equivalent, I know. Israeli air strikes are not intended to kill children. But children do get killed, and then their bodies are lifted up in anguish and a picture is taken. Never mind that Hamas or Hezbollah or the PLO hid among children. The picture shows a dead child—collateral damage, or something like that. That picture takes more than a thousand words to explain. Somewhere around word five hundred, or maybe sooner, the explanation becomes irksome.

That night, the children in a nearby kibbutz were put to bed in a special house. The children's house could be sealed in the event of a gas attack. It contained food, water, and oxygen. The walls were decorated with brightly colored pictures of the sort you see in any kid's room. An adult remained in the room, cradling his rifle.

In our hotel room, we could hear an exchange of artillery between the PLO and the Christian militia allied with Israel. My son asked me about the boom-boom. I said it was thunder. I had to lie. I needed to reassure. I needed to comfort. That was my role that night. Up there, on a border that, just days before, I had seen from the other side, I was transformed. On the Lebanese border with Israel, I was a journalist. On the Israeli border with Lebanon, I was a father. If terrorists burst through the door, I'd become something else as well.

A Jew.

The Arab side lost and lost. It lost the initial struggle, that of repulsing Jewish beachheads—the early settlements. It lost the struggle to quash the Balfour Declaration, to leave it a stillborn asterisk in Westminster's voluminous archives—a discarded plan, a wild idea smothered at birth by reality. It lost the effort to repel succeeding waves of immigrants. It failed at terrorism and then at war: the war of 1947–48 and then the succeeding ones, and then episodically at guerrilla warfare, cross-border raids, shelling, rocket attacks, and even alliances with madmen for whom the Arab cause was a sideshow in the much more important struggle against Western imperialism, capitalism, and that sort of thing—the Japanese Red Army, for instance.

At Munich in 1972, Israel's Olympic athletes were slaughtered. On the seas, ships were boarded and hostages taken. In the air, planes were seized and, once they landed, were blown up. The innocent were killed with abandon: about 1,500 civilians, 142 of them under eighteen, since the founding of the state, and not all of them Jewish. (Among the twenty-six people killed by the Japanese Red Army in the 1972 Lod Airport massacre, seventeen were Christian pilgrims.) Municipal buses were blown up, cafés and restaurants were bombed, pizza parlors were incinerated. The north of Israel was attacked indiscriminately with shells and rockets, and when those attacks finally ceased, they started in the south.

For over sixty years, the Arab world threw itself at Israel. Israel did not move. It did not retreat. It often counterattacked, sometimes disproportionately, but at the end of the sixty years or the one hundred years or however you count these things, very little had changed. Nearly four thousand Jews had been killed either in battle or by terrorists, but Israel still existed. In fact, it thrived.

The Arabs had lost. They had lost lives, time, energy, money, and, of course, territory, including Jerusalem. Most of all, the Arabs lost direction. Instead of moving forward, they remained stuck in place. A generation of leaders, wastrels all, took advantage of the diversion-cum-obsession and rallied their people to the impossible cause of eliminating Israel when they should have concentrated on their economy, their education system, tribalism, and the abject condition of women. For some, this rage was sincere. An outrage had occurred, and the land that was Muslim and Arab had been taken from them and with it the sacred city of Jerusalem. More than land had been taken. So had self-respect. What had happened?

Others were opportunists. These leaders valued the status quo. They exulted in it, denouncing the ossified situation with Israel but actually loving it to pieces. As long as Israel was the enemy, the regime could not be.

As for the Jews, Jabotinsky's prescription slowly took hold if only because events went his way. The Gandhian goodness of the liberals, the socialists, was of no avail. The Arabs would not budge. At Khartoum in 1967, eight Arab nations formulated what became known as the three nos: "no peace with Israel, no recognition of Israel, no negotiations with it, and insistence on the rights of the Palestinian people in their own country." The fourth was not a no, but since "their own country" consisted of Israel proper, it might as well have been. It certainly was a long way from a yes—recognition of Israel's right to exist.

Likud, lineally descended from Jabotinsky's Revisionists, became Israel's dominant political party. Like Jabotinsky, it espoused a robust do-nothingism and a maximalist notion of what Israel should look like. Jabotinsky wanted a Greater Israel, a much greater Israel—not just the West Bank but so much more, all the way into Jordan. That was not going to happen, but retaining the West Bank, or, if not all of it, then a good piece of it, was a different matter and it could happen. The rest unfolded more or less along the lines that Jabotinsky envisioned. Reality insisted on it. Reality's rallying cry was, Do *nothing!*

Nonetheless, Israel kept doing something. It conquered the Sinai and then pulled out. It conquered Gaza and then pulled out. It did not pull out of the West Bank—not entirely and not permanently—but the West Bank was different. It was the heart of biblical Israel. No one could *return* to Tel Aviv. That was like returning to Levittown. Hebron, though, was a different story. Abraham, Isaac, and Jacob may be buried there, so legend has it. Abraham, Isaac, and Jacob *are* buried there, or so it is fervently believed.

The mistake, the miscalculation, had been made back in 1967 when Israel took the West Bank from Jordan in a war that Israel did not seek and which it implored Jordan to stay out of. King Hussein felt he had no choice and with appropriate reluctance engaged Israel. He lost East Jerusalem, where he had been building a palace, and the rest of the West Bank. The results were calamitous. When the exultation had died down, when the thrill of finally seeing and touching the Western Wall of the Second Temple had ebbed, wise Israelis realized they had overreached. Israel had become an occupying power. It had become the custodian of seething Palestinians and in contentious command of Islam's second holiest city.

Israelis' concessions improved matters some. They brought peace with Egypt and peace with Jordan, and peace, in effect, with the West Bank Palestinians. But they could not bring acceptance. Iran, once a friend, became a bitter foe and based its enmity on a demonic brand of anti-Semitism, including for a while that staple of the dedicated Jew hater, Holocaust denial. Syria, too, was unrelentingly hostile, because it still fumed over the loss of the Golan Heights, because it had Palestinian refugees who needed to return, because it longed for Jerusalem—and because it was despotically ruled by the al-Assads, first the father Hafez, and then the son Bashar, Alawites both—a minority sect in need of a unifying cause. Israel served quite nicely.

Saudi Arabia moved into an anomalous position, a reasonable and cooperative enemy with a religious leadership that could not abide Israel but with a secular leadership that—just barely—could. As for its people, they had been subjected to generations of anti-Semitic and anti-Israel propaganda. The king-dom is a strange, ultraconservative place where the monarchy tends to respond to the fires of unrest by dousing them with money. This has worked. Still, Saudi Arabia remains anchored to fundamentalist Islam, and fundamentalist Islam cannot stomach Israel.

As for the rest of the Middle East, by 2011 it was suddenly, although not surprisingly, in flux. The steadfast regime of Hosni Mubarak in Egypt crum-pled, as the one in Tunisia did before it. Syria was in play, Yemen was coming apart, and Egypt became an Islamic republic under the Muslim Brotherhood before the military set matters straight. The Brotherhood, as it had done before, went underground. The future looked a lot like the past. A clash was most cer-tainly coming.

The longer Israel waits, and the longer it effectively adopts Jabotinsky's for-mula, the more it is clear that Jabotinsky was right in the short term—the short term being pretty long in this case—but wrong in the long term. Jabotinsky al-ways envisioned an Israel—a Jewish entity—where Jews were the majority. He allowed for an Arab minority, but one that would take orders from the major-ity. What neither he nor others could quite envision was a *large* Arab minority, maybe one-fifth of the population, coupled with about 3.8 million West Bank Arabs—in other words, a Demographic Time Bomb. The very catastrophe that Jabotinsky had warned about—the imminent Holocaust—had shredded his plan. The Jews of Europe were no more. They could not outnumber the Arabs. They were gone.

Instead, it was the Arabs who were increasing their numbers. The improve-ment in the standard of living that the Jews were always promising the Arabs was coming true. Infant mortality was down. Childbirth mortality was down. Malaria had been eradicated. The Jews had drained the fetid swaps and cleaned up the cities. The Arabs did indeed benefit. There were, as a result, many more of them. In the West Bank alone, the Arab population increased by almost two million from 1970 to 2009.

The West Bank was also home to 267,000 Jewish settlers, some of them scattered in isolated settlements but the bulk of them residents of the Jerusalem or Tel Aviv suburbs or such new cities as Ariel, a settlement in name only. With a population of about 18,000, its own university, and a concert hall, it is hardly a hilltop collection of mobile homes. It is deeply permanent.

As for Israel's Jewish population, it was growing—1.4 percent a year, on average—and that is in stark contrast to the Jewish population everywhere else in the world, with the ironic exception of Germany. Worldwide, the Jewish population has declined (0.3 percent), and this trend will persist as long as its largest component, the American-Jewish community, continues to shrink. But Israel's Jews are not what they used to be. Not only are many of them Sephardic and detached from the Yiddish-speaking Europeans of old, but a growing number of them are ultraorthodox. They make up 8 percent of the population, and they have shunned the very institution that took disparate Jews and made them into Israelis: the military. Some of them, in fact, reject Zionism on religious grounds: no Messiah, no Jewish state.

Israel has not only run out of time, but like many mature nations, it has run out of purpose. (In 1960 President Dwight D. Eisenhower appointed a "Commission on National Goals"; many Americans, too, thought their country had lost its way.) Israel has outlived the conditions that had necessitated it, and Zionism has become what Hannah Arendt called a "living ghost amid the ruins of our times." The Jews of Europe are mostly gone. They will not be coming back. The Jews of the Islamic world, never part of the original Zionist equation anyway, are depleted—they are already in Israel. The Jews of the New World will not budge. In America, anti-Semitism has gone from a threat to a family yarn. It is *fun* being a Jew, not a burden at all. In fact, Jews are leaving Israel and coming to America, where the chance of a rocket attack is nonexistent and conscription seems almost as archaic a concept as slavery.

The Jewish era—*The Jewish Century*, as Yuri Slezkine called it in his book—has come to an end. The culture that had been compressed, contained, incubated, fused, and infused in and by the ghetto is being dissipated. Intermarriage is commonplace. In America, the grandchildren of the pious are celebrating Christmas or, for the extra presents, Hanukkah, their only link to Jewishness being the cloying red twine of Kabbalah. More than half of all Jews marry a non-Jew. When the non-Jewish spouse converts, the children are likely to think of themselves as Jews. When the non-Jewish spouse does not convert—the vast majority of cases—the children are not likely to consider themselves Jewish.

Jewishness is a sand castle on the beach. Every wave, no matter how feeble, diminishes it. The tide is forever extracting converts, intermarriages, or, more recently, *indifferents*: if you're going to have no religion, it's easier to be a non-Christian—a little Christmas, a little Easter, a little Bach, and then nothing at all. The culture gets hollowed out. The Passover Seder goes from being a tough meal of indigestible religious obligation to something au courant, maybe a gourmet take on the traditional dishes and the elevation of Dr. Martin Luther King Jr. or Robert F. Kennedy to Jewish sainthood. There is no stopping this. I watch it. I rue it. I *am* it.

The moral basis for Israel—its moral imperative—has been both forgotten and soiled. The soiled part is Israel's fault. In the West Bank, it put up barriers here, there, and everywhere and built settlements where the aimless goats of the Arabs once roamed—broke arms and legs but not the spirits of the suddenly colorful and supposedly innocent natives. In a Pavlovian sense, it cannot distinguish the bell of reasonable criticism from the bell of hateful anti-Semitism. It has failed time and time again to make its case, assuming that it simply cannot make its case—the world will not listen. The ugly little war in Gaza was waged in response to the incessant shelling of the Israeli south—an unacceptable and intolerable situation—yet Gaza and Gazans became the objects of sympathy, as if the rules had been suddenly rewritten so that one side could make war with impunity, as if to wage war clumsily is tantamount to not waging war at all. For Israel, it is better to overreact than react. The response is the same.

As for the Israeli side of the story, it simply evaporated. The rocket attacks that precipitated the Gaza war were hardly mentioned or, in some sense worse, treated as if they were juvenile pranks, kids hurling dog excrement over a backyard fence and then running like hell to escape the wrath of the home owner. It was a nuisance, for sure, and in bad taste, for sure, but a mere nothing compared with the response. The home owner had gone nuts, shooting at the kids instead of chasing them with a broomstick. Once again, Palestinians were being patronized.

Things will only get worse. Who will defend Israel when its national character is no longer that of the European exile, the fighting intellectual, rifle in one hand and a volume of Kierkegaard in the other? What will happen when Jews from Islamic lands, already nearly 50 percent of the population, become a healthy majority and change the face that Israel presents to the world, particularly America?

What happens when you add to that the Arabs of the former Palestine and a healthy quotient of the ultraorthodox? Who among a younger generation of American Jews—of Americans who are barely Jewish, of Americans for whom the Holocaust is but a cinematic reference, of those who wince at Israel's West Bank policies or the antics of the very religious or the imperious demands of the ever-victimized right-wingers—will rush to Israel's defense when it is wrong or merely not quite right?

For many of these people, history did not end, in the famous (and misunderstood) formulation of Francis Fukuyama, but was consumed in the Holocaust—a conflagration so intense and furious that it devoured the hated, the hater, and even the hate, leaving a historic black hole. Two thousand years of anti-Semitism supposedly halted on the spot, stopped right there, and history started something new. Context is gone. The moment is everything. The tweet, the text, the phone call, the cell phone picture, and, if you want to get really fancy, the photojournalist garbed as if for a safari, countless pockets for this and that, but none for what went before. It is not necessary to know what went before because it cannot be seen in the picture anyway.

The Middle East of today is not the central and eastern Europe of yesterday. The differences are obvious and stark: Christianity as opposed to Islam, most of all. But the similarities are also stark. First, both regions had very little in the way of democratic institutions, not to mention democratic government, before they became democracies, if only in name and aspiration. Second, and pertinent to the theme of this book, both regions were saturated with anti-Semitism. In the Christian world, this was originally based on religious differences, the special and intense hate that a schism produces. Jesus was born and died a Jew.

In the Muslim world, anti-Semitism lacks a deicide. Muhammad was born a pagan and died a Muslim but of natural causes. Still, just as Christian anti-Semitism adapted to the times—deicide giving way to a more "scientific" bigotry—so has Islamic anti-Semitism undergone a metamorphosis. It has capitalized on the creation of Israel and Jewish control of Jerusalem to develop an anti-Semitism that is both religious and secular.

But the Jew of the Arab imagination—the anti-Semitic Arab, that is—has a corporeal quality that the European one lacked. The Jew of Europe was powerful only in myth; he was rich only by exception; he was controlling only in allegation; and, upon firsthand inspection, he was perplexingly poor, often wretchedly so. Not so the Israeli Jew. He has a gravitational force. He cannot be wished away. This Jew is real.

The old despots had wearied of Israel. The matter had been settled. The Jewish state existed. It was strong—too strong to be confronted militarily. It had the support of the United States, the great donor nation. No Arab leader was willing to break his sword on Herzl's mad creation.

The archetype for this approach was Anwar el-Sādāt, the Egyptian leader who was assassinated by Islamic extremists in 1981. He was pro-German during World War II, probably as a reflection of his strong anti-British feeling, but when he was asked in 1953 by the magazine *Al Musawwar* what he would write to Hitler if he were still alive, he began gushingly with "My Dear Hitler, I admire you from the bottom of my heart." He went on to extoll the dead dictator for, among other things, creating dissension between "the old man Churchill and his allies, the sons of Satan." If the Holocaust or any of the associated horrors troubled him, he politely did not complain to the late Mr. Hitler.

Later, Sādāt picked up where Nasser left off when it came to the vehemence and stridency of his rhetoric about Israel. Yet he wound up going to Jerusalem, addressing the Knesset, and agreeing to a cold porridge of a peace with a reluctant and obstinate Menachem Begin. For Sādāt, the existence of Israel was a settled matter. Not so for the men who killed him in 1981. Sādāt had visited Jerusalem. His killers wanted to occupy it—and another generation might turn to war to do it.

Since Egypt's last war against Israel, 1973, at least fifty million people have been added to the Egyptian population, none of them with any memories of the war or of what, in the end, was an Israeli triumph. Since then, it can and will be argued that everything has changed. Besides, do not niggle when the obligation is sacred. Jerusalem weeps.

War or the constant threat of war will degrade Jewish Israel. So, too, will the lack of economic opportunities. Israel is hardly just another Middle Eastern country, but neither is it a European one or the United States of America. The threat of terrorism or war is omnipresent. Universal conscription and a lengthy reserve commitment are no longer the rule in much of the Western world—certainly not in the United States. The Israeli economy boasts a robust hi-tech sector; scientists, programmers, and such are frequent commuters to America's several Silicon Valleys; and on the streets of New York, Hebrew is a fairly commonly overheard language. Israelis know how to do finance, too.

But the economic opportunities in America are either greater or perceived to be. Whatever the case, an astounding 36.6 percent of Israelis told pollsters for the newspaper *Haaretz* that they had contemplated or were contemplating leaving the country. Only a small percentage of these will actually leave, but those who do so will be the young with valuable talents that they can sell almost anywhere. Very few of those surveyed cited security concerns, but the poll was taken during a serene period—and before the rocket attacks on Tel Aviv from the Gaza Strip in 2012. In any case, about 750,000 Israeli Jews already live in the United States. Not all intend to stay, but some of them will stay anyway. They will succumb to the bleat of a child for yet another year in the same school or to the fear of terrorism or to the reality that life in America is good and embracing.

Secular Jews in particular will leave, as they have already been doing, because they have somewhere else to go. This will only increase the relative strength of both the Palestinian and the Orthodox Jewish communities. A tipping point will be reached. The sort of Israel that Herzl envisioned will be hollowed out. With war, it will crumble. Without war, it will inexorably be absorbed into the Middle East. (It is now only outwardly a European country.) In the short term, it could risk a deal with the Palestinians in the West Bank and take the chance that the area may become yet another Hamas stronghold—or, no less a possibility, that Jordan across the river may become an Islamic state. Or it could hold out in a Jabotinskian fashion behind an iron wall and wait for better days. They will not come.

But in writing this book, I fell in love—with Israel, yes, but mostly with Jews. In some sense, they were the world's most inept colonialists, too respectful of the native peoples, too concerned with their own self-image, too hung up on the moral obligations of Judaism, too intent on not being the anti-Semitic stereotype of lore. They just *had* to work the land. They just *had* to acknowledge the humanity of the Arabs. They shunned any official ideology to rationalize economic exploitation—they wanted nothing like South Africa's apartheid.

In writing this book, I tried my best to ignore the daily events of the Middle East. I paid attention, of course, out of interest and also journalistic obligation, but I felt that the future and fate of Israel and, to an extent, even of Jews, would be determined by the broad sweep of history and not the back-and-forth of daily events. The upheaval in the Arab world was inevitable, if not precisely predictable, and so was the Islamization of the Arab-Israeli struggle. The Middle

East was convulsing, and Israel, so tiny and with roots so historically shallow in the desert, could only hang on. It never had control, complete or otherwise. With the Arab Spring, it was becoming a bystander.

History moves incrementally, like the creep of tectonic plates. The Middle East will continue to reject Israel. It will do so because Israel is Western in origin and non-Muslim and because, above all, Israel is Jewish. A Christian nation in the Middle East might also be problematic—Lebanon, partly Christian, has been—but Christianity is merely a religion, while Judaism is both a faith and a people and, beyond that, a figment of the imagination. Anti-Semitism is an amazing, awesome thing. It is older than Christianity and much older than Islam. It may reach back to pharaonic times, which is to say about when Jews were becoming Jews. It is as durable and adaptable as bacteria. It infects the intellect and the soul, a pathogen that mimics the body's agents for belief and helps satisfy that need. Anti-Semitism cannot promise an afterlife, heaven and hell, and it cannot work miracles, but it can explain so much that is otherwise inexplicable.

Anti-Semitism provides answers. It predates God because the Jews, in a sense, do. They concocted Him. They gave Him voice and body and powers unlimited. God did not give mankind free will; the Jews gave God free will. This explains so much. This explains it all.

Anti-Semitism is a prejudice of the zeitgeist. It is now situated in the Middle East, in the Arab world. It stirs in Europe and elsewhere, but the noxious stink of the Hitlerian abattoir clings to it still, so it is a sotto voce sort of thing. Only Israel—with its alleged excesses, its alleged outrages, its allegedly unforgivable oppression of the pathetically innocent Palestinians—gives it expression, and then only in a restricted way: not Jew hatred, mind you, but resistance to Israel or—check that—Israeli *policies,* the altogether necessary criticism, no matter how harsh, of the wayward Jewish state, which is the essential duty of all thinking peoples. That sort of thing. A blah-blah-blah of indignation that Israel so eminently deserves but that next-door Jordan, for some reason, does not.

The Diaspora of old was contained by anti-Semitism. The Jew was hated everywhere, and everywhere he was hated, he remained a Jew. What deracinated him was tolerance, enlightened liberation, the progressive rejection of anti-Semitism.

Israel's enemies—hardly anti-Semitic initially and, if so, hardly the reason they made war—serve the old purpose. They contain Middle Eastern Judaism. Israel remains a place where Jew marries Jew—and if marriage is too traditional an arrangement, then at least the arrangement that succeeds it still usually involves two Jews. Anti-Semites would destroy Judaism with hate, not realizing that mere tolerance would do the trick.

This is a gloomy prognostication, for sure, and not one I relish making. But as I write, events in the Middle East—the so-called Arab Spring—more and more convince me that I am right. Pragmatic dictators have been replaced by mob-beseeching politicians or general uncertainty. The European left, once so enamored of Israel, has abandoned it, embracing a romanticized ideal of the Palestinian movement and proving, to its own satisfaction, that it has moved so far beyond anti-Semitism that it can be anti-Semitic. The European right will surely follow, although for the foreseeable future, it is better to hate European (and other) Muslims than it is to hate their enemies, among them the Jews.

America remains Israel's steadfast ally. But America has evolved. The core of Israel's support continues to be the American Jewish community, which remains, for the foreseeable future, politically potent. But the community is not what it used to be. It is both smaller and less coherent. The standard institutions—the synagogue, social-service agencies, and Israeli charities—have a weakening grip. An increasing number of American Jews are unaffiliated, belonging to no synagogue, and even some of those who are affiliated depart after a son's or daughter's bar or bat mitzvah. Even those who remain associated with an institution are sometimes highly critical of Israel, and an increasing number find fault with West Bank settlements. As for intermarriage, it has become so common that marriage within the community is no longer routine. The Pew Research Center poll commissioned by the *Jewish Daily Forward* (no longer daily and no longer in Yiddish) found that 58 percent of all Jewish marriages are not Jewish at all. For the non-Orthodox, the figure puts twentieth-century Germany in the shade. Seventy-two percent marry outside the faith.

The Pew Poll was met by a gale of vituperation and criticism, although why that was, is beyond me. (The marriage pages of the Sunday *New York Times* clearly show the trend. Jew marrying non-Jew, page after page of them.) The consequences have long been known. Sooner or later, there's a falling away from Judaism. America is unique in many respects, but not in this one. It's pre-Nazi Germany all over again.

For many of these Jews, these barely Jewish Jews, these non-Jewish Jews, the Holocaust is not even a distant memory. It's a remotely historical event that happened some time ago . . . over there somewhere. Whatever it is, it does not excuse the brutal treatment of Arabs.

For these Jews, as for so many people, there is no antecedent—no "before," no 1948, no 1967—just the moment, and the moment looks awful on TV. Israel seems extraneous, governed by religious or nationalist zealots: people difficult to like, difficult to defend, awkward subjects at cocktail parties, and necessitating a confession of primitive tribal loyalty in which somehow blood is thicker than reason or, if you will, ideology. At moments like that, my mind turns to the sawmill owner and a beach I have located a bit north of Tel Aviv.

20

The Man on the Beach

The sawmill owner reached the beach. It was 1946 or '47 or '48—it does not matter—and the man flung himself out of the surf. He was a Holocaust survivor. He had lost his whole family, his friends, his business, and, of course, the irrational belief that man is a rational being. Above all, he no longer trusted God.

He was perplexed by the hatred of Jews, but he had seen it firsthand. Several times strangers had tried to kill him. He had been in no army and in no war, and yet those people wanted him dead. It made no sense, no sense at all, yet one had to respect what had just happened. "Never again" made a nice slogan, but if something had happened once, it could happen again. "Never" is a vow; "again" is a possibility.

Anti-Semitism explicates the inexplicable. It conjures up Jews who are as fantastical as angels or the devil. No one has ever seen the devil, yet he is thought to exist because evil exists. It will be the same for anti-Semitism and Jews. If unaccountable things happen, if the powerful appear weak and the weak are powerful, if the rich seem poor and the poor are rich, if soothing explanations are needed for frightening events, then the necessary Jew will be created and shoved front and center. Herzl was wrong. It is not Jews who produce anti-Semitism; it's anti-Semitism that needs the Jew.

The man on the beach is a Jew. He is desperate, a fugitive from anyone and everywhere. He has run for his life, collapses exhausted into the damp sand, and burrows into it like a hermit crab scratching for safety. Soon he rights himself. He learns a language and writes it, as it should be written, backward. He creates a life. He creates a culture. He realizes that he has taken the place of someone who was there first, but he had no choice in the matter. Still, he gives the Palestinians the vote and seats in parliament, and, astoundingly, when he thinks he can, he withdraws from some of their lands.

The man erects an edifice of courts and philharmonic societies and research centers and gay bars. He creates a clenched fist of an army and a vaunted spy agency. He drains the swamps and drips water over thirsty desert plants and engages in cancer research. He writes novels—good ones, by the way—and creates music and film and participates in furious debates in which, it is sometimes argued, Jewish justice should trump Jewish survival, and every enemy should be treated as a friend, and all fault, almost everything that's wrong, can be righted by him, not by his adversary.

In February 1962 the prime minister of Israel, David Ben-Gurion, went to see the country's most famous philosopher, Martin Buber. Buber had asked Ben-Gurion for a meeting, but the prime minister thought it only right that he go to see the older man. So he went over to Talbieh, one of Jerusalem's nicer neighborhoods, and met with Buber, who was then eighty-four and had fled Germany some twenty-four years earlier. Buber wanted Ben-Gurion, then seventy-six, to commute Adolf Eichmann's death sentence.

Ben-Gurion recorded this meeting in his diary. He had great respect for Buber, yet it does not seem that he gave the commutation request serious consideration. (He was opposed, and so was most of Israel.) But it's what the diary does not mention that is most fascinating and pertinent. It does not ask, In what other country would there be any controversy at all about the entirely legal execution of a Nazi who had been convicted of mass murder?

In what other country could a philosopher ask for a meeting with the head of government to discuss a pending execution? In what other country would the head of government agree—and not just to a perfunctory five minutes or so, but to an actual discussion?

Ben-Gurion's visit to Buber—not the draining of the Hula swamp, not the irrigation of the desert, not the nuclear weapons program, not the Uzi or the drones or the tanks or even the compulsion to create a university and name it after an aspirational language—is the most remarkable thing about Israel, or, if you wish, the Israel of the near past. It was an astounding event.

The condemned man, *Obersturmbannführer* Eichmann, was not, as Hannah Arendt had characterized him, a dispassionate traffic manager of the doomed, but a passionate and determined anti-Semite. He had longed to kill as many Jews as he could and deeply regretted that his government had surrendered before he could finish the job. Before that happened, though, he had managed to transport over 400,000 Jews to Auschwitz.

In all the world, in any other country, such a man would have died swiftly, maybe publicly, hanged or guillotined or shot or gassed—and these would have been countries where the survivors, the relatives, the loved ones, and the friends were not a huge and vocal part of the population but maybe a scattered few clustered outside the prison gates, waiting in the rain for the signal.

And yet there was David Ben-Gurion, head of the avenging state, going to argue about justice with the aging philosopher—a (very) German Jew. (In 1927 Buber had delivered a lecture at the Hebrew University and adamantly refused to speak in Hebrew, insisting on German instead.) Buber thought that sparing Eichmann would show the world the soul and conscience of Israel. Ben-Gurion had all the usual rebuttals, including the difficulty of holding such a man in jail over a long period of time, the risk of some sort of Nazi rescue attempt, and—not mentioned—the even greater risk of a vengeance killing by a Jew (one such killing had already occurred: the 1957 assassination in Israel of the Hungarian Jew Rudolf Kastner).

Buber's position was distinctly unpopular. The poet Uri Zvi Grinberg had attended the trial and heard Eichmann describe a visit to the Yanovska camp (in Ukraine), where he had seen a jet of blood "burst from the ground." Grinberg's family had been killed in that camp. He wrote, "I am not speaking on behalf of the Jewish people and not on behalf of the millions. I am speaking for myself. The murder of my father and mother is my affair. Buber can waive retribution for his parents' death if they were exterminated by Eichmann, but neither he nor other Bubers can demand amnesty for the murder of my parents. Only I can waive retribution for their deaths. And I am not ready to do so. I demand retribution."

Much of Israel felt the same.

That meeting was—and remains—the essence of Israel. I can appreciate that a philosophical and somewhat arcane discussion between two old men, both born in the nineteenth century, does not annul what happened before and what happened afterward: the *nakba*, either in its mythological telling or in its actuality. It does not hold Israel harmless for its subsequent treatment of the Palestinians in the occupied territories or for the arguably excessive pummeling of Gaza and, before that, Lebanon. It does, though, highlight a truth: the meeting could not have taken place in almost any other nation, certainly not an Arab one. Maybe a holy man could meet with the leader. Maybe a tribal leader. Maybe . . . But not an aged philosopher, a relic of an earlier day, more German than Israeli, a Herzilian concoction.

"Would you like some tea?"

"Yes, tea. It would be nice."

Increasingly, Israel is a dilemma for American Jews. For a whole post-Holocaust generation, for the generation even beyond them, the raisons d'être for the state are obscure, homey, heirloomish. Some of them question, as the late historian Tony Judt famously did, the justification for a *religious* state, one with the word *Jewish* in its very title and with a national anthem, "Hatikva," written with a single ethnic group in mind:

> As long as deep in the heart,
> The soul of a Jew yearns,
> And forward to the East
> To Zion, an eye looks
> Our hope will not be lost,
> The hope of two thousand years,
> To be a free nation in our land,
> The land of Zion and Jerusalem.

It's hard to imagine an Arab Israeli singing that verse. In the Knesset, Arab members do not.

Other nations were founded by religious groups or came to be controlled by them. But along the way—usually after much bloodshed—they abandoned or greatly loosened those ties so that the state's association with a particular church was limited to those rare occasions when Pomp and Circumstance, or an equivalent thereof, is played. American Jews, for one, reliably oppose any effort to designate America as a "Christian nation," yet many of them see nothing wrong in insisting that Israel remain the *Jewish* state. The synagogue has less influence than the mosque does in the Arab world, but its influence is not negligible. There is, for instance, no civil marriage in Israel, and women are granted only limited access to Jerusalem's Western Wall, a site run by the government and policed by it.

This generation of American Jews has experienced no threatening anti-Semitism. Here and there some deranged teenager might scratch a swastika on some synagogue wall, but aside from that, anti-Semitism hardly exists. No American Jew carries a second passport as an insurance policy of sorts, yet 59 percent of Israelis told pollsters that they either had or were applying for a second passport—useful for business, tourism, and all sorts of things, including refuge.

The sheer utility of Israel has eroded. It is no longer *the* safe haven for Jews but something of a trap—an oxymoronic risky haven. On the political left, it is both caricatured and pilloried as nothing more than a colonialist venture. Sometimes the Nazi analogy is trotted out. Israel is accused or deemed guilty of genocide and population transfers, and the accusation, while a monumental misreading of the historic record, nevertheless has enough truth embedded in it to add some credence to what, after all, is a propagandist's effort to discredit the very basis for Israel. The country does indeed favor one religion above all others and one ethnic group over others, and it did subjugate a conquered people in ways that were occasionally brutal—and sometimes still are.

Does it matter if Israel survives? In one sense, the answer is no. Jews survived and occasionally thrived in the Diaspora. They are a Diaspora people, at home without a home, a nation of *luftmenschen*, living on the air, like Chagall's ephemeral creations. For a good deal of that time, Jews and Judaism flourished. The Talmud was compiled; rabbis took up where the temple had left off. Among European Jews, a population explosion occurred sometime around the fifteenth century and lasted until the nineteenth. (Jews went from fifty thousand to five million.) Great books and music were written. Jews were significant cultural, political, scientific, and financial actors—as well as just plain actors.

The cohesiveness of the Diaspora—the *Galut* in Hebrew—was sustained by anti-Semitism, but for whatever reason, it existed and sometimes flourished. There was an Israel without Israel.

But in another sense, the answer is yes. It is the Middle East's only democracy. It is the creation of other democracies. It represents the best of Western civilization—not its perfection, but it has handled itself pretty well under great stress. If it goes under, it will undoubtedly not be replaced by anything better, anything more democratic, anything more respectful of minority rights, or of women, or of homosexuals.

A deal was made with that man on the beach. The deal was not that he could stay for a while and then shove off for New Jersey or someplace. It was that he could build a family there, a business, a nation—an enduring legacy. He could plant a tree that could live a hundred years, and someone with his name, with his genes, with his odd ears or funny nose or red hair, could someday reach up and pluck fruit from it—and he would smile . . . and *she* would smile . . . in that characteristically shy way that an ancestor did in some shtetl now so long gone.

And something else: the world would recognize and acknowledge the resplendent virtue of this culture. It would say that in Israel something wonderful was created, and it was better—yes, *better*—than the culture that preceded it. It made better music and published better books and dispensed better justice and treated its women better. It was tolerant of gays and of minority religions and the right to argue. None of this pardons the harm done to the Palestinians, but the harm was mostly necessary, was often unavoidable, and could always have been far worse. This is not succor for the victim. Still, it is a statement of fact.

Israel's promise is great, but its future is not bright. It is the Middle East's Jewish neighborhood, affluent, ripe for looting, a land for a hated people and a despised religion, a gated community in the vast Arabian Desert. If it survives, it will not be likely to thrive—it would take an annulment of anti-Semitism, its abrupt disappearance, for that to be otherwise. It would take more Jews (instead of less and less) to reach some sort of critical mass, and it would take a groundswell of enlightenment sweeping across the impoverished and frustrated Muslim world, and it would take events unforeseen, unfolding in ways unpredictable, just as it has since Herzl met with the kaiser.

But if Israel does not survive, if historians of the future see it as this weird anomaly, hugely romantic but a sorry mistake in timing and, of course, location, then that will not be because it occupied the West Bank or besieged Gaza or smacked around some Palestinian—and not because it offended Western Europe's intelligentsia or the American left. None of that will matter. If Israel dies, it will be because its justification atrophied, because the reasons for it were no longer viable, and the world once again got morally lazy.

The wars, the incessant terrorism, the embargoes, the foul and horrible language, the persistence and growth of officially sanctioned anti-Semitism, the condemnation detached from circumstances, the historically pervasive loathing, the persistent vows of elimination, the simplicity of criticism as naive as early Zionism itself, the calls to relinquish the West Bank, the unstated call to forget the lessons of the withdrawal from Gaza, the exhortations to take a chance with security, see if the Palestinians are sincere and, if so, which ones—all this takes matters out of the hands of the Israelis and places it where it has really been all along: with the Arabs.

It does not matter now if the creation of Israel was colonialism at its rawest. (It wasn't.) It doesn't matter now if the early Zionists proceeded as if there were no Palestinians in Palestine and, if there were, it didn't matter. None of this matters any more than whether the Indians of Manhattan were rooked by Peter Minuit. What matters is how to proceed. And what matters is a simple fact: no Egyptian (Jordanian, Syrian, Lebanese, Iraqi, Yemenite, Saudi Arabian, and so on) realistically fears that his country will be wiped out by Israel. The same is not true the other way around. The Palestinians may suffer under the Israeli occupation, but they do not fear for their survival in the event that they get their own state. Israelis, however, do. What if the West Bank becomes a Hamas state? What if it is run by men determined to wipe out Israel?

If Jabotinsky was right, it was not about the Jews but about the Arabs. It is the Arabs who have effectively adopted the principle of the Iron Wall: do nothing. They're the ones who see time as an ally. They're the ones who have the requisite population. They can wait. Sooner or later, the Jews will run out of miracles.

So the question comes down to, What do we owe the sawmill owner?

He is dead, so maybe he is owed nothing. He did not actually exist anyway—he was murdered back in 1945, remember?—so he is owed even less than nothing. But as an abstraction, as an embodiment, as a device—*as a representation of others*—he is owed quite a lot. He was party to a deal. The deal was that Israel would be created, that it would be legalized, that the world would approve and pass a proper resolution that the state would not be attacked, not once and certainly not repeatedly, and that the man would be permitted to go about his business.

The man requested certain accommodations. He didn't like the borders: much too narrow in places. So when the surrounding states attacked, he kept some of what he had conquered. Everyone understood, and no one made a big deal about it. Still, the deal did not include the West Bank. A deal is a deal—and the man had to honor his part of it too.

Israel is a nation much like any other nation. It sins. It is sometimes wrong. It was conceived in arrogant disregard of the indigenous peoples, and it accumulated land and made space in vile yet ordinary ways. It did nothing that other nations have not done, and yet their right to exist is not challenged. Israel is not evil. It is merely human.

In writing this book, I discovered the past. I did it for myself—fresh, new and so very exciting. The story is thrilling, full of aspiration and goodness, brimming with all that's good about Judaism or being a Jew. My pride overwhelms my doubts, sweeps them away, and I trash the newspapers in favor of history books. The long view is what matters—back as well as forward. Israel must endure. It is the irrevocable deal made with that man on the beach.

All the rest is commentary.

Acknowledgments

As surely as no man is an island, no author works entirely alone. At least, I didn't. I had help. At a key moment Lisa Chase stepped in to create order from chaos as did, later on, Emily Loose. What chaos remains is my fault. I had fact checking assistance from Julia Kardon. Any mistakes, therefore, are my own.

James P. Rubin, a former assistant secretary of state, was an early reader of the manuscript as was Alexander Cohen, an investigative journalist and, incidentally, my son. Judith Stone, a one-time social worker in Israel and, incidentally, my sister, was another early reader.

At Simon & Schuster I'd like to thank Jonathan Karp, Jonathan Cox, Mara Lurie, Elisa Rivlin, Michael Accordino, Lewelin Polanco, Kate Gales, and Stephen Bedford.

Alice Mayhew, my editor, surely deserves a paragraph of her own. She has been my friend since she first came down to Washington as the editor of *All the President's Men,* and she has remained that through the writing of this book—a long, too-long process through which she remained both understanding and encouraging. Through countless revisions she never lost her patience or her sense of humor. I am deeply indebted to her.

Note on Sources

I *read* many books for this project; I *consulted* many more. I am not a historian, and so my research method was basically not to have one at all. I read what seemed appropriate, sometimes merely what interested me, following a footnote to yet another book and from there to still others. I employed no research assistant, but I did reach out on rare occasion for help in fetching this or that document from the ether, where almost anything can be found nowadays. The right combination of keystrokes could, within a day or two, secure almost any book—either from an internet bookseller or from the digitalized stacks of some archive.

Still, not all books are created equal. Some stand out. Among them are two by the late Amos Elon. From his biography *Herzl*, I took much of my Herzl, and from his *The Pity of It All: A Portrait of the German-Jewish Epoch*, I took away much material—and a sadness that endures. I was familiar with this tragedy, of course, but Elon's telling of it is searing.

I was not as familiar, however, with the astonishing story of the Hungarian-Jewish community, and here I owe a debt to T. D. Kramer's *From Emancipation to Catastrophe: The Rise and Holocaust of Hungarian Jewry*. It hardly seems possible, but Hungary's Jews made their German coreligionists seem like underachievers.

So many extraordinary books have been written about Nazi Germany that it seems almost tasteless to mention just a few. Yet Richard J. Evans's trilogy not only tells the whole, awful story, but does so with a verve and style that too many other histories lack. Nevertheless, the most chilling book of all remains Christopher Browning's *Ordinary Men: Reserve Police Battalion 101 and the Final Solution*, which vindicates Hannah Arendt's observation about the banality of evil—although not Arendt herself. Browning's men were hardly evil, and their work was hardly banal, but they murdered Jews from nine to five because, after all, that was what they were asked to do.

The history of Poland and Poland's Jews is always controversial. Here I relied on both Norman Davies's *God's Playground* and Celia S. Heller's *On the Edge of Destruction: Jews of Poland Between Two Wars*. Heller documents the extent and depth of Polish anti-Semitism, by no means the entirety of Polish interwar history, but an important and ugly piece of it. Jan T. Gross's *Fear: Anti-Semitism in Poland After Auschwitz* tells a similar story, adding harrowing detail.

David Fromkin's *A Peace to End All Peace* is justly praised as a wonderfully written account of Europe's slapdash creation of the modern Middle East. I found it a feast. Ari Shavit's *My Promised Land: The Triumph and Tragedy of Israel* is a well-written, anguished account of Israel's creation. Also invaluable is Anita Shapira's *Land and Power: The Zionist Resort to Force, 1881–1948*. This is a powerful rebuttal to anyone who thinks Israel's early settlers were trigger-happy land grabbers. And if Shapira doesn't convince you, Benny Morris nails it. His *1948: The First Arab Israeli War* proves that war leaves no room for saints. The Jews could be pretty bad, but not as bad as some would like it—and not, I think, as bad as the Arabs.

Yuri Slezkine's *The Jewish Century* was an inexhaustible mine of detail, data, and anecdote regarding the role European Jews played in the last century. I went back to it time and time again, and it never failed to inform, entertain, and startle. These were some people! This is some book!

Geoffrey Wheatcroft's *The Controversy of Zion: Jewish Nationalism, the Jewish State, and the Unresolved Jewish Dilemma* was informative, fair, and a pleasure to read. So was Louis Begley's *Why the Dreyfus Affair Matters*. He not only proves that it did—and does—matter but does so in charming, flowing prose.

In their *A Safe Haven: Harry S. Truman and the Founding of Israel*, Allis Radosh and Ronald Radosh converted my cinematic hero George S. Patton into an anti-Semitic horror. Had I known Patton was such a Jew hater, I would never have seen the movie.

Lawrence Wright's *The Looming Tower* is an exhaustively reported and compelling account of the role played by fundamentalist Islam and Sayyid Qutb in the attacks of September 11, 2001. There's a history to everything, even what seemed like random attacks of terror.

Stefan Zweig's memoir *The World of Yesterday* is just a joy to read. It summons up a vanished Vienna, a vanished *Mittleuropa*, and, of course, a vanished Jewish cultural class. Zweig says little about his personal life and not much about being a Jew, but like the dog that didn't bark, his silence tells much.

Finally, my hat's off to Wikipedia, the online encyclopedia. I found it almost always accurate and an invaluable tip sheet. If the article didn't suffice, the footnotes did. They led me on some fascinating journeys.

Bibliography

Alon, Yoav. *The Making of Jordan: Tribes, Colonialism and the Modern State.* London: I. B. Tauris, 2009.

Arendt, Hannah. *Eichmann and the Holocaust.* New York: Penguin Books, 2005.

———. *Eichmann in Jerusalem: A Report on the Banality of Evil.* England New York: Penguin, 1963.

Armstrong, Karen. *Islam: A Short History.* London: Phoenix Press, 2001.

Aschheim, Steven E. *Beyond the Border: The German-Jewish Legacy Abroad.* Princeton, NJ: Princeton University Press, 2007.

Aslan, Reza. *No God but God: The Origins, Evolution, and Future of Islam.* New York: Random House Trade Paperbacks, 2005.

Avineri, Shlomo. *Arlosoroff.* London: Peter Halban, 1989.

Avishai, Bernard. *The Hebrew Republic: How Secular Democracy and Global Enterprise Will Bring Israel Peace at Last.* Orlando, FL: Houghton Mifflin Harcourt, 2008.

———. *The Tragedy of Zionism: How Its Revolutionary Past Haunts Israeli Democracy.* New York: Helios Press, 2002.

Bankier, David. *The Jews Are Coming Back: The Return of the Jews to Their Countries of Origin After WWII.* Jerusalem: Berghahn Books, 2005.

Bartov, Omer. *Erased: Vanishing Traces of Jewish Galicia in Present Day Ukraine.* Princeton, NJ: Princeton University Press, 2007.

———. *The "Jew" in Cinema.* Bloomington: Indiana University Press, 2005.

Bartov, Omer, Atina Grossman, and Mary Nolan. *Crimes of War: Guilt and Denial in the Twentieth Century.* New York: New Press, 2002.

Bar-Zohar, Michael. *Ben-Gurion: A Biography*. New York: Delacorte Press, 1978.

———. *Shimon Peres: The Biography*. New York: Random House, 2007.

Begin, Menachem. *The Revolt*. New York: Nash, 1951.

———. *White Knights: The Story of a Prisoner in Russia*. Jerusalem, Tel Aviv; Haifa: Steimatzky's Agency, 1957, 1977.

Begley, Louis. *Why the Dreyfus Affair Matters*. New Haven, CT: Yale University Press, 2009.

Beinart, Peter. *The Crisis of Zionism*. New York: Time Books, 2012.

Bell, P. M. H. *The Origins of the Second World War in Europe*. Harlow, UK: Pearson Education, 1986.

Ben-Ami, Jeremy. *A New Voice for Israel: Fighting for the Survival of the Jewish Nation*. New York: Palgrave Macmillan, 2011.

Ben-Ami, Shlomo. *Scars of War, Wounds of Peace: The Israeli-Arab Tragedy*. New York: Oxford University Press, 2006.

Bender, Benjamin. *Glimpses Through Holocaust and Liberation*. Berkeley, CA: North Atlantic Books, 1995.

Ben-Gurion, David. *Memoirs*. Cleveland, OH: World, 1970.

Ben-Hur, Raphaella Bilski. *Every Individual, A King*. Washington, DC: B'nai B'rith Books, 1993.

Benvenisti, Meron. *Son of the Cypresses: Memories, Reflections, and Regrets from a Political Life*. Berkeley: University of California Press, 2007.

Berenbaum, Michael, and Abraham J. Peck. *The Holocaust and History: The Known, the Unknown, the Disputed, and the Reexamined*. Bloomington: Indiana University Press, 2002.

Berman, Paul. *The Flight of the Intellectuals*. New York: Melville House, 2010.

Bermant, Chaim. *The Cousin-Hood*. New York: Macmillan, 1971.

Beschloss, Michael. *The Conquerors: Roosevelt, Truman and the Destruction of Hitler's Germany 1941–1945*. New York: Simon & Schuster, 2003.

Bethell, Nicholas. *The Palestine Triangle: The Struggle for the Holy Land, 1935–48*. New York: G. P. Putnam's Sons, 1979.

Black, Ian, and Betty Morris. *Israel's Secret Wars. A History of Israel's Intelligence Services*. New York: Ian Black and Benny Morris, 1991.

Blumenson, Martin. *The Patton Papers 1940–1945*. New York: Da Capo Press, 1974.

Boyle, Susan Silsby. *Betrayal of Palestine: The Story of George Antonius*. Boulder, CO: Westview Press, 2001.

Breitman, Richard, and Allan J. Lichtman. *FDR and the Jews*. Cambridge, MA: Belknap Press of Harvard University Press, 2013.

Brenner, Michael. *A Short History of the Jews*. Princeton, NJ: Princeton University Press, 2010.

Browning, Christopher R. *Ordinary Men: Reserve Police Battalion 101 and the Final Solution in Poland*. New York, HarperPerennial, 1993.

———. *The Origins of the Final Solution: The Evolution of Nazi Jewish Policy, September 1939–March 1942*. Lincoln: University of Nebraska Press, 2004.

Buruma, Ian, and Avishai Margalit. *Occidentalism: The West in the Eyes of Its Enemies.* New York: Penguin Books, 2004.

Calvert, John. *Sayyid Qutb and the Origins of Radical Islamism.* New York: Columbia University Press, 2010.

Cantor, Norman F. *The Sacred Chain: A History of the Jews.* New York: Harper Perennial, 1994.

Carroll, James. *Constantine's Sword: The Church and the Jews.* Boston: Houghton Mifflin, 2001.

Carter, Jimmy. *Palestine Peace Not Apartheid.* New York: Simon & Schuster, 2006.

Carvajal, Doreen. *The Forgetting River: A Modern Tale of Survival, Identity, and the Inquisition.* New York: Riverhead Books, 2012.

Chomsky, William. *Hebrew: The Eternal Language.* Philadelphia: Jewish Publication Society of America, 1957.

Cohen, Gerard Daniel. *In War's Wake: Europe's Displaced Persons in the Postwar Order.* New York: Oxford University Press, 2012.

Cohen, Mark R. *Under Crescent and Cross: The Jews in the Middle Ages.* Princeton, NJ: Princeton University Press, 1994.

Cohen, Rich. *Israel Is Real: An Obsessive Quest to Understand the Jewish Nation and Its History.* New York: Farrar, Straus and Giroux, 2009.

Cramer, Richard Ben. *How Israel Lost: The Four Questions.* New York: Simon & Schuster, 2004.

Davies, Norman. *God's Playground: A History of Poland.* Vol. 2. New York: Columbia University Press, 2005.

Davitt, Michael. *Within the Pale.* New York: A. S. Barnes, 1903.

Dawidowicz, Lucy. *The Jewish Presence: Essays on Identity and History.* New York: Holt, Rinehart and Winston, 1960.

———. *The War Against the Jews 1933–1945.* New York: Holt, Rinehart and Winston, 1975.

Dawood, N. J. *The Koran.* London: Penguin Books, 2006.

Day, David. *Conquest: How Societies Overwhelm Others.* New York: Oxford University Press, 2008.

Dayan, Moshe. *Story of My Life.* New York: William Morrow, 1976.

Deak, Istvan, Jan T. Gross, and Tony Judt. *The Politics of Retribution in Europe: World War II and Its Aftermath.* Princeton, NJ: Princeton University Press, 2000.

De Lange, Nicholas. *Penguin Dictionary of Judaism.* London: Penguin Books, 2008.

Dershowitz, Alan. *The Case for Israel.* Hoboken, NJ: John Wiley and Sons, 2003.

———. *The Vanishing American Jew: In Search of Jewish Identity for the Next Century.* New York: Touchstone Books, 1997.

———. *Why Terrorism Works.* New Haven, CT: Yale University Press, 2002.

Dinnerstein, Leonard. *America and the Survivors of the Holocaust.* New York: Columbia University Press, 1982.

Douglas, Ann. *Terrible Honesty: Mongrel Manhattan in the 1920s.* New York: Farrar, Straus and Giroux, 1995.

Douglas, R. M. *Orderly and Humane: The Expulsion of the Germans After the Second World War.* New Haven, CT: Yale University Press, 2012.

Eban, Abba. *Personal Witness: Israel Through My Eyes.* New York: G. P. Putnam's Sons, 1992.

Eizenstat, Stuart E. *The Future of the Jews: How Global Forces Are Impacting the Jewish People, Israel, and Its Relationship with the United States.* Lanham, MD: Rowman and Littlefield, 2012.

Elon, Amos. *Herzl.* New York: Schocken Books, 1975.

———. *The Israelis: Founders and Sons.* New York: Holt, Rinehart and Winston, 1971.

———. *The Pity of It All: A Portrait of the German-Jewish Epoch 1743–1933.* New York: Picador, 2002.

Evans, Richard J. *The Coming of the Third Reich.* New York: Penguin Press, 2004.

———. *The Third Reich in Power.* New York: Penguin Books, 2005.

———. *The Third Reich at War.* New York: Penguin Press, 2009.

Feldman, Noah. *The Fall and Rise of the Islamic State.* Princeton, NJ: Princeton University Press, 2008.

Ferguson, Niall. *The Pity of War: Explaining World War I.* New York: Basic Books, 1999.

———. *The War of the World: History's Age of Hatred.* London: Penguin Books, 2006.

Fest, Joachim C. *Hitler.* New York: Harcourt Brace Jovanovich, 1974.

Finkelstein, Norman G. *Beyond Chutzpah: On the Misuse of Anti-Semitism and the Abuse of History.* Berkeley: University of California Press, 2005.

Florence, Ronald. *Emissary of the Doomed: Bargaining for Lives in the Holocaust.* New York: Viking, 2010.

———. *Lawrence and Aaronsohn.* New York: Penguin, 2007.

Frantz, Douglas, and Catherine Collins. *Death on the Black Sea: The Untold Story of the Struma and World War II's Holocaust at Sea.* New York: HarperCollins, 2003.

Fredrickson, George M. *Racism: A Short History.* Princeton, NJ: Princeton University Press, 2002.

Freedman, Lawrence. *A Choice of Enemies: America Confronts the Middle East.* New York: Lawrence Freedman, 2008.

Friedrich, Otto. *Before the Deluge: A Portrait of Berlin in the 1920s.* New York: Harper Perennial, 1972.

Fromkin, David. *A Peace to End All Peace. The Fall of the Ottoman Empire and the Creation of the Modern Middle East.* New York: Holt Paperbacks, 2009.

Gay, Ruth. *Unfinished People.* New York: W. W. Norton, 1996.

Gedye, G. E. R. *Fallen Bastions: The Central European Tragedy.* London: Victor Gollancz, 1939.

Geehr, Richard S. *Karl Lueger: Mayor of Fin de Siècle Vienna.* Detroit: Wayne State University Press, 1990.

Gelernter, David. *Judiasm: A Way of Being.* New Haven, CT: Yale University Press, 2009.

Gilbert, Martin. *Churchill and the Jews: A Lifelong Friendship.* New York: Henry Holt, 2007.

Gilder, George. *The Israel Test.* Israel: Richard Vigilante Books, 2009.

Gilman, Sander L. *Smart Jews: The Construction of the Image of Jewish Superior Intelligence.* Lincoln: University of Nebraska Press, 1996.

————, and Steven Katz. *Anti-Semitism in Times of Crisis.* New York: New York University Press, 1991.

Gitlin, Todd, and Liel Leibovitz. *The Chosen Peoples: America, Israel, and the Ordeals of Divine Election.* New York: Simon & Schuster, 2010.

Glubb, John Bagot. *A Soldier with the Arabs.* New York: Harper and Brothers, 1957.

Goitein, S. D. *Jews and Arabs: A Concise History of Their Social and Cultural Relations.* New York: Dover, 2005.

Goldberg, J. J. *Jewish Power: Inside the American Jewish Establishment.* New York: Basic Books, 1996.

Goldfarb, Michael. *Emancipation: How Liberating Europe's Jews from the Ghetto Led to Revolution and Renaissance.* New York: Simon & Schuster, 2009.

Goldhagen, Daniel Jonah. *Hitler's Willing Executioners: Ordinary Germans and the Holocaust.* New York: Alfred A. Knopf, 1996.

Goldhill, Simon. *Jerusalem: City of Longing.* Cambridge, MA: Belknap Press of Harvard University Press, 2008.

Goldstein, David B. *Jacob's Legacy: A Genetic View of Jewish History.* New Haven, CT: Yale University Press, 2008.

Goldstein, Phyllis. *A Convenient Hatred: The History of Antisemitism.* Brookline, MA: Facing History and Ourselves National Foundation, 2012.

Gorenberg, Gershom. *The Accidental Empire: Israel and the Birth of the Settlements, 1967–1977.* New York: Times Books, 2006.

————. *The Unmaking of Israel.* New York: HarperCollins, 2011.

Gross, Jan T. *Fear: Anti-Semitism in Poland After Auschwitz: An Essay in Historical Interpretation.* New York: Random House, 2006.

————. *Golden Harvest.* Oxford: Oxford University Press, 2012.

Grossmann, Atina. *Jews, Germans, and Allies: Close Encounters in Occupied Germany.* Princeton, NJ: Princeton University Press, 2007.

Haass, Richard N., et al. *Restoring the Balance: A Middle East Strategy for the Next President.* Washington, DC: Brookings Institution Press, 2008.

Hamann, Bridgitte. *Hitler's Vienna: A Dictator's Apprenticeship.* Oxford: Oxford University Press, 1999.

————. *Hitler's Vienna: A Portrait of the Tyrant as a Young Man.* New York: Tauris Parke Paperbacks, 2010.

Hamerow, Theodore S. *Why We Watched: Europe, America, and the Holocaust.* New York: W. W. Norton, 2008.

Hastings, Max. *Inferno: The World at War, 1939–1945.* New York: Random House, 2011.

Hecht, Ben. *A Child of the Century: The Autobiography of Ben Hecht.* New York: Simon & Schuster, 1954.

Hegghammer, Thomas. *Jihad in Saudi Arabia: Violence and Pan-Islamism Since 1979.* New York: Cambridge University Press, 2010.

Heinze, Andrew R. *Jews and American Soul: Human Nature in the 20th Century.* Princeton, NJ: Princeton University Press, 2004.

Heller, Celia S. *On the Edge of Destruction: Jews of Poland Between Two Wars.* Detroit: Wayne State University Press, 1994.

Herf, Jeffrey. *Nazi Propaganda for the Arab World.* New Haven, CT: Yale University Press, 2009.

Hertzberg, Arthur. *The French Enlightenment and the Jews: The Origins of Modern Anti-Semitism.* New York: Columbia University Press, 1990.

———. *The Zionist Idea: A Historical Analysis and Reader.* New York: Jewish Publication Society of America, 1959.

Herzl, Theodor. *The Diaries of Theodor Herzl.* Edited by Marvin Lowenthal. Gloucester, MA: Peter Smith, 1978.

———. *The Jewish State.* New York: Dover, 1988.

———. *Old New Land (Altneuland).* Minneapolis, MN: Filiquarian Publishing, 2007.

Hess, Moses, and Meyer Waxman. *Rome and Jerusalem: A Study in Jewish Nationalism.* New York: Bloch, 1943.

Hilberg, Raul. *The Destruction of the European Jews.* United States of America: Holmes and Meier, 1985.

Hirsh, Michael. *The Liberators: America's Witness to the Holocaust.* New York: Random House, 2010.

Hitler, Adolf. *Mein Kampf.* Boston: Houghton Mifflin Company, 1971.

Hochschild, Adam. *To End All Wars: A Story of Loyalty and Rebellion, 1914–1918.* Boston: Houghton Mifflin Harcourt, 2011.

Horne, Alistair. *A Savage War of Peace: Algeria 1954–1962.* New York: New York Review of Books, 2006.

Judaken, Jonathan. *Jean-Paul Sartre and the Jewish Question: Anti-Antisemitism and the Politics of the French Intellectual.* Lincoln: University of Nebraska Press, 2006.

Judge, Edward H. *Easter in Kishinev: Anatomy of a Pogrom.* New York: New York University Press, 1992.

Judt, Tony. *Postwar: A History of Europe Since 1945.* New York: Penguin Press, 2005.

Kassow, Samuel D. *Who Will Write Our History? Rediscovering a Hidden Archive from the Warsaw Ghetto.* Bloomington: Indiana University Press, 2007.

Katz, Dovid. *Words on Fire: The Unfinished Story of Yiddish.* New York: Basic Books, 2004.

Katz, Shmuel. *Lone Wolf: A Biography of Vladimir (Ze'ev) Jabotinsky.* Vol. 1. New York: Barricade Books, 1996.

———. *Lone Wolf: A Biography of Vladimir (Ze'ev) Jabotinsky.* Vol. 2. New York: Barricade Books, 1996.

Kepel, Gilles. *Muslim Extremist in Egypt: The Prophet and Pharaoh.* Berkeley: University of California Press, 1984.

Kershaw, Ian. *The End: The Defiance and Destruction of Hitler's Germany, 1944–1945.* New York: Penguin, 2011.

Khalidi, Rashid. *The Iron Cage: The Story of the Palestinian Struggle for Statehood.* Boston: Beacon Press, 2006.

———. *Palestinian Identity: The Construction of Modern National Consciousness.* New York: Columbia University Press, 1997.

Khan, Yasmin. *The Great Partition: The Making of India and Pakistan*. New Haven, CT: Yale University Press, 2007.

Kirsch, Adam. *Benjamin Disraeli*. New York: Schocken Books, 2008.

Kirsch, Jonathan. *The Short, Strange Life of Herschel Grynszpan*. New York: Liveright, 2013.

Koestler, Arthur. *The Thirteenth Tribe: The Khazar Empire and Its Heritage*. New York: Random House, 1976.

Kramer, Gudrun. *A History of Palestine: From the Ottoman Conquest to the Founding of the State of Israel*. Princeton, NJ: Princeton University Press, 2008.

Kramer, T. D. *From Emancipation to Catastrophe: The Rise and Holocaust of Hungarian Jewry*. Lanham, MD: University Press of America, 2000.

Kuntzel, Matthias. *Jihad and Jew-Hatred: Islamism, Nazism, and the Roots of 9/11*. New York: Telos Press, 2007.

Laqueur, Walter. *The Changing Face of Anti-Semitism: From Ancient Times to the Present Day*. New York: Oxford University Press, 2006.

———. *A History of Zionism: From the French Revolution to the Establishment of the State of Israel*. New York: Schocken Books, 2003.

———, and Barry Rubin. *The Israel-Arab Reader: A Documentary History of the Middle East Conflict*. New York: Penguin Books, 2001.

Larson, Erik. *In the Garden of Beasts: Love, Terror, and an American Family in Hitler's Berlin*. New York: Crown, 2011.

Lewis, Bernard. *The Crisis of Islam: Holy War and Unholy Terror*. New York: Random House Paperbacks, 2003.

———. *The Middle East: A Brief History of the Last 2,000 Years*. New York: Scribner, 1995.

———. *What Went Wrong? The Clash Between Islam and Modernity in the Middle East*. New York: Oxford University Press, 2002.

Lipstadt, Deborah. *Denying the Holocaust: The Growing Assault on Truth and Memory*. New York: Free Press, 1993.

———. *The Eichmann Trial*. New York: Schocken Books, 2011.

———. *History on Trial: My Day in Court with David Irving*. New York: HarperCollins, 2005.

Litvak, Meir, and Esther Webman. *From Empathy to Denial: Arab Responses to the Holocaust*. New York: Columbia University Press, 2009.

Lukacs, John. *A Historical Portrait: Budapest 1900—Of a City and Its Culture*. New York: Grove Weidenfeld, 1988.

MacDonogh, Giles. *After the Reich: The Brutal History of the Allied Occupation*. New York: Basic Books, 2007.

MacShane, Denis. *Globalising Hatred: A New Antisemitism*. London: Weidenfeld and Nicolson, 2008.

Maker, Charles S. *The Unmasterable Past: History, Holocaust, and German National Identity*. Cambridge, MA: Harvard University Press, 1988.

Mamet, David. *The Wicked Son: Anti-Semitism, Self-Hatred, and the Jews*. New York: Schocken Books, 2006.

Marcus, Amy Dockser. *Jerusalem 1913: The Origins of the Arab-Israeli Conflict.* New York: Penguin, 2007.

Marsden, Victor E. *Protocols of the Learned Elders of Zion.* York, SC: Liberty Bell, 2004.

Mart, Michelle. *Eye on Israel: How America Came to View Israel as an Ally.* Albany: State University of New York Press, 2006.

Matuscheck, Oliver. *Three Lives: A Biography of Stefan Zweig.* London: Pushkin Press, 2011.

Mazower, Mark. *Dark Continent: Europe's Twentieth Century.* New York: Vintage Books, 1998.

———. *Hitler's Empire: How the Nazis Ruled Europe.* New York: Penguin Press, 2008.

Mearsheimer, John J., and Stephen M. Walt. *The Israel Lobby and U.S. Foreign Policy.* New York: Farrar, Straus and Giroux, 2007.

Medoff, Rafael. *Militant: The Rise and Impact of Zionism: The Jabotinsky Movement in America in the United States, 1926–1948.* Tuscaloosa, AL: University of Alabama Press, 2002.

Mendelsohn, Daniel. *The Lost: A Search for Six of Six Million.* New York: HarperCollins, 2006.

Miller, Aaron David. *The Much Too Promised Land: America's Elusive Search for Arab-Israeli Peace.* New York: Bantam Books, 2008.

Morris, Benny. *1948: The First Arab Israeli War.* New Haven, CT: Yale University Press, 2008.

———. *Righteous Victims: A History of Zionist-Arab Conflict 1881–2001.* New York: Vintage Books, 1999.

Morton, Frederic. *A Nervous Splendor: Vienna 1888–1889.* New York: Penguin Books, 1979.

Muller, Jerry Z. *Capitalism and the Jews.* Princeton, NJ: Princeton University Press, 2010.

Nasaw, David. *The Patriarch: The Remarkable Life and Turbulent Times of Joseph P. Kennedy.* New York: Penguin, 2012.

Netanyahu, Benzion. *The Origins of the Inquisition in Fifteenth Century Spain.* New York: Random House, 1995.

Nirenberg, David. *Anti-Judaism: The Western Tradition.* New York. W. W. Norton, 2013.

Nusseibeh, Sari. *Once upon a Country: A Palestinian Life.* New York: Farrar, Straus and Giroux, 2007.

Oren, Michael B. *Power, Faith, and Fantasy: America in the Middle East: 1776 to the Present.* New York: W. W. Norton, 2007.

———. *Six Days of War: June 1967 and the Making of the Modern Middle East.* New York: Random House, 2002.

Ostrer, Harry. *Legacy: A Genetic History of the Jewish People.* Oxford: Oxford University Press, 2012.

Pappe, Ilan. *The Ethnic Cleansing of Palestine.* Oxford: Oneworld, 2006.

Patai, Raphael. *The Jewish Mind.* New York: Charles Scribner's Sons, 1977.

Pawel, Ernst. *The Labyrinth of Exile: A Life of Theodor Herzl.* New York: Farrar, Straus and Giroux. New York: 1989.

———. *The Nightmare of Reason: A Life of Franz Kafka.* New York: Vintage Books, 1985.

Pease, Steven L. *The Golden Age of Jewish Achievement: The Compendium of a Culture, a People, and Their Stunning Performance.* California: Deucalion, 2009.

Peres, Shimon. *Ben-Gurion: A Political Life.* New York: Schocken Books, 2011.

———. *The Imaginary Voyage.* New York: Arcade, 1998.

Peters, F. E. *The Voice, the Word, the Books: The Sacred Scripture of the Jews, Christians, and Muslims.* Princeton, NJ: Princeton University Press, 2007.

Rabinovich, Abraham. *The Yom Kippur War: The Epic Encounter That Transformed the Middle East.* New York: Schocken Books, 2004.

Radosh, Allis, and Ronald Radosh. *A Safe Haven: Harry S. Truman and the Founding of Israel.* New York: HarperCollins, 2009.

Ramadan, Tariq. *In the Footsteps of the Prophet: Lessons in the Life of Muhammad.* New York: Oxford University Press, 2007.

Reinharz, Jehuda. *Chaim Weizmann: The Making of a Zionist Leader.* Oxford: Oxford University Press, 1985.

Reitter, Paul. *On the Origins of Jewish Self-Hatred.* Princeton, NJ: Princeton University Press, 2012.

Rogan, Eugene. *The Arabs.* New York: Basic Books, 2009.

Rogan, Eugene L., and Avi Shlaim. *The War for Palestine.* 2nd ed. Cambridge: Cambridge University Press, 2007.

Rose, Jacqueline. *The Question of Zion.* Princeton, NJ: Princeton University Press, 2005.

Rosenbaum, Ron. *Explaining Hitler.* New York: Random House, 1998.

———. *Those Who Forget the Past: The Question of Anti-Semitism.* New York: Random House Trade Paperbacks, 2004.

Rosenkranz, Ze'ev. *Einstein Before Israel.* Princeton, NJ: Princeton University Press, 2011.

Rothschild, Joseph. *East Central Europe Between the Two World Wars.* Seattle: University of Washington Press, 1974.

Rowe, David E., and Robert Schulmann. *Einstein on Politics: His Private Thoughts and Public Stands on Nationalism, Zionism, War, Peace and the Bomb.* Princeton, NJ: Princeton University Press, 2007.

Roy, Rachel. *Hamas and Civil Society in Gaza: Engaging the Islamist Social Sector.* Princeton, NJ: Princeton University Press, 2011.

Rubenstein, Joshua. *Leon Trotsky: A Revolutionary's Life.* New Haven, CT: Yale University Press, 2011.

Rubin, Barry, and Judith Colp Rubin. *Anti-American Terrorism and the Middle East: Understanding the Violence.* New York: Oxford University Press, 2002.

Rubinstein, Danny. *The People of Nowhere: The Palestinian Vision of Home.* New York: Times Books, 1991.

Satloff, Robert. *Among the Righteous: Lost Stories from the Holocaust's Long Reach into Arab Lands.* New York: Public Affairs, 2006.

Scheuer, Michael. *Osama Bin Laden.* New York: Oxford University Press, 2011.

Schiff, Zeev. *A History of the Israeli Army (1870–1974).* San Francisco: Straight Arrow Books, 1974.

Schneer, Jonathan. *The Balfour Declaration: The Origins of the Arab-Israeli Conflict.* New York: Random House, 2010.

Segev, Tom. *1967: Israel, the War, and the Year That Transformed the Middle East. New* York: Metropolitan Books, 2005.

———. *One Palestine, Complete: Jews and Arabs Under the British Mandate.* New York: Owl Books, 2001.

Senor, Dan, and Saul Singer. *Start-Up Nation: The Story of Israel's Economic Miracle.* New York: Hatchette Book Group, 2009.

Sereny, Gitta. *Into That Darkness.* New York: Vintage Books, 1974.

Seton-Watson, Hugh. *Eastern Europe: Between the Wars 1918–1941.* Hamden, CT: Archon Books, 1962.

Shapira, Anita. *Israel: A History.* Waltham, MA: Brandeis University Press, 2012.

———. *Land and Power: The Zionist Resort to Force, 1881–1948.* Stanford, CA: Stanford University Press, 1992.

Shatz, Adam. *Prophets Outcast: A Century of Dissident Jewish Writing About Zionism and Israel.* New York: Nation Books, 2004.

Shavit, Ari. *My Promised Land: The Triumph and Tragedy of Israel.* New York: Spiegel & Grau, 2013.

Sherman. A. J. *Mandate Days: British Lives in Palestine, 1918–1948.* Baltimore: Johns Hopkins University Press, 1997.

Shindler, Colin. *Israel and the European Left Between Solidarity and Delegitimization.* New York: Continuum, 2012.

Shlaim, Avi. *The Iron Wall: Israel and the Arab World.* New York: W. W. Norton, 2001.

Silberklang, David, ed. *Yad Vashem Studies.* 36 (1). Jerusalem: The Holocaust Martyrs' and Heroes' Remembrance, 2008.

Slezkine, Yuri. *The Jewish Century.* Princeton, NJ: Princeton University Press, 2004.

Smith, Tom W. *Jewish Distinctiveness in America: A Statistical Portrait.* New York: American Jewish Committee, 2005.

Snyder, Timothy. *Bloodlands: Europe Between Hitler and Stalin.* New York: Basic Books, 2010.

Spotts, Frederic. *The Shameful Peace: How French Artists and Intellectuals Survived Nazi Occupation.* New Haven, CT: Yale University Press, 2008.

Stavans, Ilan. *Resurrecting Hebrew.* New York: Schocken Books, 2008.

Steinlauf, Michael C. *Bondage to the Dead: Poland and the Memory of the Holocaust.* Syracuse, NY: Syracuse University Press, 1997.

Stern, Fritz. *The Politics of Cultural Despair: A Study in the Rise of Germanic Ideology.* Berkeley: University of California Press, 1974.

Storfer, Miles D. *Intelligence and Giftedness: The Contributions of Heredity and Early Environment.* San Francisco: Jossey-Bass, 1990.

Strauss, Leo. *Jewish Philosophy and the Crisis of Modernity: Essays and Lectures in Modern Jewish Thought.* Albany: State University of New York Press, 1997.

Taylor, A. J. P. *The Origins of the Second World War.* New York: Simon & Schuster Paperbacks, 1961.

Taylor, Frederick. *Exorcising Hitler: The Occupation and Denazification of Germany.* New York: Bloomsbury Press, 2011.

Tibi, Bassam. *Islamism and Islam.* New Haven, CT: Yale University Press, 2012.

Tifft, Susan E., and Alex S. Jones. *The Trust: The Private and Powerful Family Behind the New York Times.* Boston: Little, Brown, 1999.

Tignor, Robert L. *Egypt: A Short History.* Princeton, NJ: Princeton University Press, 2010.

Wasserstein, Bernard. *On the Eve: The Jews of Europe Before the Second World War.* New York: Simon & Schuster, 2012.

Weizmann, Chaim. *Trail and Error.* New York: Harper and Brothers, 1949.

Wheatcroft, Geoffrey. *The Controversy of Zion: Jewish Nationalism, the Jewish State, and the Unresolved Jewish Dilemma.* New York: Addison-Wesley, 1996.

Wilford, Hugh. *America's Great Game: The CIA's Secret Arabists and the Shaping of the Modern Middle East.* New York: Basic Books, 2013.

Wilson, A. N. *Hitler.* New York: Basic Books, 2012.

Wisniewski, Tomasz. *Jewish Bialystok and Surroundings in Eastern Poland: A Guide for Yesterday and Today.* Ipswich, MA: Ipswich Press, 1998.

Wisse, Ruth, R. *Jews and Power.* New York: Schocken Books, 2007.

Wistrich, Robert S. *A Lethal Obsession: Anti-Semitism from Antiquity to the Global Jihad.* New York: Random House, 2010.

Wright, Lawrence. *The Looming Tower: Al-Qaeda and the Road to 9/11.* New York: Alfred A. Knopf, 2006.

Wyman, David S. *The Abandonment of the Jews: America and the Holocaust, 1941–1945.* New York: New Press, 2007.

———. *A Race Against Death: Peter Bergson, America, and the Holocaust.* New York: New York Press, 2002.

Young-Bruehl, Elisabeth. *Why Arendt Matters.* New Haven, CT: Yale University Press, 2006.

Zertal, Idith. *From Catastrophe to Power: Holocaust Survivors and the Emergence of Israel.* Berkeley: University of California Press, 1998.

———. *Israel's Holocaust and the Politics of Nationhood.* Cambridge: Cambridge University Press, 2002.

Zerubavel, Yael. *Recovered Roots: Collective Memory and the Making of Israeli National Tradition.* Chicago: University of Chicago Press, 1995.

Zweig, Stefan. *The World of Yesterday.* Lincoln: University of Nebraska Press, 1964.

Index

About the Author

Richard Cohen is a nationally syndicated columnist for the *Washington Post,* where he has covered national politics and foreign affairs since 1976. He has written for numerous publications, including the *New Republic, The Nation, Esquire, GQ,* and *The New York Review of Books.* He has received the Sigma Delta Chi and Washington-Baltimore Newspaper Guild Awards for his investigative reporting.